Front Desk Management

FRONT DESK MANAGEMENT

Arohi Kanchan

CENTRUM PRESS
NEW DELHI-110002 (INDIA)

CENTRUM PRESS
H.O.: 4360/4, Ansari Road, Daryaganj,
New Delhi-110002 (India)
Tel: 23278000, 23261597, 23255577, 23286875
B.O.: No. 1015, Ist Main Road, BSK IIIrd Stage,
IIIrd Phase, IIIrd Block, Bengaluru-560085 (INDIA)
Tel: 080-41723429
Email: centrumpress@gmail.com
Visit us at: www.centrumpress.com

Front Desk Management

First Edition, 2013

ISBN 978-93-81460-06-1

PRINTED IN INDIA

Printed at Balaji Offset, Delhi.

Contents

Preface

The front-desk job is a critical role in a company. Generally, front-desk employees are the first person customers or clients speak to or interact with. Front-desk job descriptions can vary depending on the industry. Greeting and receiving guests and customer service are usually a common thread in all front-desk job descriptions. Some front-desk jobs, in a hotel for example, not only greet and assist customers, but also ensure the details of their stay are accurate. Responsibilities for a front-desk job often include answering a multi-line phone system and greeting and directing guests, as well as staff. Furthermore, duties include responding to complaints, service issues and other general questions or concerns as appropriate. Filing, mail distribution and use of a computer usually are necessary.

A front desk manager is generally in charge of everything that goes on in the front desk. This person will hire and train new people for the front desk. They will make sure that everything runs properly and that everything is organized. This person must be able to oversee the operation along with the profits of the business. There are many responsibilities and duties that come with this job title. A front desk manager could work at a hotel, motel, fitness centre or doctor's office.

A front desk manager has many duties to perform. Hiring and firing new employees is a major duty. A front desk manager will also have to make sure that all new employees are fully trained and able to perform their job. This position requires you to lead this customer service team. Answering questions, taking difficult telephone calls, analysing the front desk budget, setting schedules and welcoming guests are a few duties that this job entails. Front desk manager is responsible for communicating with all other departments in regard to the front desk department; conduct department meetings regularly; cover all shifts that are open; deal with all complaints from customers; and reporting all manners to the hotel director. The biggest responsibility is to supervise over the front desk clerks. Each day, the front desk manager is required to monitor all finances at the front desk. You must be a highly motivated person to qualify for this job. It requires a lot of attention and time. The perfect person for this job must be able to work any shift or day of the week; have great communication and manager skills; and must be highly organized. This position requires plenty of patience with people and understanding. You will need a strong personality with leadership skills that shine. Most companies will require that you have customer service and management experience. Some will require that you have a high school diploma and some college. Computer skills are required for this position. Typing skills are required. You must be able to read and write in the language the company requires. A degree in hotel or hospitality management will likely give you a better opportunity.

The book looks at the impact hospitality has on the economic, social, and cultural status of the travel destination. Quality-, quantity-, and location-based growth management strategies are also examined, along with the role of the market.

—Author

1

Front Desk Management for Hospitality Sector

Why do we refer to strategy as a *process*? The answer is that it is never a once for all event —it goes on and on. There is a need to continually review strategic objectives because the environment is always changing. The purpose of strategy is to make an organisation to fit into its environment. By achieving this, the probabilities that it will survive and prosper are enhanced.

The first section of this book is concerned with introducing the subject matter of strategy in a specific context, namely that of travel and tourism. Thus in Part One concepts, definitions and the nature of objectives are discussed in chapter highlights the particular characteristics of travel and tourism which are relevant to understanding the way in which organisations within the industry are managed in a strategic way.

The subsequent parts of this book are concerned with examining the distinct 'stages' in the strategic process. It can be argued that strategy is a process because it contains distinct 'stages' and that there are three stages in all.

Strategic Analysis

The purpose of strategic analysis is to gather information. None of us would be wise to make an important decision about anything in life without adequate and relevant information, and neither would a travel and tourism organisation.

There are two main stages in strategic analysis. First, strategic analysis involves an examination of an organisation's internal environment (*internal analysis*). This takes the form of a thorough analysis of the internal processes and structures of a business in much the same way as a doctor might carry out a thorough medical examination on a person. The purpose of internal analysis is to establish what the organisation is good at (its strengths) and what it is not so good at (its weaknesses).

The second stage in strategic analysis is an examination of the organisation's external environment (an *external analysis*). This takes the form of a thorough analysis of two 'layers' of external environment—the micro—or 'near' environment and the macro- or 'far' environment. We will encounter the external environment in the book.

The macro-environment contains a range of influences that affect not only an organisation in an industry, but also the whole industry itself. It follows that a single organisation is usually unable to affect the factors in the macro-environment—successful strategy usually involves learning to cope and adapt to changes. This book explains the macro-environment in terms of five main areas of influence—socio-demographic, political, economic, environmental and technological influence.

The micro-environment comprises the industry in which the organisation competes. The organisation is usually affected by the factors in this environment and it may be able to have an influence upon it.

However, unlike the internal environment the organisation does not have control over its micro-environment. We sometimes refer to the micro-environment as the competitive environment because it is within this sphere that an organisation competes, both for resource inputs and to sell its product outputs.

The information gathered from the external analysis, we seek to establish which influences represent opportunities, and which are, or might develop into, threats. Once we have established the organisation's internal strengths and weaknesses, and its external opportunities and threats, the challenge becomes to select a strategy that will address the weaknesses and threats whilst, at the same time, will build upon its strengths and exploit its opportunities. It is important to understand that a detailed internal and external analysis is a necessary prerequisite for the SWOT information—it emerges from the internal and external analysis.

The process sometimes involves an additional stage of condensing the strengths, weaknesses, opportunities and threats (SWOT) into a survey of the 'key issues'. These are the most pressing or most important elements of the SWOT statement—those which require the most urgent action or which the strategy should be particularly designed to address.

Strategic Choice

The second stage in the strategic process involves taking the important information gathered from the strategic analysis and using it to make an intelligent and informed choice or selection of the most appropriate courses of action for the future. Choices are required about how the travel and tourism organisation (or its constituent parts) will compete, the strategic direction it will take and the methods which will be utilised.

It is at this stage that we come to appreciate the importance of the strategic analysis. If we have gained insufficient or flawed information from the analysis, then we cannot be sure that the strategy selection we make will be the right one.

Strategic choice therefore begins with an examination of the strategic analysis. Once we are acquainted with it, we normally generate a list of the options open to the organisation, paying particular attention to how each option will address the key issues. After this, we evaluate each option using a number of criteria. Finally, the most appropriate strategic option is selected.

Strategic Implementation and Management of Change

The third stage in the strategic process involves taking the selected strategic option and actually putting it into practice.

This is a complex part of the process as it concerns putting detailed aspects of the strategy into practice. It involves *doing* the strategy and this brings into focus a number of other managerial issues. There are a number of areas of which we need to be aware in order to effectively implement a strategy for a travel and tourism organisation.

Implementation typically involves taking into account the following:

- the adequacy of the organisation's resource base;

- the readiness of the organisation's culture and structure to undertake the proposed strategy;
- the management of any changes that are needed to implement the strategy;
- the extent to which the organisation positions itself in respect to its geographic coverage and international presence.

In implementing the strategic process it is necessary to be aware not only of changes occurring to the internal and external environment, but also of changes to the subject matter itself. Thus Chapter considers the present and future trends occurring in the study of strategic management.

The 'feedback' Link

Finally, the progress of strategy is monitored continually through feedback from the implementation stage back to the analysis stage. As a strategy proceeds, it may affect the organisation's internal environment and it may have an effect on the external environment. In addition, independent influences may have brought internal or external changes about since the strategic analysis was first carried out.

In order to ensure that the selected strategy is still appropriate, therefore, a review of the strategic analysis is necessary. If nothing has changed, then the company may decide that no amendment to the strategy is necessary. If the environment (internal or external) has changed, however, some modification to the strategy may become necessary.

Strategy and Strategic Objectives for Travel and Tourism Organisations

Strategic thinking and strategic management are the most important activities undertaken by any business or public sector organisation. How skilfully these activities are carried out will determine the eventual long-term success or failure of the organisation. In this chapter, we introduce the most basic concepts in the study of these activities. The various definitions of the word *strategy* are discussed and then we explore the levels of decision-making in successful strategic management (at the strategic, tactical and operational levels). These are defined and the links between the levels are discussed. Finally, we discuss the nature of strategic objectives—who is responsible for setting them and what they are essentially about.

Learning Objectives

After studying this chapter, students should be able to:

- define the word *strategy* using Mintzberg's five Ps frame work;
- distinguish between deliberate (prescriptive) and emergent strategy;
- explain what strategy contains in practice;
- describe what is meant by *strategic, tactical* and *operational* decisions;
- explain what is meant by *hierarchical congruence* and why it is important;
- employ the stakeholder model to explain how strategic decisions are arrived at;
- define mission and describe the purpose and typical contents of a mission statement;
- explain the most typical types of objectives that are sought through strategic management.

What is Strategy?

Definition

At the beginning of a book on strategy, the question 'What is strategy?' seems to be the most obvious starting point. The answer to the question is rather more complicated than it might at first appear. The growth of the subject has led to the use of the term strategy (and strategic management) in various ways.

Many organisations are hindered by short termism, concentrating on the most pressing immediate tasks at hand rather than looking ahead and taking a longer-term view. This is understandable given the pressures on modern business, but is not the most sensible way to manage. It is difficult to plan ahead (in the same way as it is difficult to forecast the weather) because there are so many sources of uncertainty and change, but concepts, frameworks, tools and techniques have been developed to facilitate the process. The overall aim of strategic management is thus to develop a framework for thinking ahead—for thinking strategically.

Historically, the term strategy has military roots, with commanders employing strategy in dealing with their opponents (see for example Keegan, 1988). Indeed, dictionaries often continue the military theme, defining strategy as 'the art of war'. Viewing strategy in such a way, the fundamental underlying premise of strategy becomes the notion that an adversary can be defeated (even a larger, more powerful one) if it can be outmanoeuvred using strategic skill.

Since the beginning of commercial transactions, businesses have had strategies determining their future courses of action. It is only since the 1960s, however, that the subject area has been widely considered as a topic of academic interest and hence widely taught in business schools and on business based courses. The subject is also widely taught as part of some tourism related courses and has received some attention in the tourism literature (see for example: Go and Pine, 1995; Hall, 2000; Holloway, 1998; Olsen *et al.*,1998; Phillips and Moutinho, 1998; Moutinho, 2000; Poon, 1993; Teare and Boer, 1991; Tribe, 1997).

As in the military arena so in business organisations attempt to outmanoeuvre their rivals. In so doing, strategies have to be developed that rely on various disciplines such as marketing, finance and human resource management.

It is evident then, that people use the word *strategy* in different ways. You may have heard people talk about a strategy for a business, a strategy for a football match, a strategy for a military campaign or a strategy for revising for a set of exams. It was this multiplicity of uses of the term that led Henry Mintzberg at the McGill University in Montreal (Mintzberg, 1987) to propose his 'five Ps' of strategy.

Mintzberg's 'five Ps'

Mintzberg suggested that nobody can claim to own the word 'strategy' and that the term can legitimately be used in several ways. A strategy, he suggested, can be:

- a plan;
- a ploy;

- a pattern of behaviour;
- a position in respect to others;
- a perspective.

It is important not to see each of these Ps in isolation from each other. One of the problems of dividing ideas into frameworks like the five Ps is that they are necessarily simplified. The five Ps are not mutually exclusive, *i.e.* it is possible for an organisation to show evidence of more than one interpretation of strategy.

Plan Strategies

A plan is probably the way in which most people use the word strategy. It tends to imply something that is intentionally put in train and its progress is monitored from the start to a predetermined finish. Some business strategies follow this model. 'Planners' tend to produce internal documents that detail what the company will do for a period of time in the future (say five years). It might include a statement on the overall direction that the organisation will take in seeking new business opportunities as well as a schedule for new product launches, acquisitions, financing (*i.e.* raising investment capital), human resource changes, etc.

A large tour operator, for instance, might decide that it plans to implement a strategy concerned with expanding its share of the market and that this will be achieved by setting prices at lower levels than competitors and by acquiring smaller firms. It might write its plans down in some detail and circulate them to all of its key managers so that, at any given point in time, the entire organisation can shown to be acting in accordance with the predetermined plan.

Ploy Strategies

A ploy is generally taken to mean a short-term strategy, and is concerned with the detailed tactical actions that will be taken. It tends to have very limited objectives and it may be subject to change at very short notice. Mintzberg describes a ploy as, 'a manoeuvre intended to outwit an opponent or competitor' (Mintzberg *et al.*,1998: 14) He pointed out that some companies may use ploy strategies as threats. They may threaten to, say, decrease the price of their products simply to destabilize competitors.

One example of a ploy strategy is that employed in a soccer match. If the opposing team has a particularly skilful player, then the team manager may use the ploy of assigning two players to mark him for the duration of the game. However, this tactic will only last for the one game—the next game will have a completely different strategy. Furthermore, the strategy will only operate only as long as the dangerous player is on the pitch. If he is substituted or gets injured, the strategy will change mid-game.

Thus the tour operator (introduced above) may have an overall planned strategy which includes offering lower price levels than competitors, but as a short term ploy, it might suddenly discount its prices within six weeks of departure in order to destabilize its competitors and to sell excess capacity.

Pattern Strategies

A 'pattern of behaviour' strategy is one in which progress is made by adopting a consistent form of behaviour. Unlike plans and ploys, patterns 'just happen' as a result of the consistent behaviour. On a simple level, a small specialist tour operator offering summer villa and apartment holidays to a particular Greek island to a small but loyal group of customers might be viewed as following a pattern strategy. The company is unlikely to produce elaborate plans—simply renewing contracts with property owners and transport providers annually. If offered a new villa on favourable terms, then the operator would probably contract the property and feature it in its brochure without thinking much about it. It is an opportunity that is taken, as it appears too good to miss. However, the operator would probably not feature a hotel in Majorca although it may be available to the company because that would be outside their pattern of business behaviour.

Such patterns of behaviour are sometimes unconscious, meaning that they do not even realise that they are actually following a consistent pattern. Nevertheless, if it proves successful, it is said that the consistent behaviour has *emerged* into a success. This is in direct contrast to planning behaviour.

Deliberate and Emergent Strategies

There is a key difference between two of Mintzberg's Ps of strategy—plan and pattern. The difference is to do with the *source* of the strategy. He drew attention to the fact that some strategies are deliberate whilst others are emergent. *Deliberate* strategy (sometimes called *planned* or *prescriptive* strategy) is meant to happen. It is preconceived, premeditated and usually monitored and controlled from start to finish. It has a specific objective.

Emergent strategy has no specific objective. It does not have a preconceived route to success BUT it may be just as effective as a deliberate strategy. By following a consistent pattern of behaviour, an organisation may arrive at the same position as if it had planned everything in detail.

Position Strategies

A position strategy is appropriate when the important thing to an organisation is how it relates, or is positioned with respect to, its competitors or its markets (*i.e.* its customers). In other words, the organisation wishes to achieve or defend a certain position. In business, companies tend to seek such things as market share, profitability, superior research, reputation, etc. It is plainly obvious that not all companies are equal when one considers such criteria. Some airlines, for instance, have enviable reputations for reliability and quality whilst others are not so fortunate. The competitors with a reputation to defend will use a position strategy to ensure that the reputation they enjoy is maintained and strengthened. This may even include marketing messages that point out the weaknesses in competitors' products whilst pointing out the features of their own.

Perspective Strategies

Perspective strategies are about changing the culture (the beliefs and the 'feel', the way of looking at the world) of a certain group of people—usually the members of the organisation itself. Some companies want to make their employees think in a certain way, believing this to be an important way of achieving success. They may, for example, try to get all employees to think and act courteously, professionally or helpfully.

The Elements of Strategy

Chandler's Definition

Given the foregoing definitions by Mintzberg, we might think that writers in business strategy are unable to agree on a single definition of the word strategy. This is partly true, but some have tried to sum it up succinctly to make it easier for students to understand. One such definition, still widely quoted, was offered by Professor Chandler of Harvard Business School in 1962. Given that Chandler predated Mintzberg, it is perhaps not surprising that it is rather more simplistic than Mintzberg might have accepted.

> Strategy is the *determination of the basic long-term goals* and objectives of an enterprise, and the adoption of *courses of action* and the *allocation of resources* necessary for carrying out these goals. (Chandler, 1962—emphasis added)

Three Components of Strategy

This is a useful definition because it shows the scope of what 'good' strategy is. The italics in this quote show the three important contents of strategy.

The *determination of the basic long-term goals* concerns the conceptualising of coherent and attainable strategic objectives. Without objectives, nothing else can happen. If you do not know where you want to go, how can you act in such a way as to get there?

The *adoption of courses of action* refers to the actions taken to arrive at the objectives that have been previously set. If, for example, your objective is arrive in London when travelling from Edinburgh there are various courses of action available to you. You might travel by train, by car, by coach or by plane. You might travel on certain days or at certain times of day. You might take advantage of certain concessionary fares, and you might make a booking through an intermediary such as a travel agent or book directly with the principal company (the airline or train company). Thus as a result of wanting to travel to London, a whole range of options need to be considered and detailed decisions have to be taken as to which options to select.

The *allocation of resources* refers to the fact that there is likely to be a cost associated with the actions required in order to achieve the objectives. If the course of action is not supported with adequate levels of resource, then the objective will not be accomplished.

Hence, strategy contains three things. In the example of travelling from Edinburgh to London:

1. Your *objective* is clearly stated as arriving in London at a certain date and time.

2. In order to achieve this objective certain *actions* are necessary. It is decided that flying is the best option. Thus a specified flight is booked through a travel agent, leave is taken from work and a plane is boarded at the airport.
3. However, the actions would not be possible if they could not be resourced. You need the *resources* of a plane with a suitably qualified pilot, an airport, money to pay for your flight and other such 'inputs'. If any one of these is missing, you will be unable to meet your objective.

Resources

Resource inputs (sometimes called *factors of production*) are those essential inputs that are essential to the normal functioning of the organisational process.

These are the inputs, without which an organisation simply could not continue to exist or meet its objectives. We can readily appreciate that human beings rely upon certain vital inputs such as air, water, nutrition, warmth, shelter, etc., but organisations have similar needs. An organisation's resource inputs fall into four key categories:

1. *financial resources*—money for capital investment and working capital. Sources include shareholders, banks, bondholders, etc.
2. *human resources*—appropriately skilled employees to add value in operations and to support those that add value (*e.g.* supporting employees in marketing, accounting, personnel, etc.). Sources include the labour markets for the appropriate skill levels required by the organisation.
3. *physical (tangible) and operational resources*—land, buildings (offices, warehouses, etc.), plant, equipment, stock for production, etc. Sources include estate agents, builders, trade suppliers, etc.
4. *intellectual (intangible) resources*—inputs that cannot be seen or felt but which are essential for continuing business success. *e.g.* 'know-how', legally defensible patents and licences, brand names, registered designs, logos, 'secret' formulations and recipes, business contact networks, database, etc.

Levels of Strategic Decisions

Different 'levels'

It is useful at this stage to understand what characte-rizes strategic decisions. Management decisions within any organisation can be classified in three broad (and sometimes overlapping) categories: strategic, tactical and operation. These can be illustrated as a hierarchy in which higher level decisions tend to shape those at subordinate levels. Strategic, tactical and operational decisions within an organisation differ from each other in items of:

- focus;
- the level in the organisation at which they are made;
- scope;
- time horizon;
- degree of certainty or uncertainty;
- complexity.

The Strategic Level

Strategic decisions are concerned with the acquisition of sustainable competitive advantage which involves the setting of long-term corporate objectives and the formulation, evaluation, selection and monitoring of strategies designed to achieve those objectives. Strategic decisions are made by senior managers (usually directors), they affect the whole organisation, are long-term in nature, are complex and are based upon uncertain information. Managers at the strategic level require multiconceptual skills—the ability to consider the effects of multiple internal and external influences on the business and the possible ways in which strategy, can be adjusted to account for such influences.

The decision early on in the company's history for easy jet to operate as a low cost, no frills airline is an example of a strategic decision. It was taken at the most senior level, it affected the whole competitive position of the business, it was long-term in nature and it affected all members of the business.

The Tactical Level

Tactical decisions are concerned with how corporate objectives are to be met and how strategies are implemented. They are dependent upon overall strategy and involve its fine-tuning and adjustment. They are made at head of business unit, department or functional area level and affect only parts of the organisation. They are medium-term in timescale, semi-complex and usually involve some uncertainty but not as much as at the strategic level.

The Operational Level

Operational decisions are concerned with the shorter-term objectives of the business and with its day to day management. They are dependent upon strategy and tactics. These decisions are made at junior managerial or supervisory level, are based on a high degree of certainty, and are not complex. The procedures in a sales office are typical operational activities—processing orders that have a tactical purpose in pursuit of the overall strategy.

Comparing strategic, tactical and operational decisions

	Strategic	**Tactical**	**Operational**
Focus of decision	Achieving sustainable competitive advantage	Implementation of strategy	Day-to-day operations
Level of decision making	Senior management, board of directors	Head of business unit or functional area	Supervisory
Scope	Whole organisation	Business unit or functional area (*e.g.* Marketing)	Department
Time horizon	Long-term (years)	Medium-term (months to years)	Short-term (days, weeks, month)
Certainty/ uncertainty	High uncertainty	Some uncertainty	High certainty
Complexity	Highly complex	Moderately complex	Comparatively simple
Examples	Decision to launch new product, enter new market, investment decision etc.	Decision to advertise, alter price etc.	Decision to re-order stock, scheduling of jobs

Congruency and 'Fit'

The success of strategy rests upon a very important, but rather obvious principle. Once the strategic level objectives have been set, the operational objectives must be set in such a way so that they contribute to the achievement of the tactical and strategic objectives. In other words, the operational decisions must 'fit' the higher levels of decision-making. This introduces the concept of *congruence.*

The decision-making framework can be visualised as a pyramid. The top, where the strategic decisions are made, is thin whilst the bottom (operational decisions) is fatter. This representation is meant to show that strategic decisions are taken infrequently whilst operational decisions are taken often. Strategic decisions are few and far between whilst operational decisions are taken weekly, daily or even hourly. For every one strategic decision, there may be hundreds of individual operational decisions. Tactical decisions are between the two.

Time and Planning Horizons

One of the key differences between the three levels of decision-making in organisations is the timescale with which they are concerned. It is usually considered that the higher up the organisation, the longer the timescale with which management is concerned. Certainly this is true in most manufacturing companies, but in service companies where service delivery is of prime importance relatively senior staff can often be involved in operational decision making.

On an airline flight, for example, the flight crew, including the captain, are typically concerned with ensuring that the daily schedule runs safely and to time, whilst the chief executive may be worrying about potential threats that are some years away. Meanwhile, middle managers, say those in charge of graduate recruitment or the preparation of financial statements, will be planning a few months in advance—possibly as far as one year ahead.

Strategic management involves taking account of a large number of environmental variables. The longer ahead that a manager seeks to plan for, then the more uncertainty is introduced into the analysis.

Mission and Mission Statements

An organisation's *mission* can be described as its overarching *raison d'etre.* It is the objective that subsumes all others beneath it.

For some organisations, the mission is very easy to articulate but for large commercial businesses, it tends to be more complex.

The Purposes of a Mission Statement

Some organisations attempt to frame their mission in a formal statement, which is often to be seen adorning office walls, printed on employee identity cards and published in annual reports. Mission statements are commonly found both in the commercial sector and in the non-commercial (*not for profit*) sector. Such a statement has a number of possible purposes. It can be used to clearly communicate the objectives and values of the organisation to the various stakeholder groups and it can be argued that it assists in promoting hierarchical congruence. It may also have an effect in influencing the behaviour and attitudes of employees, although this is somewhat debatable as anecdotal evidence suggests that many employees have not in fact read their organisation's mission statement.

A mission statement can be seen as the starting point for an organisation's entire planning process since it requires senior management to sit down and seriously consider where the firm is and where it should be in the future. This point was emphasized by two leading management writers, when they stated that, 'in business like in art, what distinguishes leaders from laggards, and greatness from mediocrity, is the ability to uniquely imagine what could be' (Hamel and Prahalad, 1994: 25).

However, establishing an organisation's mission is not easy or without controversy, and as a result styles and content vary enormously. Drucker (1974: 94) pointed out that: defining the purpose and mission of the business is difficult, painful and riskiy. But it alone enables a business to set objectives, to develop strategies, to concentrate its resources and to go to work. It alone enables a business to be managed for performance.

Campbell and Yeung (1998) emphasized that whilst the mission statement itself is clearly important, it is also important for managers to instil a 'sense of mission' in employees. The success of the mission requires the behaviour of employees to match the values of the company, but such harmony is difficult to achieve and requires the mission as it is implemented to become embedded as part of the organisational culture.

Effective Mission Statements

- **Clearly articulated.** The mission statement should be simple to comprehend so that employees and other stakeholders can clearly understand the principles and values that will guide them in their dealings with the organisation. The statement must be specific enough to have an impact upon the behaviour of individuals.
- **Relevant.** The mission statement should be appropriate to the organisation in terms of its history, culture and shared values. The mission should not be too broad or too narrow. Too broad may result in lack of focus. Too narrow may mean factors that are potentially important to the organisation will be overlooked.
- **Current.** An unchanged mission statement may no longer be able to act as a driving force guiding the organisation into the future.
- **Positive tone.** The mission statement should be written in such a way that encourages commitment and energizes or inspires employees.
- **Individuality.** The mission statement should set it apart from other organisations establishing its individuality it not its uniqueness through an emphasis on the advantages of the organisation based on an objective assessment of organisational strengths and weaknesses.
- **Enduring.** The mission statement cannot be continually altered, as this would be confusing, so they are likely to remain in place for a number of years. Consequently they must be written to allow for some flexibility.
- **Adapted.** Mission statements are written with various target audiences in mind, some for emplo-yees only, some for shareholders and other external groups, and others for all audiences. The information and style should reflect the relevant target audience.

What Does a Mission Statement Contain?

The style, content and terminology of mission statements vary enormously. Some are long and detailed whereas others are short and to the point. Some are focused on a particular audience (such as employees or customers) others are written with multiple target audiences in mind. There are probably no 'rights' or 'wrongs' of how it should be presented or what it should contain it all depends upon the organization and its culture.

In assessing mission statements the reader will find many examples of the use of language that is ambiguous in its meaning or is questionable in its use of 'hype' to inflate the image of the organization. In practice, mission statements usually contain one or more of the following:

- Some *indication of the industry* or business the organization is mainly concerned with.
- An indication of the *realistic market share* or market position the organisation should aim towards.
- A brief summary of the *values and beliefs* of the organisation in relating to key stakeholder groups such as customers and employees.
- An indication of the *ownership* or control of the organisation.
- A summary of the *geographical location* or scope of organisational activities.
- Specific and *highly context-dependent objectives* are sometimes expressed in the mission statement.

A selection of mission statements taken from a range of tourism organisations in various sectors of the industry is presented below.

British Airways

British Airways introduced a new mission statement after a consultation process involving employees in 1997. The mission statement replaced an existing statement which had been drawn up in 1995 in the run-up to privatisation, and many employees have received training in its meaning for their particular jobs. In introducing its new mission British Airways cited four vital challenges for change facing the company:

- What customers are asking for?
- What people want?

- The global economic climate.
- The challenge of competition.

'Whatever it is called, a vision, mission or strategic intent, its purpose is to provide a guiding light for the future. Companies without a mission are prone to opportunism, incrementalism, to constant changes of direction, to being driven by short-term budgetary pressures and to corporate confusion.

A unifying mission is especially important in large companies where staff and managers are expected to take decisions themselves, without constant referral back to headquarters or to their seniors. If everyone understands where the company is aiming, then independent decisions are more likely to be aligned with each other and with the companies' ultimate objective.

A mission also helps an organisation set stretching goals and then drive its short-term plans and budgetary trade-offs to achieve the long-term aim.'

British Airways Mission Statement Post 1997

Our Mission

'To be the undisputed leader in world travel'.

We are passionately committed to excellence and to the highest levels of customer service.

Our Goals

Customers' Choice—Airline of first choice in our key markets.

Strong Profitability—Meeting investors' expectations and securing the future.

Truly Global—Global network, global Outlook: recognised everywhere for superior value in world travel.

Inspired People—Inspired teams of people, building and benefiting from the company's success.

Our Values

Safe and Secure

Honest and Responsible

Innovative and Team-spirited

Global and Caring

A Good Neighbour

British Airways Mission Statement Pre 1997

Our Mission

'To be the best and most successful company in the airline business'.

Our Goals

Safe and Secure—To be a safe and secure airline.

Financially strong—To deliver strong and consistent financial performance.

Global leader—To secure a leading share of air travel business world-wide with a significant presence in all major geographical markets.

Service and Value—To provide overall superior service and good value for money in every market segment in which we compete.

Customer driven—To excel in anticipating and quickly responding to customer needs and competitor activity.

Good employer—To sustain a working environment that attracts, retains and develops committed employees who share in the success of the company.

Good neighbour—To be a good neighbour, concerned for the community and the environment.

Four Key Objectives

To be genuinely the world's favourite airline.

To be pre-eminent in customer service.

To be truly global.

To be the UK's best managed company by the year 2000.

Southwest Airlines

The mission of Southwest Airlines is dedication to the highest quality of customer service delivered with a sense of warmth, friendliness, individual pride and company spirit.

To Our Employees

We are committed to provide our Employees a stable work environment with equal opportunity for learning and personal growth. Creativity and innovation are encouraged for improving the effectiveness of Southwest Airlines. Above all, Employees will be provided the same concern, respect and caring attitude within the organisation that they are executed to share externally with every Southwest Customer.

Maldives Tourism Promotion Board

Vision

- Be the most exclusive destination in South Asia.
- Be the top tourism earner in South Asia.
- Be an example of sustainable tourism development in small island nations.

Mission

The Maldives Tourism Promotion Board will promote quality and sustainable growth in the tourism industry of the Maldives to foster a well utilised and financially healthy private sector industry—in this way enabling the industry to deliver long-term economic, social and cultural benefits to the people of the Maldives, whilst at the same time contributing to enhancements to the Maldives' unspoiled marine environment to the benefit of the people and visitors of the Maldives.

Objectives

- To strengthen and enhance the exclusive image of the destination in the source markets.
- To position the Maldives as the 'premium' destination world-wide.
- To achieve growth targets set for the destination in the Marketing Plan for each year.
- To diversify the source markets as well as the market segments to the destination.
- To undertake market research to monitor the world economic conditions and travel trends in order to identify market opportunities.
- To monitor and support the private sector in their operations to maintain viable bed occupancy levels and to iron out seasonal fluctuations in visitor arrivals.

Holidaybreak plc

Holidaybreak is the UK's leading operator of specialist holiday businesses. Group companies retain a distinctive identity whilst sharing expertise and exploiting opportunities in areas of common interest.

Our aim is to achieve continuing profitable growth by developing our existing businesses and market leading brands in the UK and European holiday markets and through acquisitions in the travel sector.

Certain core values will be common to all:

- High levels of customer service.
- Excellent value for money for all customers.
- An open and cooperative working environment where individual initiative and responsibility are encouraged.
- A commitment to the welfare and development of all employees.
- The maintenance of good supplier relations.
- Continuous improvement in everything we do.

How Do Businesses Set Objectives?

Earlier in this chapter, we introduced the idea that strategic objectives, since they represent the most important level of decision-making, are set by an organisation's senior management, usually the board of directors. In setting objectives, however, senior managers are likely to be influenced by a range of different groups, which have an interest in the organisation. *Who or what influences the senior management in their objective-setting?* This question cuts to the heart of an important debate that is taking place both in universities and in business circles. This debate revolves around two differing approaches towards objective-setting: the stockholder and stakeholder approaches.

The Stockholder Approach

The stockholder approach argues that businesses exist primarily for their owners (usually shareholders). Accordingly, any business behaviour that renders profit performance sub-optimal is not only theft from shareholders but will also, eventually, lead to a level of business performance that will harm all other groups such as employees, customers and suppliers.

In 1970, the Nobel Laureate Professor Milton Friedman contended that 'the moral obligation of business is to increase its profits'. Friedman argued that the one and only obligation of company directors (which are the legal agents of shareholders' financial interests) is to act in such a way as to maximize the financial rate of return on the owners' shares. The capitalist system upon which the Western economies rests in large part upon the presupposition that investments made in shares (*e.g.* in pension funds, unit trusts, etc.) will perform well. The profitable performance of shares lies in an increase in the share's value and in the rate of dividend per share—objectives that can only be served by financial profits.

The Stakeholder Approach

A stakeholder can be defined as: *Any group or individual who can affect or is affected by the achievement of an organisation's objectives.* (Freeman, 1984: 46)

This definition draws in almost everybody that is, or may be potentially involved in the life of an organisation. It consequently goes without saying that not all stakeholders are equal in their influence on an organisation's objectives.

The stakeholder approach (as advocated by Freeman, 1984; Donaldson and Preston, 1995 and Campbell, 1997a), argues that organisations, like individual people, are characterised by their relationships with various groups and individuals such as employees and customers. A group or individual qualifies as a stakeholder if it/he/she has a legitimate interest in the organisation's activities and thus has the power to affect the firm's performance and/or has a stake in the firm's performance.

The implications of this proposition are far-reaching. In essence, stakeholder theory argues that shareholders are neither the sole owners of a business nor the sole beneficiaries of its activities. Whilst shareholders are undeniably one stakeholder group, they are far from being the only group who expect to benefit from business activity and, accordingly, are just one of those groups who have a legitimate right to influence a company's strategic objectives. Some of these groups are internal to the organisation whilst others are external. Stakeholder groups, which might be able to exert an influence over the setting of objectives, are shown in Table.

Examples of internal and external stakeholders

Internal stakeholders	External stakeholders
Board of directors	Shareholders
Employees collectively	Creditors (existing and potential)
Individual employees (*e.g.* founding entrepreneur)	Suppliers (existing and potential)
Employees' representatives (trade unions, trade associations etc.)	Customers (existing and potential)
Functional business areas (marketing, finance etc.)	Trade bodies (*e.g.* ABTA)
Geographical areas of the organisation (*e.g.* Europe, Asia etc.)	Pressure groups (*e.g.* environmental)
	Competitors (current and future, national and international)
	Government (legal, fiscal and regulatory impacts)
	Private individuals
	International regulatory bodies (*e.g.* IATA)
	The local community

Stakeholders and Objectives

One widely used and useful model for understanding how stakeholders exert influence on an organisation's objectives was proposed by Mendelow (1991). According to this model, stakeholders can be 'ranked' depending upon two variables: *interest* and *power:*

- stakeholder *power* refers to the *ability* to influence the organisation;
- stakeholder *interest* refers to the *willingness* to influence the organisation.

In other words, interest concerns the extent to which the stakeholder cares about what the organisation does.

It then follows that:

Stakeholder influence = power × interest

The actual influence that a stakeholder has will depend upon where the stakeholder is positioned with respect to ability to influence and willingness to influence. A stakeholder with both high power and high interest will be more influential than one with low power and low interest. We can map stakeholders by showing the two variables on a grid comprising two intersecting.

Once constructed, we can use the map to assess two things:

1. which stakeholder is likely to exert the most influence upon the organisation's objectives, and;
2. the stakeholders that are most likely to be in potential conflict over strategic objectives (where two or more stakeholders are in close proximity in the high power—high interest part of the map).

The managing director and the board of directors are examples of stakeholders with both high power and high interest. This is because they manage the business, depend upon it for their jobs and their positions within the organisation give them power with which to implement their decisions. The local community (in most cases) will not concern itself with the setting of organisational objectives and have limited power to impose their views.

The Content of Corporate Objectives

The Importance of Objectives

In strict terms, the most important of all objectives is simply to survive as a going concern. Other objectives depend upon the type of organisation and the nature of its environment. Objectives are not necessarily mutually exclusive in that an organisation can usually pursue more than one type of objective at the same time. Juach and Glueck (1988) defined an objective as 'the end the firm seeks and the criteria the firm uses to determine its effectiveness'. The objectives can be written in a *closed* manner in that they are stated in quantitative terms and are specific in relation to form and timescale, or an *open* manner in that they are stated in qualitative terms and are general in form and timescale.

Objectives are essential to the successful accomplish-ment of the managerial function in any formal organisation in that they:

- provide a sense of direction;
- provide a standard of measurement and a means of controlling performance;
- project an image of the organisation's style.

Corporate Objectives

Corporate objectives translate the mission into specific long-term targets that can usually be quantified and measured.

Corporate objectives are strategic level objectives that can be used as a starting point in the setting business (or tactical) and operational objectives which are more detailed objectives set lower down the organisational hierarchy (see the foregoing discussion). The business objectives will usually relate to important constituent parts of the overall organisation— often termed strategic business units (SBUs), whilst the operational objectives will usually relate to smaller units or teams within each SBU.

Corporate objectives normally:

- relate to the whole organisation;
- apply to the medium to long term;
- are set by senior management;
- relate to a number of key areas of concern;
- can be pursued simultaneously.

Care must be taken in writing corporate objectives so that they are clear and easily understood. A common view is that objective writing is a *'CRIME'* in that corporate objectives should be:

- *Communicable*—capable of being easily communicated down the line to the workforce and other internal and external stakeholder groups.
- *Realistic*—capable of being achieved within the timescale.
- *Internally consistent*—consistent with the overall organisational mission, the operational objectives and the strategy for achieving the objectives set.

- *Measurable*—capable of being quantified so that they can be measured and it is possible to assess whether the objectives have been achieved.
- *Explicit*—written in clear unambiguous language, precise in relation to both targets set and to timescale.

Corporate objectives often relate to economic and social concerns and to matters of growth and competitive advantage which will now be considered.

Economic Objectives

Economic objectives are those that can be measured in financial ways. For commercial organisations, objectives will usually include measures such as *return.* Return is an accounting term to describe the proportion of either sales or investment capital that is left over as profit. In commercial organisations the economic objective is often referred to as the *primary objective,* with other objectives being *secondary* to the achievement of the financial objectives.

Return on sales, sometimes referred to as profit margin, is an indication of how well the company has controlled its costs whilst *return on assets* (or *return on capital employed*) is an indication of how efficiently the company has used its investors' money. Both of these are important business objectives—to provide sufficient return to retain some profits for future investment and to provide investors with a dividend on their shareholding.

Not-for-profit organisations also have economic objectives but they are measured in different ways. Organisations like destination marketing offices, charities and government departments tend to measure economic performance by using cost—benefit or value-for-money objectives. These organisations usually rely in large part on income over which they have little control—it may, for example, be fixed by central or local government. The objectives set will typically involve extracting the maximum benefit in terms of outputs from the income they have.

A destination marketing office for a country, a city or a resort for example, will have a certain income which it uses as carefully as possible to ensure it can deliver as many tourists of required type as possible to the destination within its allocated budget.

Social Objectives

We should not assume that all organisational objectives are financial in nature. Many exist, either in part or totally, to deliver social benefits. Many publicly funded organisations such as museums, art galleries, heritage attractions and so on exist to deliver services to society in general. Charities exist primarily to provide social benefit to one or more allegedly worthwhile constituencies. For organisations of this type, economic objectives may be secondary to their desire to deliver socially desirable ends.

Commercial organisations are also gradually adopting social objectives in their strategic planning. Although they are usually subordinate to their economic objectives, commercial organisations may espouse social or environmental causes that they purport to believe in. They may, for example, recognise the social value of supporting local community projects or seconding (at their own expense) some of their people to serve with charities.

Growth or Market Share Objectives

At some stages in the life of an organisation, objectives concerning growth and expansion become among the most important. This is especially true of businesses who must grow and maintain market position in order to 'keep up with' or 'keep ahead of' competitors.

Size and market position offer a number of advantages and it is these that an organisation seeks when growth is a key objective. Size gives an organisation economy of scale advantages in both product and resource markets. It means that a larger organisation attracts resource inputs at preferential unit cost compared to smaller concerns and its larger presence in its product markets increases its pricing power and its ability to subjugate competitors.

Competitive Advantage Objectives

Finally, and importantly, many strategic objectives concern the company's position in respect to its competitors. Competitive advantage objectives concern how the company's position compares to others—especially to competitors. The objectives are limited to ensuring simply that 'we beat you', or 'we are better than you'. Superior performance is the only objective and if a company can achieve ascendancy over its nearest competitors, then the objective will have been accomplished.

Objectives in British Airways

An illustration of the cascading of objectives is provided by British Airways.

The mission sets the long-term direction, which is used to identify the strategic goals needed to achieve the mission. The mission and strategic goals provide a planning horizon of 10 years between 1997 and 2007. The combined mission and corporate goals is provide the parameters and relevance for 3-year business plans for each of the key areas of business (the SBUs), which in turn are used to set each year's budget for each department. The business plan and budget determine the actions required by each department which in turn determine individuals' work programmes. Relevant key performance indicators (KPI) are set for each individual employee.

2

The Front Office Organisation

Introduction

The ability to make sense of an organisation's financial situation is an important part of strategic analysis. In order to carry out a financial analysis of a company's situation or of an industry, it is necessary to understand some of the fundamentals of finance and its sources. This chapter begins with a discussion of the sources of corporate finance and then goes on to discuss the costs of the various types of capital. This information helps students to make sense of a company's financial structure before the tools of conventional financial analysis are discussed. The various 'tools' for financial analysis are introduced and, finally, the concept of bench-making is explained and its use in analysis is discussed.

Learning Objectives

After studying this chapter, students should be able to:

- understand what is meant by financial analysis;
- identify the sources of funds available to companies and the relative advantages and disadvantages of each;
- assess a company's potential for further funding based on current position, future prospects and past performance;
- explain the cost and non-cost issues involved in raising and using various forms of capital;
- understand the importance of the cost of capital;

- describe the limitations of a company report and accounts as a source of data for financial analysis;
- describe the major tools that can be used to analyse a company's financial position;
- explain the nature and analysis of foreign exchange risks in travel and tourism;
- understand the nature and analysis of cash flow risks in travel and tourism.

An Introduction to Financial Analysis

The Importance of Finance

Although the travel and tourism industry covers a diversity of different organisations, including tour operators, airlines hotels and travel agencies, financial management is important to all of them.

Financial management is that part of the total management function concerned with the effective and efficient raising and use of funds. Finance, like a physical resource, has a large number of competing uses; is scarce but can be obtained at a price; and is bought and sold in markets. Financial management is concerned with managing this scarce resource so as to ensure that:

- sufficient *finance* is available at the right time;
- *finance* is obtained at the least possible cost;
- *finance* is used in the most profitable ways.

Most university business courses have an accounting and finance content. You may consequently be familiar with some of the content of this chapter and this will be to your advantage. This chapter develops the material into the context of strategic analysis.

Money, or the lack of it, is central to the strategic development of all organisations, large or small. It is one of the key resource inputs and cannot be ignored. The most original strategies and the most complex plans for the future of a business are meaningless unless management has considered the financial position of the organisation at the outset and during the period covered by the strategy. The ability of a company to finance both current and future strategies is central to any analysis of the company's position. A central theme to this chapter will be the ability of the company to finance current strategies—its ability to raise the funding required for future developments.

The success or failure of the organisation is judged by its ability to meet its strategic objectives. The financial information (in the form of annual corporate reports) produced by companies provides a quantifiable means of assessing success. It is important to recognise, however, that other quantifiable information, such as efficiency and productivity data, and non-quantifiable data such as the company's image, can also be used to make such judgements. In this chapter we will examine the value of information extracted from corporate reports as a source from which judgements can be made.

Corporate reports are, however, just one source of information about a company's financial state. Managers have a number of ways of gathering information about their own and competitors' finances and we will discuss these later in the chapter. The case of the UK tour operator International Leisure Group (ILG) illustrates the pitfalls that overcome an organisation when management makes strategic errors in the financial management of a company.

International Leisure Group (ILG)

Flying too close to the sun—anatomy of a corporate collapse

The ILG group of companies, like Icarus from Greek mythology, flew too close to the sun, got burnt and fell to earth. We can focus on four aspects of ILG and its demise.

The Company

ILG was formed in the early 1970s by the extrovert, publicity seeking Harry Goodman. It traded under various brand names, including Intasun, Club 18-30, Lancaster tour operators and the airline Air Europe. The company grew rapidly throughout the 1970s and 1980s, spurred on by Britain's apparently insatiable appetite for package holidays, the number of which trebled during the 1980s. The company was also helped by the collapse of Clarkson's, the UK's second largest tour operator, in 1974 and Laker Airways eight years after, both of which 'Harry' took full advantage of.

The growth in company sales (which in its last published figures for 1989 had a turnover of approximately £722 million) was not matched by a corresponding growth in profits and its gearing levels were extremely high.

After a relatively brief life as quoted company, the management team led by Harry Goodman took the company 'private' in the spring of 1987. The stock market, it was said, took too short term a view of the company. A Swiss financier took a 49% holding in the company, which was reduced to 29.5% in 1990.

The Strategy

ILG's financial strategy was simple. It used cash generated from its travel and charter airline businesses to finance the development of a new scheduled airline. The tour operations certainly worked on very tight margins (thanks in part to the price war Goodman himself had started in 1985), but tour operations also produced a good cash flow. Advance payments from customers (which usually stood at about £50 million) provided a source of interest-free funding.

The company was to have been a pan-European airline based on modern fuel efficient aircraft and taking advantage of European airline deregulation in the 1990s. Cash was also provided by the group's third, less visible business, trading in aircraft. By placing orders for new aircraft several years ahead, the company was at the head of the queue in the mid 1980s when aircraft demand was high. Consequently the company could sell aircraft at a profit. This source provided a third of operating profits in 1989.

The Faults

Although tour operations provided a good cash flow, it was, nevertheless, fundamentally a high volume, low margin business trying to finance a highly volatile airline development. The costs of developing the airline were considerable and were much higher than had been planned.

To develop the airline, the company negotiated inventive leasing arrangements with a handful of banking syndicates, the largest led by Citibank accounting for 10 of the company's 37 aircraft.

The first apparent weakness, then, was that in return for narrow lending margins, the banks insisted on onerous covenants (financial restrictions) and these were to prove crucial later. A second apparent weakness was an over-commitment by Lloyds Bank. Lloyds began with a £30 million working capital facility but eventually had up to £90 million at risk. A third financial weakness existed in the financial team. Goodman was highly autocratic, but his flair was largely marketing based rather than financial. Beneath him the company appeared to lack an obvious financial strategist. A fourth financial weakness was that the management was also firmly entrenched. They had only 15% of the equity but 100% of ordinary voting shares (Goodman with 53%), giving them a blocking vote.

The Collapse

By spring 1990 Goodman had already decided that the company should be sold. Some approaches were made but nothing materialised. At the end of October 1990 ILG breached the strict covenants agreed in spite of a £22 million injection of funds by the Swiss investors. The banks gave three months for the company to sort out the problems.

However, bookings in the crucial pre-Christmas period were poor with the onset of recession (down an estimated 20% on the already poor level of 1989). The Gulf War in the New Year was disastrous for package bookings, which were down 40% on a year earlier and scheduled services were operating at 35% capacity.

The writing seemed to be on the wall, but a last minute deal was agreed at the end of January with £40 million of cash from the Swiss and Lloyds converting £50 million of debt into equity. By mid February it was clear that this would not be enough. The Swiss investors were themselves in trouble. Lloyds then agreed to an additional £20 million with a further £20 million from a German investor. In early March the German investor pulled out and a syndicate of banks led by Citibank took steps to have 10 of Air Europe's aircraft 'arrested'. The following day the company was placed in administration.

The company, bought out largely with funds provided by the banks, found in the end that the banks would not support it, was ILG's flawed financial structure that was its real undoing.

Understanding Financial Structure

At the outset it is necessary to have an understanding of a business's financial structure. A company's annual accounts will contain two key statements: the balance sheet and the statement of profit and loss. We will examine each briefly.

Understanding the Balance Sheet

Assets are financed (and matched in the balance sheet) by capital and liabilities. Liabilities may be current (less than one year) or long term (over one year).

Capital + Liabilities = Assets

The principles underpinning a balance sheet.

The assets of the business are 'funded' by long-term funds (capital), comprising such items as long-term loans, share capital and reserves. Current liabilities comprise items such as overdrafts and trade creditors.

A proportion of the short-term assets are funded by long-term funding, which, unlike short-term funding (current liabilities), is difficult to take away at short notice and consequently represents a more stable form of financing. Overdrafts, for example, can be quickly recalled by banks if they choose to do so.

Long-term (or fixed) assets such as property, land, vehicles and aircraft are financed entirely by more stable financing sources, *i.e.* long-term funding.

Understanding the Profit and Loss Account

A profit and loss (P&L) account matches the revenue earned in a period with the costs incurred in earning it. A skeleton profit and loss account is shown below:

Sales or income received

Less	Cost of sales
Equals	Gross profit
Less	Expenses (such as personnel costs, head office costs, administration and distribution)
Equals	Profit before interest and tax (also called operating, trading or 'net' profit)

Less Interest and tax

Equals Profit after interest and tax (also called earnings)

Less Dividends to shareholders

Equals Retained profit (which is transferred to the balance sheet).

Sources of Corporate Funding

Financial resources, as we have already learned, are an essential input to strategic development. Capital for development can be raised from several sources and these are summarised here.

Key cConcept: Capital

Accountants use the term capital to describe one particular type of 'money'. It is usually contrasted with revenue. *Revenue* is money that is earned through normal business transactions—through sales, rents or whatever the company 'does' through its normal activities. *Capital* is money that is used to invest in the business—to buy new equipment, new capacity, extra aircraft, etc. The investment of capital enables the business to expand and, through that expansion, to increase its revenue and profits in future years. Capital can be raised from shareholders, through retained profits, through rights issues, through loan capital or through the disposal of assets.

Share Capital

For limited companies, a sizeable proportion of capital is raised from shareholders (the financial owners of the company) in the form of share capital.

Historically, share capital has comprised the majority of capital for a limited company's start-up and subsequent development. In return for their investment, shareholders receive a return in accordance with the company's performance in a given year in the form of a dividend. The dividend per share is taken as an important measure by shareholders of the company's success in its chosen strategy. Shares also confer on their holders a right to vote on company resolutions at annual or extraordinary company meetings *pro rata* with the proportion of their holding. It follows of course that a shareholding in excess of 50% confers total control over a company's strategy.

Under normal circumstances, share capital is considered to be permanent—it is not paid back by the company. It is thus unlike other forms of capital (*e.g.* loan capital). The shareholders' only 'payback' is in the form of dividends and through capital growth—an increase in the value of the shares. Shareholders who wish to divest their stock (*i.e.* shareholding) in a company must usually sell it *via* a stock exchange (in the case of shares in a public limited company) or through a private sale (in the case of a private company). In exceptional circumstances, some companies offer a 'buyback' of their own shares.

Shareholders can be individuals or 'institutional shareholders'. Some individuals hold their personal share portfolio but the vast majority of shares are held by institutional shareholders such as pension funds, life assurance companies and investment trusts. The profile of shareholders varies from company to company and from country to country.

Concepts : Share Value and Share Volume

Share value is the price of a given company's shares at a given point in time. Like any other commodity, its value is determined by the forces of supply and demand. Given that in normal circumstances the supply is fixed over the short to medium term, price is determined by how many people want to buy it. If the market has confidence in a company's prospects, demand for the share will rise and so, accordingly, will its price. If a company's prospects are considered poor, investors will sell the share, fewer will want to buy it and the price will fall.

Share volume is the number of shares issued by a company in total. This is usually determined at the foundation or flotation of a company although rights issues and similar events can increase the share volume. It is generally true that larger companies have higher share volumes than smaller concerns.

Rights Issue Capital

From time to time, a company may seek to increase its capital for expansion by means of a *rights issue.* This is when a company issues new shares to the stock market, normally giving its own shareholders the first refusal *pro rata* with their current proportion of the company's share volume.

The decision to go for a rights issue may well be a strategic decision for management because it can impact on the ownership of the company. If existing shareholders do not exercise their right to buy, then it is likely that ownership will be diluted, *i.e.* shareholders will find that they own a lower percentage of share volume than they used to.

Those shares not taken up by shareholders, who may be unable or unwilling to buy them, are normally covered by *underwriters* (institutional investors) at a price agreed, in advance. Underwriting is an important technical feature of new share issues and as such is a major cost in the process. A rights issue is sometimes seen as a reward to loyal shareholders. A variation on a rights issue is *placing.* A placing involves the selling of shares direct to a small number of investors, usually large financial institutions. This may be marginally cheaper than a rights issue, but its major advantage is its flexibility in enabling new shareholders to have significant and possibly strategic holdings. Placings take place, for example, as a part of a joint venture agreement whereby the two companies exchange placed shareholdings as a sign of their mutual commitment to the alliance.

Retained Profit as a Source of Capital

Shareholders provide other funds for development by agreeing *not* to receive all the company's profits in a given year. *Retained profit,* that element of operating profit not paid to shareholders in the form of dividend, is the most common method of funding strategic developments, particularly if the company is quite old in terms of years. By using this form of funding, organisations save on the costs involved in using alternatives such as fees to merchant banks, lawyers and accountants. It also means management do not have to reveal nor justify their strategies to others and risk their plans becoming known to competitors.

It should be recognised that retained profits do not constitute a loss to shareholders as such, because the value of the organisation and consequently the share price is normally increased when these funds are used for reinvestment. It is, however, important that companies recognise the need to balance the proportion of profits distributed and retained in order to satisfy those shareholders who need regular funds flow themselves (such as insurance and pension companies).

Loan Capital

An important consideration in the use of retained profits to find corporate development is clearly the ability of the company actually to make a profit than can be, at least in part, distributed to shareholders as dividends. Whilst a company may make a profit from its normal activities after taxation, some profits may be required to meet the cost of other forms of debt finance or loans.

Debt finance is shown in the balance sheet under two headings, *Creditors: amounts following within one year* and *Creditors: amounts falling due after more than one year.* The form of borrowing with most impact on strategic development is that falling due after more than one year—long-term debt. This type of borrowing can take a number of forms. In addition to the use of long-term bank loans, a company can use debentures, convertible loan stock or corporate bonds.

Debt finance is normally for a set period of time and at a fixed rate of interest. The interest must be paid every year, regardless of the level of profit (referred to as *servicing* the debt). The interest rate for this source is normally less than the cost of share capital (when the dividend payable on the shares is taken into account).

Comparing Share Capital and Loan Capital

Each of the types of capital described above has its *pros and cons*. Share capital has the advantage that the amount paid on the capital is dependent upon company results. A company can decide not to pay a dividend if profits are poor in any given year. Loan capital, by contrast, must be serviced regardless of results in much the same way that a mortgage on a house must be repaid regardless of other commitments.

Offsetting this advantage is the fact that share capital is permanent. As long as the company exists, it has an obligation to repay a dividend to its shareholders. Loan capital has the advantage to the company that it is time-limited. Servicing the capital is restricted to the term of the loan (like a mortgage on a house) and when it is finally repaid in full, the business has no further obligation to the lender.

The fact that the repayment of debt finance takes precedence over dividends on shares means that shareholders bear an increased risk. If the company performs badly, their return on investment will be small or non-existent in a given year. Against this possibility, they usually expect to receive higher returns compared to providers of loan capital in the years when profits are good.

The major advantages and disadvantages of share and loan capital are set out in Table 6.1.

Table 6.1—Summary of the major advantages and disadvantages of share and loan capital

	Advantages	**Disadvantages**
Share capital	No fixed charge or legal obligation to pay a dividend No maturity date Issue of equity increases credit worthiness Marketable, *i.e.* can be traded	Extension of voting rights High issue costs May increase average cost of capital Dividends not tax deductible
Loan capital	Known and often lower cost No dilution of equity Interest payable is tax deductible	Increase in risk which may cause value of equity to fall Need for repayment Limit to amount of available funding

In practice, business profits can vary significantly over time. In some years, it is preferable to use loan capital, especially when interest rates are low and profits are high. In other years, when profits are lower and interest rates are higher, share capital works out cheaper. The fact that the benefits are so finely divided means that most companies opt to use an element of both. The relationship of debt capital to shareholder capital is referred to as the company's *gearing ratio.*

Gearing is an indication of how the company has arranged its capital structure. It can be expressed as either: Borrowed capital (*i.e.* debt)

Total capital employed (*i.e.* borrowings plus shareholders' capital)

or, as

Borrowed capital (*i.e.* debt)

Shareholders' capital (*i.e.* equity)

Both are usually expressed as percentages by simply multiplying the quotient by 100. It is not important which one is used unless we are comparing the gearing of two or more companies.

Other Sources of Capital

Whilst the foregoing are the most common mechanisms of raising capital for development, others are available under some circumstances. One such method is to dispose of existing fixed assets. This can range from selling of an aircraft to selling a subsidiary to a third party.

Finally, marginal improvements in a company's capital situation can be achieved by improving the management of working capital. Over the course of a financial year, small savings can accumulate to significant proportions, increasing both profitability and capital for reinvestment. This can be achieved by:

- extending the time taken to pay creditors;
- getting debtors to pay sooner; or,
- spreading payments through leasing rather than purchasing assets.

Working capital is the amount of money that a company has tied up in the normal operation of its business. Working capital comprises money tied up in:

- stocks;
- debtors (money owed to the business);
- creditors (money the company owes);
- cash or current bank deposits.

A company's objective is usually to minimize this figure, or to manage the working capital in such a way that minimizes financing costs or maximizes earnings on cash balances. This is an important source of earnings for many travel and tourism companies.

Working capital is needed to pay for goods, services and expenses before money can be recovered from creditors. The ability of a business to pay its cash commitments as they fall due shows that it has sufficient *liquidity.*

Inefficient management of working capital can lead to over-investment in working capital—*over-capitalisation.* Conversely *under-capitalisation,* also known as overtrading, often occurs when a company tries to do too much, too soon with too little long-term capital. A company can be trading profitably but run out of cash to make payments, *i.e.* it can become *insolvent.* Warning signs of overtrading include: a rapid increase in sales, a rapid increase in current assets, small increase in share capital, a deterioration in liquidity ratios such as the acid test ratio which measures the proportion of current assets less stocks to current liabilities.

Cost of Capital

Availability of capital (where to get it from) is one issue when examining a company's capital funding, but another equally important consideration is its cost. We learned above that providers of loans or share capital (equity) both require a return on their investments. Management therefore need to know what return (profit) they need to make in order to meet the minimum requirements of capital providers. Failure to achieve this minimum will make the raising of future funds all the more difficult. The cost of capital can be seen as the minimum return required on the company's assets, which in turn may influence the objectives of the company.

At its simplest, the cost of capital can be viewed as the annual amount payable (as a percentage) against the principal amount of money. Most of us will be aware that the return payable on such things as loans varies between lenders and over time as interest rates rise or fall. The cost of loans on a credit card is, for example, much higher than a mortgage loan (where the security against the loan is mainly responsible for the difference). Some fortunate people are able to borrow money interest-free (at zero cost of capital).

Cost of Debt Capital

The costs of debt capital are relatively easy to calculate as they tend to correspond closely to the prevailing rate of interest. If the loan is to be repaid at a fixed rate, the calculation is even more straightforward. It is generally the case that the rate of interest attached to a loan will be strongly influenced by the risk of default. Unsecured loans attract the highest rates whilst those that can be recovered by the sale of the asset against which the loan is taken out (such as a property) will attract a lower rate. The history of the business in dealing with lenders (its credit rating) will also be a factor.

Cost of Share Capital

Calculating the cost of share capital is slightly more complex as it contains more variables. Acconting academics spend a great deal of time discussing what should and should not be included in this calculation and how each component should be weighted. Reasons for this complexity include the indefinite nature of the funding, the opportunity cost of undistributed profits and shareholders' expectations. These mean that some models try to include components for inflation, industry averages and attitudes towards risk.

At its simplest, the cost of share capital can be calculated as follows:

Cost of share capital (equity) as a percentage =

Current net dividend per share

Current market price of share

+ average percentage annual growth rate

Example

If the market price for shares were 400p per share and the annual dividend was 20p. If growth in profits average 10% per annum, this gives

$$\text{Cost of share capital} = 20/400 \times 100 + 10\% = 15\%$$

Models of Capital Costing

The CAPM Model

The *Capital Asset Pricing Model* (CAPM) is a more complex but widely this model used for calculating the cost of share capital.

$$\text{Cost of share capital} = Ri + \beta\ (Rm - Ri)$$

The model takes into account the competitor financial products available to potential investors. These range from the percentage return on virtually risk free government bonds (Ri) to a component covering the average interest for the share (equity) markets overall (Rm). The final element of the model represents the company itself, or more correctly its position relative to the market overall. The β coefficient is a measure of the volatility of the company's financial returns.

The CAPM model does have a number of drawbacks, which need to be recognised. First, the shares of the company need to be traded on a stock market. This means that the cost of equity in private companies cannot be calculated using this model. Secondly the volatility of share prices in recent years causes problems in arriving at a date for 'acceptable' returns. The dynamic and complex nature of many industries and markets also suggest that historical data has limited value.

Example: CAPM Model

Assume that risk free government bonds were trading at 4% and the average return on the market was 10%. Also assume that the volatility of the company had been calculated at 1.1, (meaning the shares fluctuated slightly more than the market average).

Cost of share capital (equity) = 4% + 1.1 (10% – 4%) = 10.6%

The WACC Model

Whereas the CAPM model is used to calculate the cost of share capital, the *Weighted Average Cost of Capital* (WACC) can be used to determine the overall cost of funding to a company. The calculation of this information is relatively simple.

WACC = (Proportion of loan finance × Cost of loan finance) + (Proportion of shareholders' funds × Cost of shareholders' funds)

Example: WACC Model

Assume that a company had £30 million of loan capital and £70 million equity funding. The cost of each type had been calculated as 5% and 15% respectively, the calculation would be as follows:

Type of capital	Proportion	Cost (after tax)	Weighted cost
Loan finance	0.3	5%	1.5%
Shareholders' funds	0.7	15%	10.5%
Total	1.0		12.0%

Why Calculate the Cost of Capital?

The cost of capital is usually an important figure to calculate because if it works out to be too high, the development that it is intended to fund may not be viable. Given that both debt and share capital attract servicing costs, the profit returns must exceed these servicing costs to the extent that the proposal is economically attractive.

If the projected returns on a strategic development (such as a new factory facility) are not much more than the projected servicing costs, then management will have to make a judgement as to whether the investment is actually 'worth the risk'.

The whole situation is rendered more complex if debt capital is obtained at a variable rate of interest. Interest rates can vary substantially throughout an economic cycle and depend upon such things as government inflation targets, the currency exchange value and the national rate of capital deposition.

There are no guidelines as to the ideal capital structure—the balance between debt and equity finance. The optimal structure will vary from company to company, from industry to industry and from year to year. Some companies will calculate their WACC and include factors which are difficult to quantify, such as the degree of risk faced by the industry trends in interest rates and even the cost and availability of funds to competitors.

Financial Analysis

The Basics

We would usually employ an analysis of a company's financial situation as part of an internal strategic analysis. We may wish to understand a company's finances in order to make an assessment of its 'health' or its readiness to undertake a phase of strategic development.

Three key areas of financial analysis are:

- longitudinal analysis (sometimes called trend analysis);
- cross-sectional analysis (or comparison analysis);
- ratio analysis.

A comprehensive analysis of a company's financial situation would normally involve an element of all three of these analyses.

The one thing to bear in mind when looking at accounting statements is that they contain numbers in isolation. An accounting number on it own is just that—a number. In order to make any sense of it, we must compare it with other accounting numbers. In the next few sections Air New Zealand will be used to illustrate some of the 'tools' of financial analysis.

Air New Zealand is an airline providing services to, from and within New Zealand, Australia and the South West Pacific. In June 2000 Air New Zealand achieved full ownership of the Australian carrier Ansett, giving the combined Air New Zealand —Ansett Group, which is a member of the 'Star' strategic alliance, the scale of a world top 20 airline. Note, the airline subsequently sold its Ansett stake.

To many organisations in travel and tourism two further areas of finance are key to considering the overall financial situation, namely analyses of the organisation's exposure to:

- foreign exchange risks analysis;
- cash flow risk analysis.

Longitudinal Analysis

The simplest means of assessing any aspect of a company's finances is to compare the data for two or more years and see what has increased and what has decreased over that time period, and by how much. It goes without saying that the longer back in time we look, then the better idea we will get as to the organisation's current position in its historical context. Many company corporate reports provide a five or ten years record and this can help us in constructing a longitudinal analysis.

The easiest way to perform this form of analysis is conduct an initial scan of the figures to identify any major changes between the years. This involves simply looking along each line in turn, and highlighting any larger than normal increases or decreases, for example a scan along five years of fuel expenses shown below clearly indicates that large increases in these costs occurred over the period 1996 to 2000 and particularly between the years 1999 and 2000.

Year	2000	1999	1998	1997	1996
Fuel costs (NZ$000)	464	322	347	356	318

Anomalies like these may need further investigation. The impact of the 'blip' on the year's performance must be assessed as must its impact on current performance. Further investigation of the balance sheet or profit and loss account, together with any notes to the accounts, may provide some clues.

The initial scan may need to be followed by a more detailed analysis, which might, for example, calculate the year on year increase / decrease in percentage terms. It is sometimes helpful to plot trends on a graph against time. This can help to highlight changes at particular points in time.

The identification of trends, in terms of say turnover, costs or of some items of a balance sheet (such as debtors) can therefore be valuable in our financial analysis. such trends should, however, be seen in their context. An organisation operating in a static or slow growth market may judge a 1% year on year increase in turnover as a great success, whereas for a company in a buoyant market would judge a 1% increase as a failure.

Cross-sectional Analysis

Whilst longitudinal analysis helps us to assess performance against a historical trend, it tells us nothing of the company's performance against that of competitors or of companies in other industries. If we were, for example, to identify strong sales growth of 10% a year in a longitudinal analysis of Company A's financial statements, we might be tempted to think that the company was performing well. If we were then to compare this company with one of its competitors only to find that the industry average rate of growth was 15%, then we would wish to modify our initial assessment of Company A's performance.

Intercompany comparison or financial *benchmarking* is a variation on cross-sectional analysis. It usually involves an analysis of 'like' companies, usually in the same industry but it can occasionally be an inter-industry analysis.

In order to make the benchmarking analysis meaningful, the company selection should usually be guided by similarity by:

- company size (*i.e.* they should be comparable in terms of turnover, market value or similar);
- industry (in that the companies produce similar products);
- market (*i.e.* the companies share a similar customer base).

In practice, sample selection for benchmarking study always involves some compromise because no two companies are in all respects directly comparable. Many companies, for example, operate in more than one industry and this may render problematic any comparisons with another company that operates in only one industry.

Accountants and financial analysts have undertaken the practice of inter-company (cross-sectional) analysing using financial data for many years. Benchmarking, however, can be used to compare financial and, importantly, non-financial information between two or more companies.

Benchmarking is now used to compare the effectiveness of various processes, products and procedures against others. The objective is to identify where superior performance is found in whatever variable that is being used for comparison. Once the company with the highest performance is identified, the exercise becomes to explore the reasons behind the superior performance.

The benchmarking process therefore involves decisions on:

- What are we going to benchmark? (financial or non financial data)
- Who are we going to benchmark against? (sample selection)
- How will we get the information?
- How will we analyse the information?
- How will we use the information?

The value of benchmarking is in identifying not only which company has the superior performance in a sector but also why this is the case. Our analysis, for example, might highlight the fact that Company X enjoys a return on sales significantly higher than the other companies in the sector. Company X thus occupies the profitability benchmark in the sector. The other companies may then wish to examine the practices within Company X that give rise to this level of performance.

For non-financial indicators, our analysis may highlight the fact that Company Y is able to attract the best-qualified people within a key category of personnel, for example the best scientists or computer programmers. In this case, Company Y demonstrates the benchmark in successful recruitment. Other companies who are unable to attract the best personnel would usually wish to examine Company Y to see why it is so successful in this regard.

Commonly sized accounts are particularly useful in cross-sectional analyses but it can also be used to analyse the same company's accounts from year to year. If we were, for example, to examine the P&L or balance sheets of two companies in the same industry, we may at first be unable to make sense of differences between the two. We can sometimes make sense of the two separate accounts by making the totals of both equal 100 and then dividing each entry by the resultant quotient accordingly. A simplified example of commonly sized accounts.

Simplified profit and loss accounts for two hypothetical companies

	Company A		Company B	
	£m	Common size	£m	common size
Sales	113.4	100	224.6	100
Cost of sales	65.0	57.32	112	49.87
Gross profit	48.4	42.68	112.6	50.13
Administrative and other costs	33.7	29.72	67.0	29.83
Operating profit	14.7	12.96	45.6	20.3

We can make comparisons between the cost structures of the two companies despite the fact that Company B has approximately twice the turnover of Company A. We can tell, for example, that overall, Company B is better at controlling overall costs that Company A evidenced by the fact that its operating profit is 20.3 compared to Company A's. We could draw comparable conclusions from other commonly sized components of the accounts.

Concept: Financial Statements

One of the conditions placed upon limited companies is the requirement to file an audited annual report and accounts. There are five compulsory components to this document as set out in the UK in the Companies Act (1985 as amended): chairman's statement, auditor's report, profit and loss statement, balance sheet and cash flow statement. The accounting rules by which they are to be constructed are prescribed in financial reporting standards (FRSs) to ensure that all companies mean the same thing when they make an entry in one of the statements. When they are completed (following the company's financial year end), they become publicly available. Each shareholder receives a copy, and a copy is lodged at UK Companies House in Cardiff or London.

It is for the purposes of comparisons of this nature that cross-sectional analyses are important. As well as comparing accounting numbers like turnover, it is often helpful to compare two or more companies' ratios (see next section), such as return on sales or one of the working capital ratios.

Ratio Analysis

The third important tool in the analysis of company performance is *ratio analysis.* A ratio is a comparison (by quotient) of two items from the same set of accounts. Given that there are a lot of numbers in a set of accounts, it will not come as a surprise to learn that a large number of ratios can be drawn—some of which are more useful than others.

Ratio analysis is an area of some academic debate, and accordingly, the way in which ratios are expressed may vary between accounting and strategy textbooks. What is important therefore is to employ a consistent approach to ratio analysis, especially in longitudinal and cross-sectional analysis.

For most purposes, we can divide ratios into five broad categories:

1 Performance ratios

2 Efficiency ratios

3 Liquidity ratios

4 Investors' ratios

5 Financial structure ratios

Performance Ratios

As their name suggests, performance ratios test to see how well a company has turned its inputs into profits. This usually involves comparing *return* (PBIT or profit before interest and tax) against either turnover or against its capital. This is because the rates of tax and interest payable vary. Using profit after interest and tax would distort the performance.

Return on capital employed (ROCE) is perhaps the most important and widely used measure of performance. It indicates the return being made compared to the funds invested. At its simplest, it is this figure that tests the gains of investing in a business as opposed to simply placing capital on return in a bank.

Where an organisation can break down its figures by divisions or subsidiaries, individual performance can be measured and decisions relating to continued ownership made.

Return on equity or *Return on ordinary shareholders' funds* gives an indication of how effectively the share capital has been turned into profit (*i.e.* it does not take account of loan capital). This ratio should be used carefully as the capital structure of the company can affect the ratio.

Return on sales, or *profit margin,* either net or gross, is a popular guide to the profitability of a company. This ratio assesses the profit made per £ (or other currency) sold. Return on sales tends to vary from industry to industry and between companies within an industry. Airlines and tour operators, for example, typically make returns of under 10% whilst companies in the pharmaceuticals sector rarely make less than 20%. Figure shows a graphical representation of return on sales for Air New Zealand.

Efficiency Ratios

These ratios show how efficiently a company has used its assets to generate sales. We can use any one of a number of a company's inputs to test against sales or profits. Common efficiency ratios include *sales per employee* and *profit per employee,* both of which test the efficiency with which a company uses its labour inputs.

Concept: Efficiency

The term efficiency is used in many ways—not just in accounting. We may speak of an efficient engine or the efficiency of a heating system in a house. At its simplest, efficiency is a comparison of a systems output to its inputs with a view to testing how well the input has been turned into output.

Other commonly used efficiency ratios are *asset turnover* and a variant of this, *fixed asset turnover.* A high level of asset turnover indicates that the company is using its assets efficiently and, conversely, a low level may indicate that the company is suffering from overcapacity. Stock turnover gives an indication of how well the company controls its stocks. A company that keeps stock moving will generally have a higher stock turnover than one that has piles of unsaleable or obsolete materials.

Liquidity Ratios

These ratios test the company's ability to meet its short-term debts—an important thing to establish if we have reason to believe the company is in trouble. Essentially, they ask the question, 'has the company enough funds to meet what it owes?'.

The *current ratio* is the best-known liquidity ratio. It is a measure of a company's total liabilities in comparison to its total assets and is thus calculated entirely from balance sheet figures. It is used to assess the company's ability to meet its liabilities by the use of its assets such as stock, debtors (receivables) and cash.

The *acid test ratio* is a variant of the current ratio and tests the company's ability to meet its short term liabilities using its cash or 'near cash' assets. Many textbooks suggest a ratio of 2:1 should be a target for this ratio and a target of 1:1 should be sought for the acid test ratio. These are simple guides and should not be taken as the norm for all industries. For example, many companies in the travel industry have low levels of stock and, as a result, their current ratio will be well below 2:1, and consequently the acid test ratio provides a better guide in such cases.

Investors' Ratios

This family of ratios test for things that are important to a company's investors—usually its shareholders or potential shareholders. There are three that are widely used.

Earnings per share (EPS) are calculated by dividing profit after interest and tax (called earnings) by the number of shares. It shows how much profit is attributable to each share.

The *price earnings ratio* (P/E) gives an indication of the stockmarket's confidence in a company's shares. It is the current market price of the company's ordinary shares divided by its EPS at the last year end and it follows therefore that the P/E varies with the share price. Broadly speaking, it is a way of showing how highly investors value the earnings a company produces. A high P/E ratio (where the price is high compared to the last declared EPS) usually indicates growth potential whilst a low P/E suggests static profits. The P/E ratio for quoted companies is regularly published in the financial press.

Dividend yield is the third widely used investors' ratio. Potential shareholders often, want to know what the most recent return on the share was in terms of percentage. Dividend yield is calculated by dividing the dividend per share at the last year end by the current price (and then multiplying by 100 to arrive at a percentage).

Financial Structure Ratios

We encountered financial structure above when we discussed the relative merits of loan and share capital. The way in which a company 'mixes' these forms of capital is referred to as its financial (or capital) structure.

The *gearing ratio* looks at the relationship between all the borrowings of the company (including short-term borrowings), and all the capital employed by the company. This provides a view of the extent to which borrowing forms part of the total capital base of the company and hence the risk associated with rising interest rates.

The *debt—equity ratio,* a variation on the gearing ratio, uses the shareholders' funds in the calculation rather than the total capital employed. This ratio provides a more direct comparison between the funds attributed to shareholders and liability of the company to loan providers.

Using Ratios in Financial Analysis

Compared to simply looking at accounting numbers, ratios, provide a way of making some sense of published accounts. However, if we place a ratio within its longitudinal or cross-sectional context, its usefulness is maximized.

If we take return on sales as an example, we would usually want to know how Company A's figure this year compares not only with last year's (*i.e.* is it more or less), but also with Company

A's competitors. This enables us to assess how Company A is performing over time and to make a judgement on its competitive position in its industry. This is because profitability is an important indicator of competitive success.

Limitations of Financial Information

For most purposes in strategic analysis, we can accept the proposition that the data we collect from a company's annual accounts are accurate and provide a truthful statement on its financial position. From time to time, however, we may need to qualify our analysis because of one or more reasons.

First, whilst the financial statements are audited for accuracy, other parts of the annual report are not. If our financial analysis consists of an examination of the entire document and not just the accounting sections, then we would need to be aware of this. Additional disclosures made in corporate reports may serve a number of purposes. Some commentators have suggested that such disclosures may be something of a public relations and marketing exercise.

Second, we should remember that the financial information in a corporate report is historical, often published up to three months after the period they represent. Whilst this historical information can be used to judge past performance, it may have limited use in predicting future performance. The balance sheet shows the financial position at 'a moment in time' (at the year end). It does not (unlike the P&L) summarize a full year's trading and things can sometimes change quickly after the year-end.

In an attempt to avoid this potential problem, Stock Exchange quoted companies are required to produce interim reports, normally half yearly and unaudited, which show their profit and turnover for that period. Quoted companies are also required to provide the Stock Exchange with information that may have a significant impact on its prospects such as changes on the Board or anything that gives rise to a 'profits warning'.

Third, those who prepare a company's financial statements (the financial accountants) sometimes have cause to 'hide' bad news so as to avoid alarming the company's investors. It is possible to employ legal financial restructuring so as to make some figures appear better than perhaps they are. A year on year increase in the value of fixed assets, for example, may appear at first glance to be healthy, but it may be that the company has accumulated a high amount of debt to finance it. It is for this reason that we sometimes need to examine all parts of a company's financial statements to spot any countervailing bad news that has been obscured by the company in its reporting.

Finance and Risk in Travel and Tourism

Foreign Exchange Risk Analysis

The travel and tourism industry operates internationally, producing international flows of funds in various currencies. Tour operators and airlines, for example, typically have a very large exposure to movements in foreign exchange rates, almost certainly far larger than for most companies of a similar size engaged in other areas of the economy (manufacturing companies, for example). The very purpose of these companies implies that they are international in their activities, thereby leaving them exposed to international risks associated with foreign exchange transactions.

The profitability of any company that trades internationally is affected by changes in foreign exchange rates. As Lockwood (1989) stated: 'as a large part of the travel and tourist industry is concerned with persuading and assisting people to cross national boundaries and thus to buy goods and services priced in a foreign currency, the identification and management of exchange rate exposures is vital to the profitable operation of a travel and tourist business'.

Thus foreign exchange management is very significant for many travel and tourism businesses. The lack of stability caused by the continual changes in exchange rates between currencies creates uncertainty. Specifically, uncertainty is created as to:

- what foreign income will be worth when it is received;
- what payments will cost when they have to be made;
- what the value of foreign assets and liabilities might be in the future.

British Airways' Foreign Exchange Exposure

The overall foreign exchange position of a company may be complicated as illustrated by the position of British Airways: 'The group does business in approximately 140 foreign currencies which account for approximately 60% of Group Revenue and approximately 40% of operating expenses. The Group generates a surplus in most of these currencies [*i.e.* revenues are greater than costs]. The principal exceptions are the US dollar and the pound sterling in which the Group has a deficit arising from capital expenditure and the payment of some leasing costs, together with expenditure on fuel, which is payable in US dollars and the majority of staff costs, central overheads and other leasing costs, which are payable in pounds sterling'.

It is imperative to the profitability of many companies operating in the travel and tourism industry that this exposure to foreign exchange rate movements is recognised and managed appropriately.

In all cases risk attributed to foreign exchange rate movements arises out of uncertainty about the future exchange rate between two currencies. This risk would be minimised if it were possible to predict future rate movements. Unfortunately, it is not possible to do so with any degree of accuracy, and for a company to try to do so can be financially dangerous. If foreign exchange rates cannot be predicted, another option might be to pass on to the customer the effects of any adverse movements in exchange rates, and hence the company would incur to impact. In most cases, however, the highly competitive nature of the travel and tourism business prevents higher costs being passed on to the customer in this way. Clearly then it is prudent to manage these risks, although it is common in the industry for the risks to be ignored, especially by smaller companies.

Types of Risk Exposure

We can identify three different types of foreign exchange risk or exposure a company may be faced with:

Transaction Exposure

Transaction exposure arises, 'because the cost or proceeds (in home currency) of settlement of a future payment or receipt denominated in another currency may vary due to changes in exchange rates' (Buckley, 2000).

Transaction exposure relates to the foreign exchange exposure where contracts have already been entered into. When a company has contracted to receive or pay an amount of money in a foreign currency at some time in the future a risk is incurred. The specific risk is that adverse exchange rate movements between now and the time of the eventual cash receipt/payment will increase the amount to be paid out or decrease the amount to be received.

For example, a UK tour operator selling holidays to America would receive its income in pounds sterling but have to make payments to hoteliers and other suppliers in US dollars. In order to make the payments at some stage the company would have to convert sterling into US dollars. This would entail a risk that the US dollar might rise in value (appreciate) against sterling, thereby making the payments more expensive in sterling terms. Assume, for instance, the company had costed its hotel beds in its American programme at a rate of $1.50 to the pound (*i.e.* 1 pound buys 1.50 US dollars), and that the total cost to purchase the required bed spaces was $1500 000. The cost in sterling to the company would be $1500 000/1.50 = £1 000 000. Now if the rate subsequently fell to $1.40 the cost would increase to $1500 000/1.40 = £1071429.

Translation Exposure

As Buckley (2000) states, 'Translation exposure arises on the consolidation of assets, liabilities and profits, denominated in foreign currency in the process of preparing consolidated accounts'.

The concept is also known as *accounting exposure.* For example, if a UK hotel company purchases a hotel in Australia, it acquires an asset priced in Australian dollars. Each year when the balance sheet of the business is prepared, the value of the hotel would be translated into sterling at the prevailing rate on the balance sheet date. The hotel might therefore be worth less in sterling terms as shown in the balance sheet of the company.

Economic Exposure

Economic exposure (sometimes referred to as political exposure) arises from the effect of adverse exchange rate movements on future cash flows, where no contractual arrangement to receive or pay money has yet been made. This kind of exposure is longer term in nature and often difficult to quantify exactly and forecast accurately.

For instance, suppose a specialist tour operator operates most of its programme to one country, perhaps Gambia for example.

The company will have a high economic exposure to that country and its currency. In some countries the political and economic circumstances are very uncertain, and if, for example, the government should be replaced in a violent way, (as occurred in recent years in Gambia), customers will be reluctant to book holidays to that country, thereby severely limiting the revenues of the specialist tour operator.

Thus, movements in foreign exchange rates lead to a number of different problems or exposures for travel and tourism companies. These exposures can be dealt with in a number of ways. The most obvious ways of dealing with such exposures are to avoid the exposures altogether, either by trading in domestic markets only, or by passing the exposure over to suppliers or customers. These alternatives are seldom possible in international travel and tourism, so other management methods such as the use of forward foreign exchange contracts or foreign exchange options have to be employed in order to reduce the risks. For a full discussion of these methods see Samuel, Wilkes and Brayshaw (1995) and Ross (1996).

Cash Flow Risk Analysis

Travel and tourism has one of the most highly seasonal patterns of demand for any product, with less variation than the demand for Christmas cards or air conditioners, but more than nearly all high value individual purchases (Bull, 1995). This seasonality is largely due to climate, but is also related to factors such as school holidays, festivals and historic travel patterns. Seasonality of demand for the product leads to a highly seasonal pattern of cash inflows and outflows. Consequently, at certain times of the year companies may have large cash balances to invest and at other times of the year many companies need to borrow money in order to maintain payments to suppliers (creditors). The industry is also *cyclical* in nature, in that cash flows are very responsive to changes in the general level of economic activity.

In terms of cash management, tour operators, travel agents and airlines are typically low margin businesses, deriving important parts of their income, not from operating profits (through the selling of travel arrangements), but from interest income derived from investing cash surpluses they may be holding at certain times of the year.

Seasonality of Cash Flow for a UK Tour Operator

If we take as an example a typical UK outbound tour operator selling mass-market package holidays largely to Europe, it is greatly affected by the seasonality of the product and this directly affects its cash flow and in turn its management.

Such an operator may have a number of operating characteristics:

- the bulk of holidays sold would be summer sun, with the season lasting from April to September, but with the peak months being July and August during school holidays.
- Summer sun holidays are typically booked in three distinct periods:
  - (i) The *early booking period starting in August or September,* when a significant number of people book. This applies especially to families, and those who are tied to taking holidays between certain dates, or are trying to take advantage of particular offers such as 'free child places', or low deposits.
  - (ii) *The post Christmas period from January to March,* which is usually the largest booking period, and during which customers may be targeted with a second edition of the brochure.
  - (iii) *The late booking period, from April onwards,* which has become increasingly significant in recent years, and may be a time of intense competition as operators try to sell remaining capacity and vary prices in order to do so.
- Many tour operators have attempted to widen their range of activities, and reduce the effects of seasonality, by, for instance, introducing winter sun and skiing programmes. The winter sun season normally lasts from October to April, whilst the skiing season normally lasts from December to April with peaks in February and at Easter. In most cases the combined size of these programmes is far smaller than the summer programme, representing perhaps 25% of the summer programme in terms of receipts. Bookings for the winter sun and skiing programmes are taken throughout the summer and

autumn, but the winter ski programme in particular is subject to a great deal of late booking in late autumn and early winter as customers wait to see what snow conditions are likely for the season.

- The tour operator will have a number of seasonal costs such as airline fuel, staff working at resorts, and accommodation charges. However, the tour operator will also have a high level of costs that have to be met throughout the year, such as the costs of head office staff aircraft maintenance and computer facilities.

The characteristics of the tour operating business outlined in the box entitled 'Seasonality of cash flow for a UK tour operator' have certain implications for cash flow analysis and cash management. Cash builds up and declines in a seasonal way. During certain times of the year, particularly in the spring, large surplus cash balances are free to be invested until the cash is needed to pay bills during the summer season and for the remainder of the year. The size and timing of the cash balances, and the interest to be earned from the invested balances will vary from year to year, since the profile of bookings and level of interest rates also vary from year to year.

The period of greatest risk for many travel and tourism companies, however, usually comes in the autumn and winter. Cash balances have been run down as seasonal payments have been made during the preceding summer season and the bulk of bookings for the subsequent season have yet to be made. The position is often exacerbated by companies offering favourable payment terms to customers whereby a low initial deposit is required. Companies often have to rely on bank support to help them through this period.

The problems of cash flow may be compounded, however, if the early summer booking period for the forthcoming season and winter ski and sun bookings are poor, and post Christmas bookings are delayed.

In a case where a bank (or other party) fails to lend the necessary support, insolvency is the inevitable result. Insolvency (the inability to pay bills as they become due), has often befallen companies in this sector when revenue from expected bookings has failed to materialise.

When a company reaches an insolvent position it normally leads to the company's failure and liquidation. A company can sometimes survive for many years without making profits or making very low levels of profit, but if they run out of cash it is difficult for them to survive, because employees and creditors must be paid. Many travel and tourism companies routinely rely on banks to provide short-term finance for a part of the year, but it is when these negative cash balances are larger or more prolonged than usual and banks feel unable to provide finance that problems occur.

Illustrates the cash flow problems described above for Interjet, a fictional small outbound UK tour operator with ambitious plans. The company plans to increase its sales turnover by around 25% each year. However, like many tour operators, travel agents and other tourism businesses, the company experiences annual seasonal cash flow difficulties. A cash flow forecast has been prepared for the following financial years.

On analysing the cash flow, the following may be necessary:

- Insert all known income and payments for each period on to a cash flow schedule.
- Income and payments should be totalled to produce a balance carried forward to next period.
- Forecast future cash flow using available information.
- Produce 'sensitivity' analyses, *i.e.* what if, for instance sales were 10% lower/higher than expected or jet fuel prices rose by 50%?
- Produce a graph showing monthly or weekly balances may help indicate trends.

Analysis of the cash flow should prompt certain questions such as:

- How easily predictable are the cash flows?
- How seasonal or cyclical are the cash flows?
- Can the company keep within its borrowing limits?
- Is the company generating enough cash to ensure its survival?
- Does the company require further credit facilities?

- How long does it take customers to pay the company?
- How quickly does the company pay suppliers and others?

There are a number of actions a company may wish to consider to alleviate perceived cash flow problems including:

- Postponing capital expenditure.
- Accelerating cash inflows
- Postponing or reducing cash outflows.
- Selling assets.
- Negotiating new lines of credit.
- Leasing rather than buying equipment.

3

Government Liasoning and Tourism

Introduction : The Essence of Politics and Government

Politics can sometimes be a bit of a dirty word. Most 'ordinary' people seem to love to have it. 'They should keep politics out of sport'; 'they bring politics into everything these days' or 'politics and business don't mix' are typical, sincere laments. Such refrains, however, reveal a profound misun-derstanding of the nature of politics and its all-pervasive, everyday significance. Times of war remind us that there's only one thing worse than too much politics, and that's too little.

A frequently heard grumble is that politics is too adversarial, with politicians squabbling and arguing with each other 'like children', instead of pooling the best minds for the good of the country. Politics, however, *is* a 'dispu-tatious' (Crick 1995) or 'quarrelsome' (Gilliatt 1987) activity. It is an adversarial business. the configuration and organi-sation of the House of Commons—its opposing front benches separated by two swords' length and one foot—symbolically reminds us so. The cut and thrust of debate is intended to be a more acceptable currency of political discourse than more violent ways of of expressing purposive choice. The party-system has tended to produce a more 'temperate politics' than some of its early observers feared (Humphreys 1992). However, that is not to ignore the reality that the institutio-nalised politics of 'London SW1', in the case of England, are perceived by apparently large numbers of the population to be of decreasing interest and relevance in their own lives; their belief in the capacity of the institutions of representative democracy to deliver has diminished. In the political science literature, politics, being about choices, competing preferences and alternative priorities, informs many typical definitions. However, it should be noted that politics is not only about arranging for these more-or-less legitimate differences to be articulated, expressed, heard and debated, but also involves making collective decisions and together agreeing ways forward. Without this second dimension, politics would indeed be a dark and destructive pursuit.

Definitions of Politics

- Politics 'considers conflicts of interests and values and how they are or can be conciliated' (Crick 1995: 3).
- 'Political activity is a ...universal phenomenon. It involves disagreements and the reconciliation of those disagreements (Ball and Peters 2000: 27).
- 'People or groups of people who want different things - be it power, money, liberty, etc. - face the potential or reality of conflict when such things are in short supply. Politics begins where their interests clash' (Jones *et. al.* 2001: 8).
- 'Politics may be defined briefly as a process whereby a group of people, whose opinions or interests are initially divergent, reach collective decisions which are generally regarded as binding on the group, and enforced as common policy' (Miller 1987: 391).
- 'Politics is the activity by which groups reach binding collective decisions through attempting to reconcile differences among their members' (Hague and Harrop 2001: 3).
- 'Choice, preference, priorities, they are the currency of politics, and those who translate them into practical policies are politicians' (Wilson and Game 1998: 219).

The business of tourism and leisure throws up practical examples on an almost daily basis. In the wake of terrorist atrocities in New York, Washington and Pennsylvania on September 11, 2001, was it right to postpone golf's Ryder Cup competition? Should motor-racing's Formula 1 circus have raced in Indianpolis or not? At the same time, was it right to switch Glasgow Rangers' European football tie from Dagestan to 'neutral' Poland on account of the former's proximity to war-torn Chechnya? Should the former undis-puted world heavyweight boxing champion and convicted rapist Mike Tyson have been allowed into the UK in 2000 to fight in Manchester? And what about the Miss World context in India in 1996, when protesters from the Indian Forum for Awakening Women announced their intention to set fire to themselves at the pageant as an expression of opposition? What should have been the response of the Indian Authorities to such a clash of culture and values? Should Miss World have been banned? Should the protestors have been permitted to go ahead with deliberate and public self-immolation? Should protestors have been taken into protective custody for 'their own good'? Should the authorities have done nothing and allowed events to take their course? Are there any right or wrong answers at all? Such questions take us to the heart of classical political theory.

In the advanced liberal democracies of the socalled 'free' world, politics tend to be a secular business (Crick 1995). The currency of politics is different from that of religion; there is no holy writ, neither eternal truth nor tablets of stone - only complex problems capable of relatively temporary resolution in terms of shifting political values. Conditions and attitudes change. In this sense, there are no right or wrong answers for at the heart of secular politics lies the 'principle of uncertainty'.

Politics and Tourism

The travel and tourism industries, arguably the largest of global business, raise many virtually intractable political issues, such as the balance between development and conservation, the relative distribution of positive and negative external effects, the relationship between host, indigenous cultures and incoming visitors, and long-term sustainability—all at the global, national and local levels. Therefore, given : *(i)* the nature of politics both as an activity and as a field of study, and *(ii)* the nature of the global business of tourism and its consequences, a prominent place for tourism on the political agenda would seem assured. However, this has tended not to be the case (Hall 1994).

'Tourism is widely regarded as the world's largest industry. However, despite the significant role of tourism in national and regional economies, and its social and environmental effects, the political aspects of tourism are rarely discussed in the tourism literature. Given the vast seasonal intra and international movements of people which modern travel represents and the impacts of tourism on many destinations, it must therefore strike the student of tourism that the rarity of academic research on the political dimensions of tourism is somewhat surprising' (Hall 1994: 3).

There are several reasons for this state of affairs. For one thing, governments and politicians tend to play down the intensely political nature of tourism. This is reflected in, for example, their historic reluctance to develop systema-tically clear policies for tourism (clearly connected with other policy fields such as energy, environment or transport), as well as their disinclination to commission fundamental research (as opposed to collecting visitor numbers or developing marketing strategies). Academics and scholars are also to blame, for they are not inclined to view tourism as a serious subject of enquiry - more to do with holidays than proper, serious work. There are also significant methodological challenges (Hall 1994).

Nevertheless, the hand of the state is ever discernible in the scale, distribution, character and organisation of tourism. Each aircraft flight, or package holiday or overnight hotel stay bears witness to the extent of governmental influence. Take a typical tour operator's brochure from any 'high-street' travel agency, for example. The hand of government is likely to be evident in the choice of available holiday destinations, points of departure, prices, resort information, the use of photographs, textual content, codes of practice, consumer protection provisions, currency regulations, travel advice and so on. Indeed, as discussed in Chapters, tour operations are highly regulated at both the national and European levels. The purpose of this chapter, therefore, is look at the relationship between tourism and government, focusing in particular on the influence of changing 'styles' of government on tourism. the first task, however, is to review the public administration of tourism in the UK (for a detailed account, see Holloway 1998).

Government and Tourism: Aspects of the Administrative Architecture in the UK

In everyday parlance, the term 'government' may be used to convey several different meanings. These include a vague sense of authority, power and order, control by a political party such as the 'Labour Government' or a particular administration, may be as in 'the Blair Govern-ment', or a collective of official institutions such as 'government departments' and 'local government'. It may even be used when referring to particular organisations, such as the Ministry of Defence or the Treasury. All of these uses are legitimate. Underlying them all, however, is a deeper meaning, for 'government' conveys a sense of the settled (but not permanent) and agreed formalisation of power and authority which provides a framework within which political discourse can be managed, disagreements can be debated, collective choices made and policy directions set out. In a sense, but not entirely, it's the problem-solving end of politics.

Not entirely though, for government policies can themselves cause their own problems. Some would argue, for example, that Mrs Thatcher's economic policies in the 1980s created major problems of social distress and civil unrest whilst, more generally, Dunleavy (1995) has written of the catastrophic unintended consequences of 'policy disasters'.

The United Kingdom is a relatively small centralised (albeit of late increasingly devolved) unitary state. Even so, governmental arrangements for the tourism, leisure and cultural industries are characterised by a high degree of organisational pluralism and institutional fragmentation. Indeed, many governmental bodies are involved in the tourism business, although many of these are not primarily or exclusively concerned with the business of tourism. Therefore, many of the effects of their policies or influence are indirect. Let us take central government as one example.

Central Government and Tourism

Central government has, for the past couple of centuries at least, exercised significant indirect effects on the develop-ment of the tourism industry. For example, nine-teenth century legislation providing for Bank Holidays and paid leave for industrial workers (together with the development of the railways of course) contributed to the development of the Victorian seaside resort. The official promotion of education, literacy and other 'self-improving' pursuits, coupled with the suppression of 'undesirable' leisure activities, such as gambling, drinking or cock-fighting (Henry and Bramham 1989), also shaped the infant leisure and cultural industries. Moreover, nine-teenth century foreign, penal and agricultural policies still exert discernible effects in present day patterns of international tourism, especially in the Visiting Friends and Relatives (VFR) sector. For example, condoning, in the name of agricultural improvement, the clearance of crafting communities in Caithness, Sutherland and elsewhere in favour of the Cheviot sheep (Prebble 1969) was no more an instrument of tourism policy than was British penal policy in the nineteenth century.

However, in 'forcibly' relocating British nationals in Australia, Canada, New Zealand, the United States and elsewhere, a significant contribution would be made to the future VFR market. More recently, in the 1980s and 1990s, employment policy, the deregulation and privatisation of the transport sector, as well as the policies of the Europeans Union on consumer protection or monetary integration and the single market, have all had very major consequences for the travel and tourism industries.

Government's first formal support for tourism came about in 1929 when the Department of Overseas Trade made a grant of £5000 to the Travel Association of the Great Britain and Northern Ireland (TAGBNI), successor to the Come to Britain movement (Cooper *et. al.*, 1998). TAGBNI would, in the inter-war years, become the British Travel Association, though still a voluntary as opposed to a statutory body. Apart from continuing grant-aid to this voluntary body, providing extra funds for local authorities which were seaside resorts and a piece of legislation in 1948 relating only to Northern Ireland, nothing too much changed in terms of central government's interest in tourism until 1969 (Harrop and Long 1994). It was in that year that the Development of Tourism Act 1969, was passed.

Hailed as the first piece of comprehensive legislation systematically to address the needs of the tourism industry, the Act provided for the creation of several new statutory boards—the British Tourist Authority (BTA), the English Tourist Board (ETB), the Scottish Tourist Board (STB) and the Wales Tourist Board (WTB)-as well as development grants and an accommodation grading scheme. It was a turning point, heralding as it did the creation for the first time of national arrangements for developing tourism and allocating public funds. However, the Act was articulated against a background of economic crisis and the need to generate earnings and income from wherever; tourism was seen as a major source of 'invisible' earnings and the 1969 Act may have owed as much to this imperative as to a clear commitment to tourism.

This would help to explain one of the apparent paradoxes of the past thirty years. One the one hand, there has been no shortage of central government involvement in tourism, at least not if measured by the number of departments either directly involved. On the other hand, policy has tended to remain general and vague - long on 'motherhood and apple pie', but short on specifics.

Government Institutions and Tourism

With reference to the first point above (the number of departments involved in tourism), Central Government in the UK has a number of institutional forms, especially:

- The large, well-known Departments of State, such as the Home Office, the Foreign and Commonwealth Office, the Treasury, the Department for Education in its various names and, similarly, Environment and Transport, to name but several. Many of these are relevant to an understanding of the Travel and Tourism business. Some examples might include:

Foreign Office	:	conduct of foreign and international relations, travel advice
Home Office	:	immigration and security matters
Environment	:	the countryside, local government and planning
Agriculture	:	countryside matters
Trade and Industry	:	hotels, travel agents, business.

Indeed, it would be more difficult to think of Central Government Departments without consequences for tourism than to draw up an inventory of those which do have.

- Secondly, there are the Executive Agencies. These were created after publication of the Ibbs or 'Next Steps' Report in 1988 on management and efficiency in the Civil Service. These Executive, or 'Departmental', Agencies are semiautonomous organisations which carry out many of the routine, administrative functions of central government - 'freeing-up' the centre to concentrate on policy-making. Well-known examples include the Social Security Benefits Agency and its former sister, the Contributions Agency, now merged with the Inland Revenue. They are by no means all based in London, let alone in Whitehall. Many Agencies are relevant to the business of tourism. These include the UK Passport Agency (set up in 1991); the Meteorological Office (1990); Historic Royal Palaces (1989); the Ordence Survey (1990); CADW Welsh Historic Monuments (1991); and Historic Scotland (1991).

- In addition, the territorial Departments—the Northern Ireland, Scottish and Welsh Offices—traditionally exercised responsibility for tourism in their respective geographical areas until devolution took effect.

In the absence of a dedicated Tourism Ministry, until 1992 responsibility for tourism lay with a designated 'lead' Department. Until 1985, this was the Department of Trade and Industry (tourism means business being the message), when responsibility then passed to the Department of Employment (tourism means jobs). There it remained until the creation of the Department of National Heritage in 1992 and now, the Department for Culture, Media and Sport (DCMS) following its creation after Labour's General Election victory in 1997.

The debate leading up to the creation of the Department of National Heritage in 1992 was an interesting one. It brings us to the second element of our paradox; that is, despite extensive government involvement, overall policy direction remained vague and uncertain. The commons' own Trade and Industry Committee in 1985 commented:

The truth is that the Government cannot quite decide what its own role is... The Government minimises the appearance of involvement by reducing policy aims to statements of the obvious but maintains the fact of involvement in the tourist boards and the grants provided through them. The trouble is that this actual financial commitment is then left without there being any clear specific strategy to guide its use (House of Commons Trade Committee, quoted in Cooper *et. al.*, 1993 : 148).

In the same vein, a retiring Chair of a Regional Tourist Board felt compelled to write in the Board's 1993-94 Report that central government had 'failed to provide the leadership necessary to encourage the development of the tourism industry... there is still no coherent national policy on tourism'.

Reflective of such concerns and criticism, the case for a single, integrated 'Department of Leisure' had gained momentum during the 1980s (Adams 2000; Harrop and Long 1994). It culminated in the creation, after John Major's General Election victory in 1992, of the Departnent of National Heritage. In rather rapid succession is Secretaries of State were David Mellor, Peter Brooke, Stephen Dorrell and Virginia Bottomley. Tony Blair, on the back of 'New Labour's' May 1997 General Election triumph, recast it as the Department for Culture, Media and Sport—partly because the word 'heritage' is backward-looking ('heri' in Latin, like hier' in French, means yesterday) and sent out inappropriate messages for the modernising Mr Blair. The Secretary of State for Culture, Media and Sport throughout the Blair government's first term (1997-2001) was Chris Smith. After Labour's return to office in June 2001, he was replaced by Tessa Jowell.

The Department for Culture, Media and Sport is responsible for:

- the arts
- museums and galleries
- broadcasting
- the national lottery
- cultural objects
- new media and information services
- film
- the press
- the government's art collection
- the royal estate
- heritage
- sport and recreation
- libraries
- tourism
- the millennium

The Department for Culture, Media and Sport's overall aim was to improve the quality of life for all through cultural and sporting activities, and to strengthen the creative industries. In doing so, it was expected to:

- bring excitement into the life of the nation and the work of government;
- make things of quality available to the many, not just the few; and
- create the jobs of the future.

On the tourism front, the setting-up of the Tourism Forum in November 1997 was interpreted as signalling a re-positioning of tourism at the centre of the Góvernment's cultural initiatives and in honouring of its promise in *Breaking New Ground*, published whilst still in opposition, to 'implement a committed strategy to assist the development of tourism and hospitality'. In February 1999 appeared *Tomorrow's Tourism*, the Government's strategy for tourism. Recognising tourism as 'one of our most important industries...(because)... it generates wealth, it creates jobs, it promotes entrepreneurship, it provides social and environ-mental benefits, and supports local diversity and cultural traditions' (DCMS 1999: 8), the need for a government strategy for tourism was explicitly acknowledged. Characte-rised by, firstly, diversity and fragmentation, secondly, seasonal and sometimes fickle demand, thirdly, an inadequate understanding of its market and, fourthly, a reliance on infrastructure determined by central and local government in other policy fields, such as transport or planning, the tourism business needs a clearly articulated and joined up strategy (DCMS 1999: 9). Committing itself to work in partnership with the industry towards shared objectives and common targets, the publication of *Tomorrow's Tourism* probably marked the most comprehensive governmental arrangements for tourism since the Development of Tourism Act thirty years earlier. It is a significant attempt to address the policy vacuum for tourism and to deliver on the very least that the industry might reasonably expect of governement, namely the enunciation of a clear overall policy:

At the national level, tourism is in the first instance a government responsibility to formulate a tourism policy, which may be translated into a plan... when the role of tourism is defined, the policy provides a statement of the means by which the objectives are to be attained... such... as the administrative arrangements, the respective rules of the private and public sectors and the fiscal arrangements. (Burkart and Medlik 1992)

Tourism : Other Institutional Arrangements

Despite the complexity of the arrangements described above, there are other relevant items of the administrative 'furniture' to be cited. These ay be briefly summarised as:

- sub-national government
- public bodies
- supra-national government

(i) Sub-national Government

In the absence of constitutional guarantees to the regions of the UK, sub-national government has tended to focus on local government. During the past decade, however, the picture has become more complicated. The Conservative government, for example, created Government Offices for the Regions (such as the Government Office for the North East (GONE)). Bringing together the work of some, but by no means all, central government departments on a regional basis, these Offices are involved in local economic develop-ment strategies, often with a strong cultural dimension, and the administration of European funds. Additionally, the Blair government's agenda of democratic modernisation has seen the introduction of devolved structures. The Scottish Executive, for example, exercises responsibility for tourism as part of the work of its Department for Enterprise and Lifelong Learning. The organisation of the Scottish Executive does not, however, reflect the configuration of responsibilities of the Department for Culture, Media and Sport for in Scotland, sport, the arts and culture lie within the Education portfolio. Wales now has its own National Assembly and Northern Ireland its Executive. In London, there is an Elected Mayor (Ken Livingstone, who has not always been at one with his own party in national government, as evidenced by disagreement over the future of the London Underground for instance) and a 25 member Greater London Assembly. All English regions have appointed (not elected) Regional Development Agencies and non-statutory Regional Chambers. Fully elected Regional Assemblies for the English

Regions remain a possibility. For the student of tourism, the reformed administrative architecture of government beyond Whitehall perhaps serves to compound an already complex picture.

As for local government, there is a comprehensive cover of directly elected, multi-purpose primary local authorities. Again, the arrangements are complex and a review of local government structures in the mid-1990s made the pattern even more complicated than before. In England, Wilson and Game (1998) drew up a list of 387 principal authorities as follows:

- 34 Non-metropolitan Country Councils, e.g., Northumberland or Hampshire.
- 238 Non-metropolitan District Councils, e.g., Carlisle, Tynedale or The Wrekin.
- 36 Metropolitan District Councils, e.g., Newcastle upon Tyne, Birmingham or Liverpool.
- 46 Unitary Councils, e.g., Stockton, Stoke-on-Trent or Bristol.
- 32 London Borough Councils, e.g., Tower Hamlets, Kensington and Chelsea or Islington.
- 1 City of London Corporation.

In Scotland, 1996 saw a two-tier system of regional and district councils replaced by 32 unitary authorities. Examples include Perth and Kinross. Argyll and Bute or City of Aber-deen. In the same year, Wales similarly adopted a system of 22 unitary authorities, such as Blaenau Gwent, Wrexham or Ceredigion. Northern Ireland has an arrangement of district councils, such as Belfast and Armagh.

In very general terms, local authorities have been the principal public service providers of leisure services in the arts, sport and physical recreation, and tourism (Harrop and Long 1994). They provide an extensive range of facilities, venues and activities, from orchestras to football pitches, ice-rinks to caravan sites and lifeguards. However, their activities relating to tourism fall under two main headings. First are their statutory responsibilities, such as physical planning, development control, inspection and regulation, environmental health or licensing, for example. Additionally, however, they provide many discretionary services, including promotion and publicity, information centres, conferences facilities, heritage attractions and social tourism schemes. For the twenty years, local authorities have engaged in tourism development development as a means of economic regeneration in, for example, Bradford, Glasgow, Sheffield, Sunderland and Wigan. They provide financial support to the Regional Tourist Boards and, in partnership with other agencies, increasingly participate in the development and implementation of tourism development strategies. Recent trends have seen development strategies increasingly integrated into broader economic development or local and regional cultural strategies.

Public Bodies

There are many other public bodies which are relevant to an understanding of government and tourism. Sometimes misleadingly referred to as 'quangos', these are part of the 'non-elected' state, including NHS Health Trusts or Learning and Skills Councils. Their members are appointed, not elected.

There are two main types relevant to an understanding of tourism. First, those organisations specifically concerned with the tourism business. Several of these were created by the 1969 Development of Tourism Act, including the British Tourist Authority, the English Tourist Board, the Scottish Tourist Board and the Wales Tourist Board (Adams 2000; Harrop and Long 1994). Focusing on the development of tourism within their particular territorial jurisdiction, these Boards are heavily involved in promotion, marketing and publicising the tourist product. After an increasingly controversial political history, the English Tourist Board was recast in 1999 as the English Tourism Council as part of the new support structure for tourism in England referred to in *Tomorrow's Tourism.* The national Boards and Council work in close partnership with the network of Regional Tourist Boards (Adams 2000).

In addition, there are many other public bodies which are not specifically or primarily concerned with tourism (their principal roles lie elsewhere) but which nevertheless have engaged in tourism development for a number of reasons, or which exert indirect effects. These fall into three main areas:

- arts, culture and heritage;
- environment and the countryside; and
- economic development.

They include the Arts Council, Regional Arts Boards, English Heritage, the Countryside Agency and (in Scotland and Wales) the Countryside Councils, English Nature and Scottish Natural Heritage, the Forestry Commission and various economic development bodies. The legacy of the Urban Development Corporations, wound up in 1998, is also clearly evident. All are significant elements in the overall picture.

Supra-national Government

Last, but by no means least, mention must be made of the work and and influence of the European Union (EU), an example of supra-national government in the form of an economic and political union. Its overall purposes—to restore economic prosperity to a war-ravaged Western Europe after 1945 and to win lasting peace in a world region which had twice within a generation embroiled the rest of the world in almost total warfare - went far beyond tourism. Indeed, no powers relating to tourism were conferred upon the European Commission (and its predecessors) either by the founding Treaty of Rome in 1957 or subsequent Treaties, such as Maastricht. This was not the case with agriculture, fisheries, transport, regional, energy or competition policies, where specific powers were conferred. Nevertheless, the European Union has had major effects in travel and tourism in member states. These can be classified under three headings:

- measures following from the pursuit of the internal market;
- indirect measures from other policy concerns; and
- specific tourism initiatives.

(i) The Internal Market

In this first category, one might note:

- the role of the Single European Act 1987, in providing for the free movement of goods, persons, services and capital and moving by 1993 towards a frontier-free Europe. This has progressively led to the relaxation and abolition of frontier controls and a relatively passport-free 'Schengenland'.
- deregulation of air transport.
- abolition of duty free sales for travellers between EU member states.

- mutual recognition of training and educational qualifications.
- deregulation of coach transport.
- a Union-wide framework of company law.
- the single currency, or 'Euro'.

(ii) Indirect Measures

From other policy commitments include:

- consumer protection initiatives including the package travel directive in 1993.
- denied-boarding compensation (aircraft).
- competition and its effects on civil aviation including transatlantic mergers.
- environmental standards such as bathing water quality.
- cultural tourism, including the European City and Capital of Culture initiatives.

(iii) Specific Tourism Initiatives

Which include:

- Initial Guidelines on Tourism, 1982.
- European Year of Tourism, 1990.
- Community Action Plan to Assist Tourism, 1991.
- Philcxenia - the proposed First Multiannual Programme to assist European Tourism, 1997-2000.

Competitiveness, quality and sustainability have increasingly become the watchwords of EU thinking.

Towards Governance?

Governmental involvement with the business of travel and tourism is, therefore, complex and multi-layered, exten-ding from the local to the supra-national. This multi-level governance is the outcome of several pressures, including globalisation and Europeanisation. For the UK, there have also been internal pressures which have impacted on govern-mental arrangements.

Government in the UK has undergone considerable change over the part twenty-five years or so. These changes have not only led to a new operating code in the public services but also to the partial break-up of the unitary state, with powers being devolved from Westminster to the Scottish Parliament and to the Welsh and Northern Irish Assemblies. These constitution-changing moves have resulted in a further loss of central government control and renewed calls for regional government in England. Some of these have clearly been noted in our review of the administrative furniture. Here, we assess these changes in greater detail and consider some possible consequences of, and for, a 'Disunited Kingdom'.

The Westminster Model

For many years, the Westminster Model provided an organising perspective for understanding British Govern-ment, a way of characterising its main features (Rhodes 1997a). Through its longevity, it became the traditional way of thinking about the describing British government. Most lay people would use it unwittingly in any discussion of how the British state functions. Its survival has been perpetuated by the lack of a viable alternative organising perspective.

In the political science literature, the Westminster Model is defined in various ways. Its essence, however, has been concisely captured by Rhodes, who identifies the defining characteristics are focusing on: parliamentary sovereignty; strong Cabinet government; accountability through elections; majority party control of the executive (that is, Prime Minister, Cabinet and the civil service); elaborate conventions for the conduct of parliamentary business; institutionalised opposition, and the rule of debate (Rhodes 1997a: 3).

The Westminster Model's mainstream status has been strengthened by its applicability to other countries which have developed systems of government similar to Britain's. In other words, the Westminster Model has applicability beyond the parliament which gave it its name. The perspective is transferable and portable.

However, the dominance of the Westminster Model is now being challenged. It is argued that it no longer fully or accurately describes the organisation and operation of the state and power in Britain. It is unlikely that the model will ever completely disappear from political science as an organising perspective. It may not accurately capture the move to governance, but will continue to have relevance to understanding the institutions of UK government.

From Government to Governance

The role and power of the British State has changed. We talk today not of *government* but of *governance.* Gover-nance is about a new way of governing, a changed order. This changed order means a new way of thinking about British government is required, a new way of thinking about and defining the various power relationships. One such way of thinking which has been suggested as overcoming the weaknesses of the Westminster Model is the concept of a 'Differentiated Polity'.

Rhodes (1997a) characterises the Differentiated Polity as 'functional and institutional specialisation and the fragmentation of policies and politics'. He argues that the Differentiated Polity perspective has several advantages over the Westminster Model for conceptualising and understan-ding the governance of Britain:

- the Differentiated Polity allows fuller appreciation of the limits of the Westminster Model;
- it raises important and distinct questions about government in Britain;
- it identifies and explains the major issues and problem facing policy makers today.

The Differentiated Polity framwork, therefore, has a value beyond academic debate concerning the organisation and management of British government. It is about the state, in its manifest and manifold complexity, affects everyday lives.

For many years, the Westminster Model may have been the dominant perspective. During the past quarter of a century, however, much has changed. The very conception of a public sector, its purpose and role, structures, institu-tions, resourcing and management practices have all been radically transformed in a process which continues under Mr. Blair's premiership (Harrop 1999). Although the signs were there to see long before 1979, it was Mrs. Thatcher who set about public service reform with energy and enthusiasm. Partly because of the Westminster Model itself perhaps, the overly bureaucratic state could be lampooned as self-serving, conceited, wasteful, inefficient, disabling, hidebound and insufficiently attentive to the public who, shared and entangled, struggled in deadly web of 'red tape'. Riding the ideological chariot of the 'New Right' into battle, for Mrs. Thatcher the moment was opportune. And after the so-called 'winter of discontent' in 1978-79, there was little popular support for much of the public sector. They may not have liked Mrs Thatcher very much, but they had no affection either for local government, for example.

Contemptuous of the performance of the public sector, Mrs. Thatcher embarked upon her wide-ranging reform agenda. Nothing less than wholesale change would do. Particular emphasis was laid on 'rolling back the frontiers of the state' and lifting the yoke of public bureaucracies from the people, on reducing the burden of public expenditure and making efficiency savings. Clear themes became discernible and a guiding ideological rationale (Rhodes 1997a):

- the large-scale privatisation of public assets (including for example British Airways in 1986 and the British Airports Authority in 1987);
- the marketisation and compulsory commercialisation of what remained in the public sector (including the purchaser - provider split in the National Health Service and compulsory competitive tendering and contracting out in local government);
- the break-up (and in some cases abolition) of public sector bureaucracies and the introduction of alternative delivery systems;
- the introduction and adoption of private sector methods and styles of management;
- de-concentration and devolution of the administrative work of central government (by creating the Executive Agencies, for example);
- a growth in regulation though output control; and
- tighter central resource control.

In the whirl of furious activity, however, not everything was well or carefully thought through. Some of the reforms may have been less than successful because insufficient attention was given to the underlying values and purpose of public services, and the complex challenge of their manage-ment. The result was an interesting mix of unplanned, as well as planned, outcomes. The concept of a Differentiated Polity captures something of the unintended, as well as intentional, results of the reforms as the authority of the unitary state diminishes and the ability of central govern-ment to control the system is reduced. This may not have been Mrs. Thatcher's intention.

Under Tony Blair the genie of devolution has been uncorked. The result has been the emergence of real policy differences geographically. In Scotland, for example, there are no tuition fees for students in higher education and financial arrangements for care of the elderly are less punitive. Nor do arrangements for the public administration of cultural services reflect those in England. It may be impossible to recork the bottle. 'Balkanisation' of the policy could be unintended consequence of the honourable devolution of power and authority. The balance between freedom and order, always difficult to strike, has shifted.

The Consequences of Reform

There are several unintended consequences of public sector reform which have important implications for democracy and how the British public is governed, and which also impact on government's management of travel and tourism. The impact of these consequences is augmented by the fact that they will not be easy to undo, meaning that today central government is governing with imperfect control, a situation which looks likely to continue well into the new millennium. The most serious unintended conseque-nces concern accountability, steering and fragmentation (Rhodes 1997b).

Accountability, Steering and Fragmentation

One of the main objectives of the Thatcher reforms was the break up of public sector bureaucracies, a fragmentation which would free mangers from the constraints of rule-bound administration. However, fragmentation has led to a situa-tion which is harder for the centre to control. Within a framework of networks and 'collaborative governance', may organisations provide public services. The challenge of devising an overall strategy and securing its implementation becomes more difficult for central government. Another stated reason for pursuing a policy of public sector fragmen-tation was to improve accountability. With smaller organisations, the role of individuals and organisations in policy outcomes would be more easily identifiable and, consequently, they could be more easily held to account. However, an opposite outcome may be identified; that is, fragmentation has blurred accountability. The myriad of organisations now involved in the provision of public services means that it is harder to distinguish the precise influence on policy outcomes. The buck stops where? Accountability is as slippery as a bar of wet soap.

Furthermore, the fragmentation of the public sector means that control and steering are major problems facing government. The numbers of interested parties involved in service provision means that the centre cannot clearly control their actions. Moreover, implementing parties will interpret policy to suit best their own purpose. Policy outcomes are, therefore, diluted. This dilution of policy may also result in more policy being generated to plug the gaps in policy outcomes. A vicious circle thus develops. The centre cannot steer the system through traditional means. It is arguable that, under Mrs. Thatcher, these unintended consequences led to a situation of decentralisation to centralise—in other words, in order to control the system, central government had to increase control over resources, thus defeating a main aim of the reform programme. There are no easy solutions to the problems of governance.

As far as the territorial settlement is concerned, the creation of the Scottish Parliament and Welsh and Northern Ireland Assemblies has already moved the UK from the traditional understandings of a unitary state towards disunity. The consequences of these moves are, to a certain extent, dependent on the resultant degree of disunity. It has been argued above that the creation of these devolved structures may add to the problems already apparent in the move from the Westminster Model to a Differentiated Polity. Any further realisation of regionalisation or regionalism through the establishment of regional government in England would necessarily compound the problem.

Regionalisation may ultimately result in the break up of the UK, but what of the standing of the separate emerging administrative units? Scotland may have difficulties in asserting itself in negotiations with the EU and other governments. What chance have the English regions? A more likely outcome is, perhaps, the creation of a regional tier of government in the UK, but then where would this leave Scotland and Wales? Would there be calls for Scottish and Welsh reginalisation? After all, the Highlands and Islands of Scotland may consider its claims for a degree of self-government as valid as that of, say, the South West of England. The ultimate irony, however, would be a situation where the regions of the UK achieved devolved government and found themselves more constrained as a result. The greater the differentiation the greater the integration needs to be to maintain the whole. Again, checks and balances, freedom and order.

Government and Governance, Travel and Tourism

What, then, are the implications of this shift towards governance for travel and tourism?

The UK is no longer the unitary state it once was (perhaps it never was all that united?). Goverment has undergone, and is likely to continue to undergo, great change. The way we think about and explain British government has shifted away from the Westminster Model towards the organising perspective of a Differentiated Polity. Regionali-sation is alive, if not always well. The haste to reform has, however, raised new challenges of governance. Publish in haste, repent at leisure was the warning of the wise; reform in a rush and rue the wreckage might be the advice to the legislator. The privatisation of the railways is not the only example—remember dangerous dogs? For tourism policies, what are the implications?

Ironically, in some ways, the history of policies for tourism and travel in the UK displayed many of the features and problems which are now being identified as problematic in the differentiated polity—namely fragmen-tation, lack of accountability and steering. Undoubtedly, many elements of government and the public sector were relevant to understanding the overall picture. However, the development and implementation of clear policies, systematically connected to other considerations and integrated into other policy fields such as energy, environment or transport, remained weak. The effects of public policy were largely unknown and business lamented the lack of a guiding framework for action. Indeed, various organisations, such as the Tourism Society, have long called for a more cohesive policy framework for tourism.

New Labour's chosen solution, within its general modernisation programme for government, was to think in terms of joined up solutions for joined up problems—joined-up governance, in fact.

The publication in February 1999 of *Tomorrow's Tourism*, its new strategy for 'a growth industry for the new millennium', has already been mentioned in this context. Its raft of recommendations, proposals and action points revolved around a number of key themes:

- to provide a new support structure for tourism in England, including the creation of the English Tourism Council to replace the English Tourist Board;
- to develop and promote quality tourism experiences;
- to provide better information about tourism;
- to promote improved career opportunities including a careers festival;
- to promote the wise growth of tourism through sustainable development; and
- to widen access to tourism, especially for those on low incomes, families, the elderly and the disabled.

One of its provisions was for convening, each March, an annual Tourism Summit of Ministers, officials and senior representatives from the industry. Its papers and proceedings, publicly available, provide a picture of joined-up governance in action. The second Tourism Summit (March 6, 2001) reviewed progress on the initiatives and action points agreed by Ministers at the first Summit. Chaired by then Secretary of State for Culture, Media and Sport, Chris Smith, the Summit participants (16) included another seven Ministers, representatives of the National Assembly for Wales, the Northern Ireland Executive and HM Treasury, as well as the Chairmen of the English Tourism Council, the British, Tourist Executive and senior officers of the British Hospitality Association and the Better Regulation Task Force. The following progress updates were presented:

- *Ministry of Agriculture, Fisheries and Food :*
  - Foot and Mouth disease outbreaks and the effects of restrictions
  - Rural Enterprise Scheme
  - Local food promotion

- *Department of the Environment, Transport and the Regions:*
  - Signage of tourist attractions
  - Spending Review
  - Rural Bus Challenge
  - 'Traveline', the new information system
  - Alternatives to the car for leisure travel
  - 'Waterways For Tomorrow'
  - Bathing Water Directive Standards
  - Rural White Paper
  - Urban White Paper
- *Department for Education and Employment :*
  - Standards in further education
  - Learning Skills Council
- *Foreign and Commenwealth Office*
  - Leave and multi-entry visas
  - UK portable website
  - Sustainable tourism
- *Home Office*
  - Modernisation of licensing laws
  - Sunday dancing
  - Gambling review
  - Easing UK entry procedures
- *Department of Trade and Industry*
  - Small Business Service
  - Knowledge Economy White Paper
  - Best practice forum to strengthen competitiveness through management skills and business procedures.
- Other progress reports were made by HM Treasury, the National Assembly for Wales, the Nothern Ireland Executive, the English Tourism Council and the British Tourist Authority.

New agenda items focussed discussion on resort regeneration, better regulation of hotels and restaurants and the BTA's *First Impressions* survey. The Tourism Summit, in the words of its

Chairman, 'had demonstrated its worth in concentrating minds on the needs of tourism', and would reconvene one year hence, although officials would meet more frequently in order to maintain the momentum. 'Joining-up' is not, however, a simple task. One preferred way of going about it is to create co-ordinating organisations and mecha-nisms (the Tourism Summit may be an example of the latter). However, such arrangements may add to the complexity by increasing the number of interests to be joined-up.

There are some possible strategies, however, for overcoming the challenges of governance. These strategies are as applicable to travel and tourism policies as to any other policy area. Stoker (2001) suggests three ways of improving co-ordination in an effective system of multi-level governance:

- the use of contracts or concordats can express joint commitments to spend money and achieve improvements;
- joint budget holding can guarantee co-ordination of policy working; and
- summits or regular meetings of key actors can dissipate conflicts between different levels of government.

He contends that the agenda is not about choosing between these options, but about finding space and scope for them all. The future lies not in establishing exclusive areas of jurisdiction, but in finding ways to co-operate.

Such new ways of governing will not appear, however, without change in the behaviour of key actors. Crucial to New Labour's modernisation programme and prospects for good multi-level governance are the key skills of diplomacy and negotiation. These lie at the root of the new governance and are skills which need to be developed and effectively deployed. Mindsets have to move on. The distance to be travelled may be significant. The travel and tourism busi-ness, however, demands effective policy co-ordination. A complex and fragmented business in a labyrinth of multiple interdependencies, the portfolio cannot be detached from other concerns. Itself a sensitive barometer of economic and political factors, such as economic well-being or safety and security, tourism in turn exerts its own external effects (on the planning process, for example, on transport networks, pollution and congestion, land use, environment or the physical infrastructure such as water supply and sewage disposal to name only a few) and, in addition to its obvious purpose such as offering good holidays, pleasure, relaxation and enjoyment, it can contribute to so many other concerns of public policy, including economic development or regene-ration and social inclusion initiatives. It deserves and dem-ands joined-up governance. The historical baronies of policy making and implementation have not tended to serve it well.

The modernisation of government is generally to be welcomed, but how effective will the emerging arrange-ments be? The past couple of years have been interesting and challenging ones of tourism. The year 2000 saw a fuel supply crisis, major disruption to rail travel and widespread flooding in the UK. The following year, 2001, was marked by major outbreaks of foot and mouth diseas at home and the terrorist events of September 11 in New York, Washington and Pennsylvania. How well was government able to cope? Were its responses qualitatively improved? That is the acid test of it all for government and the tourism business must make their way together in a real world not always of their own choosing, and one in which there are no easy answers.

4

Law and Hospitality

Introduction

This chapter is divided into two sections. the first describes briefly the English legal system and is intended to provide a basic understanding of the legal framework within which the travel industry must operate. The second gives a broad outline of some of the most important areas of law that are of particular relevance to the package travel industry.

The English Legal System

The purpose of this first section is to explain the sources of English law and, in particular; to differentiate between civil and criminal law. In other words, it explains where laws come from and the different kinds of law that exist.

Sources of Law

Broadly speaking, there are two sources of law in England—legislation and case law. Legislation is law made by Parliament and is the collective name for what are also known as Acts of Parliament or statutes. Case law is law made by the courts and is also known as the common law or judicial precedent.

(a) Legislation

An act of Parliament, or a statute, is a law which has been passed by Parliament after being subjected to a rigorous scrutiny by both the House of Commons and the House of Lords (often after an equally rigorous consultation process outside Parliament). This process includes a formal intro-duction into one House by means of a first reading of what is then known as bill. Then there is a full scale debate on the merits of the bill during the second reading. After the second reading the bill goes through the committee stage where it is looked at in some detail—often clause by clause. Finally, it is returned to the floor of the House where, after a report stage, it receives its third reading. Then the bill is sent to the other House where it undergoes a similar process. If it survives all this it then receives the royal assent and becomes law.

Parliament only has time to deal with about 70 or 80 new statutes a year. Examples of statutes passed in recent years that have had a direct bearing on the regulation of the travel industry include the Trade Descriptions Act 1968, which concerns false trade descriptions, and the Consumer Protection Act 1987, which is about misleading price indications. Further examples are the Unfair Contract Terms Act 1977 and the Misrepresentation Act 1967.

(b) Delegated Legislation

Apart from Acts of Parliament, another very important form of legislation is delegated legislation. For a variety of reasons, including lack of time, lack of technical expertise of the need for speed, Parliament often delegates the making of legislation to an inferior body-usually a minister but sometimes a local authority. Much law is therefore made without proper Parliamentary consideration and is usually done by way of an enabling Act—an Act of Parliament which contains a power enabling a minister, or whoever, to make delegated legislation.

One example of delegated legislation of direct relevance to the travel industry is the Civil Aviation (Air Travel Organisers' Licensing) Regulations 1995, otherwise known as the ATOL Regulations. These Regulations provide that tour operators who offer air-inclu-sive package holidays must be licensed and boned by the CAA. Although they were first passed in 1972 they have been amended on a number of occasions. However, the most important example of delegated legislation relevant to the travel industry is the Package Travel, Package Holidays and Package Tours Regulations 1992. In this instance, the enabling Act is the European Communities Act 1972 which was passed when the UK joined the EEC and provides that European legislation can be enacted in the UK by means of delegated legislation. This was how the EC Directive on Package Travel, Package Holidays and Package Tours 1990 became part of English law.

(c) European Legislation

Increasingly, much English law comes from Brussels rather than Westminster and it is necessary, therefore, to give a brief explanation of the types of legislation that we are subject to as members of the European Union.

(i) ***Treaties:*** The European Community Treaty (the Treaty of Rome), as amended by Treaty on European Union (the Maastricht Treaty) and the Treaty of Amsterdam, are all primary sources of European law and are directly applicable in the UK by virtue of the European Communities Act 1972 s.2(2). This means that they create rights in English law without the necessity for legislation by *Parliament.*

(ii) ***Secondary sources:*** These include Directives which in general are not directly applicable in the UK unless Parliament gives effect to them by statute or delegated legislation. As explained above this is how the Package Travel Regulations came into being. Regulations are a form of European legislation which, in general, are directly applicable.

Occasionally, European secondary sources of law are regarded as being directly applicable without Parliament having implemented them by means of domestic legislation. For instance, if the UK had not complied with its European obligations by bringing the Package Travel Directive in force by 31 December, 1992, the Directive would nevertheless have been directly applicable in the UK. What this means is that a UK citizen who was adversely affected by the failure of the UK government to bring the EC Directive into force could *sue the government* for the losses caused by the failure. Thus, if a tour operator had become insolvent before the Govern-ment had implemented the requirements about security, the consumers harmed by this failure could claim compensation from the Government. This situation actually arose in Germany in 1993, as illustrated by the following case.

Dillenkofer and others v Germany: A German tour operator became bankrupt before the German government had implemented the Directive. German consumers who lost out as a result sued the

German government to recover their money. The European Court of Justice held they were entitled to be compensated by the government which had failed to implement those provisions of the Directive which would have protected consumers in the event of a tour operator's insolvency.

Note that the Directive is directly applicable against the state - known as vertical applicability - but it does not create rights as between individuals (horizontal applica-bility).

(d) Case Law

A large part of English law is to be found not in statues but in case law—decisions made by the judges in individual cases which create *precedents* which are then *followed* by other judges. A system of *binding precedent* (otherwise known as stare decisis) has evolved, whereby once a court has decided a case then the rule or principle that it establishes is binding in later cases. The rule that the case establishes is also known as *ratio decidendi*—the reasons for the decision. The judge in a subsequent case has no choice in the matter, he *must* follow the previous *ratio* no matter how much he disagrees with it. The reason for this is to establish consis-tency in the law. If a judge could decide a case according to whatever principles he chose then it would be difficult for anyone to know where they stood in any particular situation.

It could be argued that a disadvantage of such as system is that lacks flexibility and, consequently, the law is unable to grow or adapt to changing circumstances and unjust decisions are perpetuated. However, the system in general does posses sufficient flexibility to overcome the problems of excessive rigidity. Firstly, it is possible for a court higher up in the hierarchy of courts to *overrule* a previous decision of a lower court. For instance, the Court of Appeal can overrule decisions of the High Court, and the House of Lords can overrule decisions of the Court of Appeal. (A case is *overruled* when a court in a later case decides that the ratio of the first case is wrong. A case is *reversed* when a court to which that case is appealed decides that the decision of the lower court was wrong.) Note that it is higher courts that bind lower courts, not *vice-versa.*

Secondly, a subsequent court can *distinguish* the decision of a previous court and refuse to follow it. To distinguish a previous case is not to disagree with the principle or rule that it lays down but simply to say that the sufficiently different to justify coming to a decision which is not based on that principle. For example, the case of *Jarvis v Swans Tours* [1973] 1 All ER 71 establishes that in holiday cases a plaintiff is entitled to damages for distress and disappointment. But how far does this principle extend? *Hayes v Dodd* [1990] 2 All ER 815 decided that, where a contract is not for the purpose of providing peace of mind or freedom from distress, damages for distress and disappointment are not recoverable.

So what about a 'flight-only' contract to a holiday destination? Is this to be decided according to *Jarvis* or *Hayes?* It would be possible for a judge, if he so wished, to distinguish the facts of such a case from either *Jarvis* or *Hayes* - giving him the freedom to decide the case as he saw fit. This would not require him to ignore or overrule these decisions—merely to say that the factual situation he is dealing with does not fit comfortably within the principles established by those cases and therefore need not be followed. One County Court case does address just this issue.

Lucas v Avro [1994] CLY 1444. The plaintiff had bought 'flight-only' tickets from the defendants. The return flight returned almost 24 hours later than the plaintiff expected because of a mistake on the ticket. Avro admitted breach of contract and paid damages of £165 for hotel, taxi and telephone expenses and loss of earnings. However, the plaintiff also claimed damages for distress and disappointment. It was held that, as the contract was not one to provide either freedom from distress or to provide peace of mind, such damages were not recoverable.

It remains to be seen whether the reasoning in this case will be adopted by the higher courts.

Finally, it is possible, if all else fails, for legislation to be passed to overrule inconvenient or unjust precedents. This is effectively what the Package Travel Regulations have done to large parts of the common law relating to package holidays. For instance the decision in *Wall v Silver Wing Surface Arrangements* (1981, unreported), a High Court decision which was followed in a number of County Court cases, laid down that a tour operator was not liable to clients who were injured on holiday by the negligence of the hotel they were booked into. Now, Regulation 15 of the Package Travel Regulations provides that a tour operator is responsible for the negligence of suppliers.

Civil and Criminal Law

Broadly speaking, the criminal law is concerned with offences that are regarded as being sufficiently serious or anti-social that, when they occur, the state should intervene to maintain order to protect citizens who may be unable or unwilling to protect themselves. This intervention will usually take the form of an individual being prosecuted by the State in a criminal court and, if the *defendant* is found *guilty,* then *punishment* such as a fine or imprisonment will be imposed. This clearly applies to 'traditional' crimes such as murder, manslaughter, arson, rape or theft, but the criminal courts also deal with large numbers of 'regulatory' offences, such as parking on double yellow lines or failing to label the contents of processed food properly. These are not criminal offences in the traditional sense but, in order to regulate a complex modern society, it has become necessary to categorise such activities as criminal and to impose criminal penalties simply in order to ensure that the traffic on our roads can flow freely or we can eat food confident in the knowledge that it is properly labelled.

A number of statutes that impact heavily on the travel industry fall into this latter category, including the Trade Descriptions Act 1968, the Consumer Protection Act 1987 and many of the provisions in the Package Travel Regula-tions 1992 relating to the provision of information. Lord Scarman has said of the Trade Descriptions Act:

"....it is not a truly criminal statute. Its purpose is not the enforcement of the criminal law but the maintenance of trading standards. Training standards, not criminal behav-iour are its concern.".

The civil law, on the other hand, is largely concerned with disputes between individuals. Two of the most important areas of civil law are contract law and the law of torts, in which the dispute will often resolve itself into a situation where a *claimant,* formerly called a *plaintiff* (the person with the grievance) is *suing a defendant* in a civil court. If the defendant is found *liable,* then the will endeavour to find a *remedy* - usually financial compensation called *damages* but, occasionally, an *injunction* or an award of specific *performance.*

Frequently, the same set of facts can give rise to both criminal and civil liability. For example, if a tour operator describes a hotel in a misleading fashion, such as stating that the hotel has a children's swimming pool when it doesn't this may give rise to a criminal prosecution under s.14 of the Trade Descriptions Act 1968 or Regulation 5 of the Package Travel Regulations. It may also give rise to a civil action for breach of contract or misrepresentation. If the misrepresentation was deliberate, then this amounts to the tort of deceit. The tour operator may end up paying both a hefty fine for the criminal offence and substantial damages for the civil liability.

Package Travel Law

Building upon the overview of the English legal system, this second looks at those aspects of the law, both civil and criminal, that have most bearing on the package travel industry. More specifically, it considers, those parts of the law that govern the relationship between tour operations and their clients. Some of this law, such as the of contract, is of general application in that it applies to all business but some, such as the Package Travel Regulations 1992, is specifically aimed at the travel industry.

This section covers four main areas:

- The civil liability of tour operators as defined by the Package Travel Regulations (PTR).
- The law of contract and its relation to the Package Travel Regulations 1992.
- Tour operators' criminal liability under the Package Travel Regulations, the Trade Descriptions Act 1968 and the Consumer Protection Act 1987.
- The protection the law gives to consumers when their tour operator becomes insolvent.

The liability of hotels, airlines, railways, ferry operators, coach operators and other travel industry business who do no come within the ambit of the Package Travel Regulations are not covered here as they fall outside the scope of this chapter.

Scope of the Regulations

The purpose of the Regulations is to regulate conventional package holidays, such as two weeks of sun, sea and sand in the Mediterranean and other similar arrangements. On this everyone is agreed but, unfortunately, the scope of the definition of a 'package' in Regulation 2 is so wide that it goes far beyond conventional package holidays.

There is an amazing variety of travel and holiday arrangements over which fierce arguments rage about their inclusion in the definition of package, such as overnight ferry tips to the continent; business travel; holiday camps and caravan sites; 'tailor-made' packages put together by travel agents; sleeper accommodation on the newly privatised railways; holidays provided by local authority social services departments for their pensioners; and activity holidays provided by schools or local education authorities. Interes-tingly, the Association of British Travel Agents (ABTA), the main trade association, has issued guidelines on the scope of the Regulations which disagree fundamentally on the extent of the definition.

We are concerned here with examining the scope of the definitions in the Regulations with a view to determining what falls within the Regulations and is subject to its regime and what falls outside and remains regulated solely by the common law.

(i) The Definition of 'Package'

The Regulations define 'package' in the following manner:

2(1) *'Package' means the pre-arranged combination of at least two of the following components when sold or offered for sale at an inclusive price and when the service covers a period of more than twenty-four hours or includes overnight accomodation:*

(a) transport;

(b) accomodation;

(c) other tourist services not ancillary to transport or accomodation and accounting for a significant proportion of the package. and

(ii) the submission of separate accounts for different components shall not cause the arrangements to be other than a package;

(iii) the fact that a combination is arranged at the request of the consumer and in accordance with his specific instructions (whether modified or not) shall not of itself cause it to be treated as other than pre-arranged.

Thus, for there to be a package there has to be :

- a pre-arranged combination
- sold at an inclusive price
- consisting of two of the following:
  - transport
  - accomodation
  - other tourist services

At the margins, all these terms cause difficulties. For instance, is a 'fly drive' package caught by the Regulations because it is only two forms of transport? Or what about package put together by travel agents? Are they 'pre-arranged' combinations? Does the term 'other tourist services' include services for businessmen? Despite the fact that the Regulations are now several years old, many fundamental questions like this remain unanswered. However, the vast majority of holidays sold by major tour operators, like Thomson, Airtours, JMC and First Choice, undoubtedly fall within the Regulations.

(ii) Upon Whom is Liability Imposed?

The regulations impose liability on 'the organiser' and 'the retailer'.

1. The Organiser

2(1) 'Organiser' means a person who, otherwise than occasionally, organises packages and sells or offers them for sale, whether directly or through a retailer.

The test here is how frequently the organiser arranges packages, not, as in other consumer protection legislation. whether the organiser acts in the course of a business. The definition will clearly catch conventional tour operators but, importantly, it will also catch most travel agents in its net. If 'tailor-made packages' are regarded as 'pre-arranged', then it will be very rare indeed that a travel agent can say that he does not 'otherwise than occasionally' put a package together. In this context it is important to note that the term organiser cuts across the more conventional terms of principle and agent. That is, to be an organiser it is not necessary to be a principle and, by the same token, an agent is not precluded from being an organiser simply because he is an agent; the criterion is whether a person 'organises' a package, not whether they act as principal.

The chief significance of being labelled an organiser is that the liabilities are much greater that those of a retailer. The organiser is responsible for the performance of the whole package but the retailer's liabilities are much more narrowly defined. There are also additional criminal offences for organisers to fall foul of.

2. The Retailer

2.(1) 'Retailer' means the person who sells or offers for sale the package put together by the organiser.

The definition clearly covers the activities of travel agents. Under the Directive, member states had the option of imposing liability on either organisers or retailers or both for failures in the package itself. It is generally believed that the Regulations do not impose such extensive liabilities on retailers but they do make them subject to the provision of information regime (Reg. 5 and possibly also Regs 7 and 8) and they incur civil liability under Reg. 4 for providing misleading descriptive matter. However a recent case has imposed liability on a travel agent.

Hone v Going Places (2001, Court of Appeal). The claimant, who was on a package holiday, was injured during an emergency evacuation of an aeroplane following a bomb scare . Both the tour operator which organised the holiday and the airline which provided the flights were bankrupt and not worth suing so the claimant sued the travel agent through whom the holiday had been purchased. During the purchase of the holiday the travel had not made it clear that they were only acting as an agent for the tour operator; they had given the impression that they were the principles selling the holiday. The Court of Appeal held that they would be treated as 'organisers' because they had held themselves out as such. (Note that although the travel agents could be sued as organisers they were ultimately not liable because the court said that there was no failure to take reasonable care of the claimant.)

As previously stated, a travel agent who puts a package together and sells it in his own name falls within the definition of organiser rather than retailer and is, therefore, subject to the more stringent liabilities in the Regulations. Similarly, the agent who packages extra elements with a conventional packages is likely to be classified as an organiser rather than a retailer.

(iii) In Whose Favour is the Liability Imposed?

The Regulations impose civil liability on the organiser and, in some cases, the retailer, in favour of 'consumers'.

2(2) ... 'consumer' means the person who takes or agrees to take the package ('the principal contractor) and elsewhere in these Regulations 'consumer' means, as the context requires, the principal contractor, any person on whose behalf the principal contractor agrees to purchase the package ('the other beneficiaries') or any person to whom the principal contractor or any of the other beneficiaries transfers the package ('the transferee')

Traditionally in English Law, only a party to a contract is entitled to take the benefit of it. In other words, there have been doubts as to the extent to which members of a client's family who are named on the booking form but who may not be party to the contract would be entitled to the benefits of the contract. All 92 and *Wooder v wimpey* [1980] 1 All ER 571. The problem also extends to members of a party where one person has made the booking on behalf of others.

However, the definition of 'consumer' in the Regulations, making what amounts to a revolutionary change to a long established rule of English law (which still applies to all but package holiday contracts) goes some way to eliminating these problems. Furthermore, if a consumer transfers his booking to another person, as he is sometimes entitled to do now under Regulation 10, the transferee stands in the same position as the original consumer.

Contract

(a) Making the Contract

A contract can be defined as a *legally binding agreement*. Legally binding simply means that it is an agreement recognised by the law which can be enforced if necessary by the courts. Briefly, the elements of an enforceable contract are that:

- the parties have come to an agreement;
- the agreements is intendent to be legally binding;
- each party has provided the other with consideration;
- the contract is in the right form; and
- the parties each have the legal capacity to make the contract.

Apart from the first of these requirements, we can dispose of the other elements briefly because they do not cause much problem in holiday contracts. However, it is important to look at how agreement is arrived at in more detail.

Intention: as far as intention to create legal relations is concerned, in general most commercial transactions are intended to be legally binding and certainly a contract between and individual and a tour operator for the provision of a holiday would be enforceable.

Consideration: consideration means that each party has given something or done something of value for the other. Consideration is the price one party pays to enforce the promise that the other party has made. So, in a holiday contract, the consideration provided by the consumer is the price he pays, or promises to pay, for the holiday. The tour operator's consideration is his promise to provide the holiday in exchange for the price.

Capacity: if a party does not have the legal capacity to make a contract, it is not binding on him. Persons falling into this category would be drunks, the insane and minors. The former two categories are of marginal legal importance and as for minors they do not in practice create problems for tour operators.

Form: some contracts must be in the right form. As far as package holiday contracts are concerned, the Package Travel Regulations 1992 provide in Regulation 9 that all the terms of a contract must be reduced to writing and a copy given to the consumer before the contract is made, unless this is impracticable. Even where it is impracticable to do it before the contract is made, a copy must be provided to the consumer in every case. If this is not done, the consumer has the right to cancel the contract.

Offer and Acceptance

Turning now to *agreement,* before there can be a legally binding contract the parties must have reached an agreement. Lawyers break down the process of agreement into two parts. One of the parties must have made an *offer* to the other party which the other party has *accepted.* An offer can be defined as a statement by one party he is prepared to be bound by the terms of his offer if the other party accepts his offer. An acceptance is an unquivocal agreement to the terms of the offer. An offer must be distinguished from an *invitation* to treat. An invitation to treat is where a party sets the ball rolling by indicating that he is prepared to consider offers from the other party. In other words, he is not yet prepared to commit himself to making a firm offer but he wishes to enter into negotiations. In a package holiday context, the tour operator usually makes an invitation to treat when he publishes his brochure. In effect, he is saying that he has holidays available for sale and if members of the public come forward and make an offer to buy a holiday then the tour operator may then accept the offer.

In this process of offer and acceptance, there are a number of other rules:

- an offer can be withdrawn at any time before it is accepted but the withdrawal of the offer must be communicated to the other party before it is effective.
- an offer will lapse after a stated time, or after a reasonable timer or after it has been rejected.
- a counter offer amounts to a refusal to the offer, which then lapses.
- silence does not amount to consent; for example, the statement 'I will assume we have a contract unless I hear to the contrary' will not bind the other party, even if they do not reply.

(b) The Contents of the Contract

As part of the bargaining process, before a contract is concluded the two parties will make a variety of statements to each other, either orally or in writing. Some of these statements may end up as part of the contract and some may not, and those which end up as part of the contract may vary in importance. This section is concerned with how to classify these statements. It is important to be able to do this because the rights of the parties clearly depend upon whether a statement is part of the contract or not, and if it is, the relative importance to be attached to it.

(i) Terms, Representations and Mere Puffs

The task of classification is complicated by the fact that English law distinguishes between three different types of statement. Firstly, there are those statements which end up as *terms of the contract* which, if broken, give the victim a straightforward action for *breach of contract.* These are the things which the other party has promised you will get. In a package holiday context, it will be a term of the contract, for instance, that it is a four state hotel, that the clients will get a balcony and private facilities, that there are three pools and two bars, that it has a children's club, and so on. Generally, these are all statements which are printed in the brochure and are what the operator has *contracted* to provide.

Secondly, there are statements which *induce* the other party to enter into the contract but do not become terms of the contract. These are known as *representations* and, if they are *false,* they give rise to an action for *misrepresentation.* An action for misrepresentation is not as straightforward as an action for breach of contract and the remedies available may be inadequate in some circumstances.

Often it is difficult to distinguish between a term and a representation but, for example, it would probably only be a representation if an operator, having described the hotel, then went on to describe the resort as having a 'wide range of shops'. The operator is contracting to provide an hotel with particular facilities but then, in order to encourage the client to enter into the contract, he makes other statements which will influence the client's decision but which do not form part of the contract. If the resort turns out not to have a wide range of shops, the client can sue for misrepresentation but not for breach of contract.

Thirdly, there are statements which have no legal force at all. These are known as 'puffs' or 'mere puffs' and a victim of such a statement has no redress at all. In one case, *Hoffman v Intasun (1990,* High Court, Unreported), the plaintiff tried to make out that because of the extravagantly worded statements made at the beginning of 'Club 18-30' brochure, the defendants, Intasun, had *contracted* that they owed her an especially high standard of care. The judge rejected this approach. He decided that the satements had no contractual effect at all. This is what he said:

"I am asked to say that because of the advertising—what lawyers call "puff"—in the early part of the brochure, the Defendants were undertaking to give an especially high standard of care. That is an argument that I reject. Puff is Puff, and if that is what lawyers call it, lay people have their own expressions for it which are perhaps less flattering. Everybody knows that travel agents (sic) set out to create an atmosphere on paper of a wonderful holiday and marvellous value for money. It cannot possibly be said that a visitor to the Tyrol can sue the travel company for breach of contract if he fails to have any respiratory defect in regarding the breathtaking views of the mountains there - and so on. I look for example at how the Club reps are described on page 8 of the brochure.

Mr Eccles (counsel for Intasun) in his opening drew my attention to it specifically saying that the reps were the life and soul of the party, hard working, good timing, trouble shooting, guitar playing, beach partying, smooth operators. I do not know if Miss Gail Tarburn [the Intasun rep] can even play the guitar and I am certain that it could not form any part of a breach of contract if she cannot."

Much of the advertising hype that goes into the front of brochures falls into this category, with satements that make the holiday sound good but do not amount to specific contractual promises. Examples are to be found in most borchures—'picturesque villages set amidst glorious scenery'—'quality hotels'—'the number one choice for families'—'the holiday of a lifetime'—'the most beautiful locations around the Mediterranean'—'hand picked accommodation'—'a luxury cruise around the glittering Caribbean', and so on.

Thus, not only do terms have to be distinguished from representations, they both have to be distinguished from mere puffs.

(ii) Conditions, Warranties and Innominate Terms

Terms can be classifieds into either *conditions or warranties*. A condition is a major term of the contract which if broken provides the victim of the breach with not only a right to damages but also the right, if they wish, to terminate the contract altogether. A warranty, on the other hand, only gives rise to an action for damages. There is no right to terminate the contract for what is regarded as a breach of a minor term of the contract. There is also an intermediate form of term - called an *innominate* term - which cannot immediately be classified as either a condition or a warranty. Its classification depends upon the nature and severity of the breach.

(iii) Express and Implied Terms

Terms can be further classified into *express terms* and *implied* terms. An express term, as its name suggests, is one which is expressed in some way, either in writing or orally. An implied term is one where the term is not expressed but can nevertheless be implied into the contract. Terms can be implied either *in fact* or *in law.* The following travel law case, decided before the Package Travel Regulations were passed, revolved around the issue of implied terms and illustrates the problem vividly.

Wall v Silver Wing Surface Arrangements (1981, Unreported), A party of holidaymakers were injured in a hotel fire in Tenerife. They had been unable to escape down the fire escape because the hotel owners had padlocked the gate at the bottom. In the contract between the clients and the tour operators nothing was expressly stated about safety at the hotel but the clients alleged that there was an implied term in the contract that they would be reasonably safe in using the hotel for the purposes for which they had been invited to be there. Ultimately the court held that there was no such term but it had to make a difficult choice between protecting the interests of the clients by implying a term relating to their safety and the interests of the tour operator by not extending its liability to all the components of the package.

(iv) The Package Travel Regulations and the Classifi-cation of Terms

The classification of terms in a package holiday contract is no longer simply a matter for the common law, but is heavily affected by the Package Travel Regulations. For instance, Reg. 6 states that all the particulars in the brochure (whatever that means) are implied warranties. On the face of it this has two major effects. Firstly, it potentially upgrades just about every statement in the brochure to at least a term of the contract - representations and puffs alike. Secondly, it appears to classify all statements as minor terms of the contract.

As far as this second effect is concerned, closer examination of the Regulations shows that this is not entirely so. For instance, Regulation 9 explicitly states that it is an implied *condition* that certain information must be supplied to the consumer before the contract is made. In addition, there are other regulations which have the same effect. Reg. 12 permits a consumer to withdraw from the contract if significant alterations have been made to the contract before departure and Reg. 14 effectively gives the consumer the right to terminate a contract if, atter departure, a significant proportion of the services cannot be provided.

(v) Exclusion Clauses

One very important type of term, which will be looked at in more detail in a subsequent section, is the exclusion clause—also known as an exemption clause or an exception clause. These are clauses where one party to the contract endeavours to escape liability for breach of contract by inserting a clause into the contract excluding his liability.

(vi) Liability under Regulation 15

Until 1992, the position at common law was that tour operators were not liable for the defaults or negligence of their subcontractors (or suppliers as they are often called). This was the issue which was at the heart of the *Wall* case referred to above. Although it had been the fault of the hotelkeeper that the fire escape gate had been padlocked, no blame could be attributed to the tour operator in the case. On the contrary, the judge said that the tour operator was a reputable company that had acted properly throughout. It had selected a modern hotel and monitored it for safely and there was nothing more that could reasonably be expected of them.

In practice, this approach meant that because most of a package is made up of elements subcontracted to others—airlines and hotels—much of what went wrong with a package could not be made the legal responsibility of the tour operator. This often left clients either without a remedy or the difficult task of suing a foreign hotel or airline. However, regulation 15 of the PTR changes all that. It provides:

15(1) *The other party to the contract is liable to the consumer for the proper performance for the obligations under the contract, irrespective of whether such obligations are to be performed by that other party or by other suppliers of services but this shall not affect any remedy or right of action which that other party may have against those other suppliers of services.*

15(2) *The other party to the contract is liable to the consumer for any damage caused to him by the failure to perform the contract or the improper performance of the contract unless the failure or the improper performance is due neither to any fault of that other party nor to that of another supplier of services, because :*

(a) *the failures which occur in the performance of the contract are attributable to the consumer*

(b) *such failures are attributable to a third party unconnected with the provision of the services contracted for, and are unforeseeable or unavoidable, or*

(c) *such failures are due to :*

(i) *unusual and unforeseeable circumstances beyond the control of the party by whom this exception is pleaded, the consequences of which could not have been avoided even if all due care had been exercised;*

or

(ii) *an event which the other party to the contract or the supplier of services, even with all due care, could not foresee or forestall.*

The effect of this is that if part of what the tour operator has promised to the client is to be performed by subcontractors, the tour operator is nevertheless held responsible if things go wrong unless he can prove one of four things:

- It was the consumer's own fault.
- It was the fault of a third party unconnected with the contract.
- It was caused by *force majeure.*
- It was caused by some other event which the tour operator couldn't predict or avoid.

(c) *Misrepresentation*

In the previous section, we saw that some pre-contractual statements did not become terms of the contract but were only *representations.* If these representations turn out to be false. Then the victim may have an action misrepresentation. To succeed in an action for misrepre-sentation it must be established that:

- One party to the contract
- Made a false statement of fact

- To the other party to the contract
- Which induced the other party to the contract to enter into it

Statement of Fact

Statements of opinion, or intention, or statements as to the future are not statements of fact and are therefore not actionable. Thus, if a tour operator prints in his brochure a statement that all clients will be accommodated in twin rooms with ensuite bathrooms and he fully intends to fulfil this promise (and has contracts with hotels to substantiate his statement), then he cannot be sued for misrepresentation if, for instance, the hotelier lets him down and his clients are all accommodated in single rooms with no bathrooms. At the time the statement was made it was neither true nor false, merely a statement of intention. It would be different, however, if the tour operator had never intended to fulfil his promise. In those circumstances, he would be making a false statement (albeit implied) about his intention to fulfil the contract. In the words of one judge "The state of a man's mind is as much a fact as the state of his digestion."

Inducing the Contract

The victim of the misrepresentation only has a remedy if he can show that the statement induced the contract. If the statement had no effect upon his decision to make the contract, it is not actionable. Thus, if an 85 year old booked a holiday at an hotel where the tour operator's brochure indicated that water sports were available, when in fact they were not, he would not be able to claim for misrepresentation unless he could show that the statement influenced him to book the holiday—which seems most unlikely.

(i) Types of Misrepresentation

Once it has been established that a misrepresentation has been made, it is necessary to determine what type of misrepresentation it is. This is because the remedies for misrepresentation are determined according to the type of misrepresentation. There are three types of misrepresen-tation.

- *Fraudulent misrepresentation*—where the representor made the statement knowing it was false or was reckless as to its truth.

- *Negligent misrepresentation*—where the representor made the statement honestly believing it to be true but reasonable grounds for that belief.
- *Innocent misrepresentation*—where the representor made the statement honestly believing it to be true and having reasonable grounds for that belief.

Putting it more broadly, the difference between the three types depends on whether the person making the statement acted carelessly or innocently.

(ii) Remedies for Misrepresentation

There are two remedies for misrepresentation, damages and rescission. Rescission is a drastic remedy which involves calling the contract off altogether and restoring the parties to the position they were in before the contract was concluded. It is available for all types of misrepresentation automatically but can be lost in certain circumstances, such as by lapse of time, by affirmation or if the parties cannot be restored to their original position because for instance the subject matter of the contract has been consumed. This would apply in a holiday case if the clients only discovered the misrepresen-tation when they arrived in resort.

For fraudulent misrepresentation, damages are awarded at common law because a fraudulent misrepresen-tation amounts to the tort of decit. For negligent misre-presentation damages are awarded under s.2(1) of the Misrepresentation Act 1967. There is no right to damages for innocent misrepresentation except in one case. Under s.2(2) of the Misrepresentation Act the court has a discretion to award damages in lieu of rescission if it thinks it just to do so. Thus, if a represented has a right to rescind the contract for innocent misrepresentation, he may be awarded damages instead—but only if he has not lost his right to rescind for other reason, such as lapse of time.

(d) Regulation 4

Regulation 4 creates a statutory right to compensation for the consumer that cuts across the traditional boundaries of the common law. It imposes civil liability on both organisers and retailers if they supply misleading infor-mation. It states:

4(1) No organiser or retailer shall supply to a consumer any descriptive matter concerning a package, the price of a package or any other conditions applying to the contract which contains any misleading information.

4(2) If an organiser or retailer is in breach of paragraph (1) he shall be liable to compensate the consumer for any loss which the consumer suffers in consequence.

There is liability if the plaintiff can show that :

- a tour operator or travel agent,
- supplied,
- to a consumer,
- a brochure,
- that contained misleading descriptive matter,
- concerning a package or its price,
- and the consumer suffers as a consequence.

The liability is imposed for supplying misleading descriptive matter. The implication here is that it will cover written matter but not oral statements. The word *matter* suggests something tangible. It will obviously cover borch-ures and other brochure-like leaflets and it would most probably extent to videos of holiday destinations. It probably does not extend to window displays or window cards because the requirement is that the matter be supplied to the consu-mer and it cannot be said that such matter is supplied to the consumer. Press advertisements are a different matter. It is a moot point whether it can be said that the operator or the retailer have supplied the matter. It comes in a paper or journal supplied by a publisher or newsagent.

The other qualification is that liability is only imposed where the consumer, as a result of the misleading infor-mation, suffers in consequence. For the consumer to show that as a consequence of the descriptive material he suffered loss, there will have to be some evidence of cause and effect. He will have to show that he relied upon the information, otherwise how can it be said that he suffered loss as a consequence? In this respect, it is similar to an action for misrepresentation.

A significant point is that the travel agent, as well as the tour operator, could incur liability, thus making them strictly liable for brochure errors they might know nothing about - and with no defence. The only way to combat this liability is to ensure that the agency agreements they have with operators contain indemnity clauses. Whether they do may very well be a matter of bargaining power.

(e) *Exclusion Clauses*

In this section, we will look at the extent to which it is possible for a party to exclude his liability for breach of contract. In other words, can a party who is in breach of contract escape liability by relying upon a term in the contract stating that in the event of a branch he will be under no liability?

As far as tour operators are concerned, the legal obstacles that have been created mean that, for all practical purposes, they are unable to exclude their liability to consumers and can only limit their liability in very restricted circumstances. Both the common law and statute have combined to produce this situation.

(i) Common Law

Although the judges bulked at striking out exclusion clauses simply on the grounds that they were unreasonable, they nevertheless created a number of hurdles before an exclusion clause could be relied upon.

Notice: for an exclusion clause to be effective it has to be incorporated in the contract. Failure to do so means that it cannot be relied upon.

Olley v Marlborough Court Hotel Company [1949] 1 KB 532. A guest had valuables stolen from her room because of the negligence of the hotel. The hotel relied upon an exclusion clause on the bedroom wall to avoid liability. It was held that the contract for the room had been made downstairs at the reception desk at which time the guest had no notice of the exclusion clause. It was held that the clause was ineffective as it had not been incoporated into the contract .

Construction: if the words used by the party trying to escape liability do not cover the kind of breach that occured the clause will not help them.

Spencer v Cosmos, The Times, December 6th, 1989; LEXIS, CA. The plaintiffs had been expelled from their hotel for alleged rowdy behaviour. They sued their tour operator for breach of contract. The tour operator could not prove that the plaintiffs had been rowdy. In their defence they argued that an exclusion clause in their contract protected them even against wrongful expulsions. It was held by the Court of Appeal that "... the clause does not even set out to exclude claims in contact for failure to provide the services comprised in the holiday" and they permitted the plaintiffs' claim.

(ii) The Unfair Contract Terms Act 1977

The Unfair Contract Terms Act 1977 (UCTA) regulates exclusion clauses in most types of contract, not simply holiday contract. It has the effect of making some exclusion clauses void altogether and many others valid only if they can satisfy a reasonableness test. The main provisions are found in sections 2 and 3.

Section 2 provides:

2(1) A person cannot by reference to any contract term or to a notice given to persons generally or to particular persons exclude or restrict his liability for death or personal injury resulting from negligence.

2(2) In the case of other loss or damage, a person cannot so exclude or restrict his liability for negligence except in so far as the term or notice satisfies the requirement of reasonableness.

Thus, if a tour operator negligently causes death or personal injury to a client, this cannot be excluded at all. Even if the damage is not death or personal injury, for example, loss or damage to baggage, this liability can only be excluded if the tour operator can establish that it would be reasonable to exclude this liability - which might prove difficult.

Thompson v LMS [1930] 1KB 41. The plaintiff was injured when she stepped down from a train which had pulled up short of the platform. The defendants escaped liability because their exclusion clause had been incorporated into the contract by means of a notice on the back of her ticket. The case was decided in 1930. Today, the railway would be found liable because s.2(1) of UCTA would prevent them from relying on an exclusion clause which protected them against negligence causing death or personal injury.

Section 3 provides:

3(1) This section applies as between contracting parties where one of them deals as consumer or on the other's written standard terms of business.

3(2) As against that party, the other cannot by reference to any contract term -

(a) *when himself in breach of contract, exclude or restrict any liability of his in respect of the breach, or*

(b) *claim to be entitled -*

(i) *to render a contractual performance substantially different from that which was reasonably expected of him, or*

(ii) *in respect of the whole or any part of his contractual obligation, to render no performance at all, except in so far as (in any of the cases mentioned above in this subsection) the contract term satisfies the requirement of reasonableness.*

A holidaymaker will benefit from the protection of this section if they can demonstrate that :

- either they dealt as consumer, or
- they dealt on the other party's written standard terms of business, and
- they suffered from one of three types of exclusion clause:
  - one which excludes or restricts the liability of the other party, or
  - one which the other party claims entitles him to offer a substantially different kind of performance, or
  - one which permits the other party not to perform at all, and
- the tour operator cannot prove the term is reasonable.

The first and third types of exclusion clause are relati-vely straightforward to understand. The second is illustrated by this case:

Anglo-Continental Holidays Ltd v Typaldos Lines (London) Ltd. (1967) 2 Lloyd's Rep. 61. The plaintiffs were travel agents who had booked a party onto the defendant's ship, Atlantica, for a cruise to Israel. With less than two weeks to go, the defendants substituted a much inferior ship, the Angelika, and an equally inferior itinerary. The plaintiffs cancelled the cruise, refunded their clients' money and sued the defendants for breach of contract. The defendants relied on an exclusion clause which stated: "Steamers, Sailing

Dates Rates and Itineraries are subject to change without prior notice". The case was decided at common law in favour of the plaintiffs but today it would be decided under UCTA and the decision would probably be the same. The defendant's would not be permitted to substitute an inferior ship and itinerary because this would be substantially different from that which was reasonably expected'.

Deals as consumer: this is further defined in section 12. It covers persons who do not make the contract in the course of a business contracting with someone who does make it in the course of a business. Thus, it would cover holidaymakers contracting with tour operators but not business who purchase packages. Note that the definition of consumer in this legislation differs from the definition in the PTR and in other consumer protection legislation, such as the Consumer Protection Act 1987, which will be examined later.

Dealing on written standard terms of business: this simply means that the business relying on the exclusion clause uses a standard set of terms and conditions on which to contract. Given that most tour operators have a set of such terms, then most people who contract with them will get the benefit of s.3.

The rationale for both s.2 and s.3 is to offer protection to those classes of contractor who find themselves at a disadvantage or where the ability to negotiate is virtually non-existent-private individuals and those who have to contract on someone else's pre-printed terms and conditions.

(iii) The Package Travel Regulations

The provisions in the PTR relating to exclusion clauses are to be found in Reg. 15. Reg.15(5) contains a blanket prohibition on exclusion clauses.

15(5) Without prejudice to paragraph (3) and paragraph (4) above, liability under paragraphs (1) and (2) above cannot be excluded by any contractual term.

However, there are two major exceptions found in Reg. 15(3) and (4).

Reg. 15(3) provides

15(3) In the case of damage arising from the non-perfor-mance or improper performance of the services involved in the package, the contract may provide for compensation to be limited in accordance with the international conventions which govern such services.

There are international conventions covering carriage by air (The Warsaw Convention), carriage by sea (The Athens and London Conventions) and carriage by rail (The Berne Convention). Under these conventions, the carriers are entitled to limit their liability for death and injury and loss or damage to baggage to relatively modest sums. However, under Reg. 15(1) and (2), the tour operator is responsible not only for the actions of themselves but also their suppliers, such as air and sea carriers. The immediate practical effect of this would be that if, say, an airline carrying a tour operator's clients crashed, the airline could limit its liability but the tour operator could not. Thus, the main burden of comprehension would fall on the tour operator rather than the airline, even though it would be the airline that actually caused the crash. To redress the balance, the PTR permits the tour operator to limit his liability in the same way that the airline (or cruise line, or railway) could. Of course, this will only happen if the tour operator incorporates an appropriate term in his contracts. It does not happen automatically.

Reg. 15(4) provides

15(4) In the case of damage other than personal injury resulting from the non-performance of improper performance of the services involved in the package, the contract may include a term limiting the amount of compensation which will be paid to the consumer, provided that the limitation is not unreasonable.

Fortunately, most complaints about package holidays are 'quality' complaints that do not concern death or personal injury. In those circumstances, the PTR permits tour operators to limit their liability to sums which are 'not unreasonable'. Tour operators take advantage of this provision in two different circumstances. Firstly, they often print tables of compensation to cover situations where they make major changes before departure. The compensation offered rises as the date of departure approaches. The amounts vary from operator to operator but often the sums are quite derisory and would quite clearly fail the test, leaving the tour operator exposed to a larger claim. Secondly, there is often a 'catch-all' clause stating that the tour operator limits its liability to a maximum of, say, twice the price of the holiday. Such a sum would, in fact, compensate consumers for all but the most disastrous of holidays and, given that the legislation permits the operator to *limit* his liability (i.e., it envisages that the tour operator will be able to escape paying full compensation in some circumstances), this would probably be regarded as a reasonable sum.

(iv) The Unfair Terms in Consumer Contracts Regulations 1994

Unlike UCTA and the PTR, the Unfair Terms in Consumer Contracts Regulations (UTCCR) cover not only exclusion clauses, but also terms which are simply unfair. In this respect, the UTCCR is much wider than the other two. For instance, if I promise that you will be accommodated at a four star hotel but insert a clause into the contract saying that I will not be liable to you if you are accommodated in a lower rated hotel then I am *excluding* my liability. On the other hand, if I say that in the event of you wishing to cancel your holiday you must pay 100% cancellation charges no matter how long before departure it is you cancel, then I am not excluding my liability but imposing a term on you which is unfair. The UTCCR covers both type of term but UCTA and the PTR only cover the former.

To gain the protection of the UTCCR it has to be established that

- a consumer
- made a contract with a supplier
- which contained unfair terms
- which were not individually negotiated

Consumer: this term is defined to cover any natural person who makes a contract for purposes that are outside his business (Reg.2(1)). Thus, business and companies are outside the protection offered by the Regulations.

Supplier: this means anyone supplying services in the course of a business (Reg. 2(1)). Tour operators would fall within the ambit of this definition.

Unfair terms: these are terms which contrary to the requirement of good faith cause a significant imbalance in the parties' rights and obligations to the detriment of the consumer (Reg.4(1)).

Individually negotiated: terms which have not been individually negotiated are subject to the Regulations. This correspondents to the requirements in UCTA relating to written standard terms of business.

Illustrative terms: Schedule 3 to the Regulations contains an 'indicative and illustrative' list of terms which may be regarded as unfair. Contained in this list are examples of standard exclusion clauses which would also be caught in most cases by UCTA, but one type of term that is potentially unfair which is listed in the Schedule is a clause 'requiring any consumer who fails to fulfil his obligation to pay a disproportionately high sum in compensation'. Tour operators are in the habit of requiring consumers who cancel their holidays to pay cancellation charges, usually on a sliding scale that rises to 100 per cent as the date of departure nears. Some of these scales might be open to attack under the UTCCR on the grounds that they are disproportionately high.

Consequences of finding a term unfair: if a term is unfair then it is void and the tour operator cannot rely upon it.

The role of the Office of Fair Trading (OFT): the OFT is given powers under the legislation to investigate unfair terms in contracts drawn up for general use and in appropriate cases he may bring an action for an injunction against the person using the term to have it restrained. Currently the OFT is in the process of investigating cancellation clauses in tour operators contracts.

Terms which reflect other legislation: one drawback for consumers wishing to employ the UTCCR against tour operators' contracts is that, under Reg. 3(1) and Schedule 1, the Regulations do not apply where the contract incorporates a term which is there to 'comply with or which reflects' other legislation. However where contract terms go beyond what is permitted in this other legislation the UTCCR can be invoked. The OFT has already used its power to require airlines to amend their standards conditions of carriage where they have not complied with the Warsaw Convention and they have made numerous requests for tour operators to change their terms and conditions.

(f) Remedies

If one party to the contract breaks it, then the other party is entitled to a remedy. The usual remedy in contract is damages, that is, financial compensation designed to put the victim of the breach in the same position as if the contract had been performed (*Robinson v Harman* (1848) 1 Ex 850). However, package holidaymakers also benefit from a range of other remedies created by the PTR which are in addition to damages and are not available in other areas of contract. These include the right to be offered an alternative holiday if, before departure, the tour operator makes a substantial change to the holiday booked, and the right to be repatriated if the tour operator cannot provide what he promised.

(i) Damages

In order to compensate the consumer for breach of contract, three heads of damage are recognised

- Damages for difference in value.
- Consequential loss.
- Damages for distress and disappointment.

Damages for difference in value: where the tour operator has provided a holiday which is worth less than the holiday he contracted to provide, the holidaymaker is entitled to the difference in value. A straightforward example of this principle is the following case.

Mcleod v Hunter [1987] CLY 1162. The tour operator promised a luxurious villa but what they provided was a cramped apartment. The court assessed the difference in value as £439. This was in addition to damages for distress and disappointment.

Consequential loss: when the breach of contract results in the holidaymaker having to expend further sums in order to rectify the breach, damages for consequential loss can be claimed. Sometimes these damages are referred to as out of pocket expenses.

Harris v Torchgrove [1985] CLY 944. The court awarded £40 damages for parking expenses because the promised parking at the apartment was not available and a further £300 for the cost of extra meals taken in restaurants because the apartment had no oven and the fridge was 'eccentric'.

Note that difference in value claims and consequential loss claims cannot be combined to give double compensation. For instance, if a tour operator promises full board but no evening meals are provided, the consumer cannot claim both the difference in value between half board and full board and also the out of pocket expenses for purchasing restaurant meals in the evening.

Damages for distress and disappointment: Holiday contracts are almost unique because in appropriate cases the courts will award damages for distress and disappointment caused by a breach of contract. Such damages are not available generally in the law of contract. The rule was established in the following case.

Jarvis v Swans Tours [1973] 1 All ER 71. The plaintiff booked a holiday in the Tyrol at Christmas. He was promised a 'house-party' atmosphere; 'gemutlichkeit'; fondue parties; yodler evenings; afternoon tea and cakes; etc. The hotel was virtually deserted, the skiing was very restricted, almost none of the services were provided and the hotel proprietor spoke no English. The Court of Appeal awarded the plaintiff £125 damages on a holiday that cost £64. Lord Denning said, "In a proper case damages for mental distress can be recovered in contract ... One such case is a contract for a holiday, or any other contract to provide entertainment and enjoyment. If the contracting party breaks his contract, damages can be given for the disappointment, the distress, the upset and frustration caused by the breach.

The rationale behind the decision is that where the purpose of the contract is to provide peace of mind and enjoyment then such damages can be claimed, but not for everyday commercial transactions where the provision of pleasure is not the essence of the contract.

Mitigation of loss: A victim of a breach of contract cannot simply sit back and collect damages. They must take reasonable steps to mitigate their loss and failure to do so can mean that they will lose their damages. In holiday cases, one of the simplest ways to mitigate your loss is to complain to the tour operator or its representative who may then be able to put things right. Reg. 15(9), in fact, requires tour operators to put a term into their contracts obliging consumers to complain at the earliest opportunity if they have a problem.

Czyzewski v Intasun (1990) County Ct. Unreported. The plaintiff complained of an 'offensive' toilet. After several unsuccessful attempts to repair it the hotel offered him an alternative room but for some reason he declined to take it and remained in his room for the rest of his holiday. The court awarded him only £50 damages based on the limited amount of time he would have had to spend in the room if he had accepted the alternative.

(ii) Remedies for Pre-departure Changes

Under Regulations 12 and 13, a consumer is entitled to remedies other than damages. These Regulations provide

12 *In every contract there are implied terms to the effect that*

(a) *where the organiser is constrained before the departure to alter significantly an essential term of contract, such as the price (so far as regulation 11 permits him to do so), he will notify the consumer as quickly as possible in order to enable him to take appropriate decisions and in particular to withdraw from the contract without penalty or to accept a rider to the contract specifying the alterations made and their impact on the price; and*

(b) *the consumer will inform the organiser or the retailer of his decision as soon as possible.*

13(1) *The terms set out in paragraphs (2) and (3) below are implied in every contract and apply where the consumer withdraws from the contract pursuant to the term in it implied by virtue of regulation 12(a), or where the organiser, for any reason other than the fault of the consumer, cancels the package before the agreed date of departure.*

13(2) *The consumer is entitled -*

(a) *to take a substitute package of equivalent or superior quality if the other party to the contract is able to offer him such a substitute; or*

(b) *to take a substitute package of lower quality if the other party to the contract is able to offer him one and to recover from the organiser the difference in price between the price of the package purchased and that of the substitute package; or*

(c) *to have repaid to him as soon as possible all the monies paid by him under the contract.*

13(3) *The consumer is entitled, if appropriate, to be compensated by the organiser for non-performance of the contract except where-*

(a) *the package is cancelled because the number of persons who agree to take it is less than the minimum number required and the consumer is informed of the cancellation, in writing, within the period indicated in the description of the package; or*

(b) *the package is cancelled by reason of unusual and unforeseeable circumstances beyond the control of the party by whom this exception is pleaded, the consequences of which could not have been avoided even if all due care had been exercised.*

Thus, under Regulation 12, if a consumer can establish that a tour operator has

- altered significantly
- an essential term

he has the choice of either

- withdrawing from the contract, or
- accepting the change with a rider to the price.

Presumably, if there is such a major change, then the consumer will withdraw unless the tour operator offers enough by way of compensation. If the consumer does withdraw, or if the operator cancels the holiday for any reason other than the consumer's fault, then the consumer is entitled to the following choices:

- a substitute holiday of equivalent or superior quality, or
- a substitute holiday of inferior quality plus the difference in value, or
- a full refund, and
- compensation, except where the contract was cancelled for *force majeure* or because of lack of minimum numbers.

(iii) Remedies for Post-departure Changes

where problems arise with the holiday after departure this is dealt with by Reg. 14 which provides

14(1) *The terms set out in paragraphs (2) and (3) below are implied in every contract and apply where, after departure, a significant proportion of the services contracted for is not provided or the organizer becomes aware that he will be unable to procure a significant proportion of the services to be provided.*

14(2) *The organizer will make suitable alternative arrangements, at no extra cost to the consumer, for the continuation of the package and will, where appropriate, compensate the consumer for the difference between the services to be supplied under the contract and those supplied.*

14(3) *If it is impossible to make arrangements as described in paragraph (2), or these are not accepted by the consumer for good reasons, the organizer will, where appropriate, provide the consumer with equivalent transport back to the place of departure or to another place to which the consumer has agreed and will, where appropriate, compensate the consumer.*

Thus, if the consumer can show that

- A significant proportion of the services are not to be provided, or
- The tour operator becomes aware that they cannot be provided the tour operator must,
- Make suitable alternative arrangements for the continuation of the holiday, or
- If it is impossible to make alternative arrangements transport the consumer home again,
- And, in both cases, compensate the consumer where appropriate.

Criminal Liability

This section of the chapter is concerned with the criminal offences that a tour operator might commit. There are three pieces of legislation that are relevant, the Trade Descriptions Act 1968 which regulates false trade descriptions, the Consumer Protection Act 1987 which regulates misleading prices, and the Package Travel Regulations which regulate both descriptions and prices. The offences are usually tried in a magistrates' court where the maximum penalty is £5,000 per offence but, in extreme cases, an offence under these provisions could be tried in the Crown Court before jury and the maximum penalty would be an unlimited fine. The offences fall into a category of criminal offence labelled as regulatory offences; that is, they are not concerned with traditional types of criminal behaviour but are intended to improve trading standards.

(a) *The Trade Descriptions Act 1968*

Section 14 of the TDA sets out two offences:

14(1) *It shall be an offence for any person in the course of any trade or business—*

(a) *to make a statement which he knows to be false; or*

(b) *recklessly to make a statement which is false;*

as to any of the following matters, that is to say—

(i) *the provision in the course of any trade or business of any services, accommodation or facilities;*

(ii) *the nature of any services,. accommodation or facilities provided in the course of any trade or business;*

(iii) *the time at which, manner in which or persons by whom any services accommodation or facilities are so provided;*

(iv) *the examination, approval or evaluation by any person of any services, accommodation or facilities so provided; or*

(v) *the location or amenities of any accommodation so provided.*

To put it another way, for the prosecution to succeed it must prove that the tour operator:

- made a statement,
- in the course of a business,
- relating to one of the categories in section 14 (for example, the facilities or the accommodation),
- that was false,
- and the statement was made knowingly or recklessly.

In the course of a trade or business: most tour operators, when they sell holidays, are doing so in the course of a trade or business. As with most busines, there will be those who only participate at the margins and there are those who organize holidays for groups of friends and, therefore, questions may be raised as to whether they are acting in the course of a business. However, for most tour operators, this is not an issue.

The statement must fall within the categories listed in section 14: only if a tour operator makes a false statement falling into one of the categories listed in Section 14 can a prosecution succeed. The list, however, is quite comprehen-sive and most of the statements that a tour operator makes in a brochure would be covered by the list. For instance, *Herron v Lunn Poly* SLT 2 was a prosecution under s.14(1)(b)(i) for a false statement relating to the provisions of any services, accommodation or facilities. That case concerned an hotel and its facilities which were incomplete when the clients arrived. *R v Clarksons* 57 Cr App R 38 was prosecution under both s.14(1)(b)(iii) for a false statement as to the time at which any services are provided. (See also *R v Avro plc* (Court of Appeal, 14th January 1993)).*R v Sunair* 1 WLR 1105, included a count for contravenings. 14(1)(b)(v) relating to the location and amenities of any accommodation provided. The prosecution concerned the non-availability of promised facilities.

The statement must be false: clearly, a statement that the hotel is only 100 metres from the beach when, in fact, it is 500 metres is a false statement and a tour operator would be rightly convicted, but some statements are much more difficult to label as true or false.

Thomson Travel Ltd v Roberts (1984) 148 JP 666. A tour operator published a brochure which described and hotel as having a 'beach'. The so-called beach was man made construction consisting of an area of sand approximately 51 yards long and 17 yards wide retained behind a concrete wall bordering the sea. Access to the sea was the ladders down to water level at which point the depth of the sea was equivalent to the shallow end of a swimming pool. Before it could be decided whether the tour operator had made a false statement about the beach the court had to decide what was meant by the word 'beach'. Only after deciding that what existed at the hotel could not be described as a beach could the court then go on to say that a false statement had been made about a beach.

It has also been held that statements as to future intention are not capable of being either true or false. At the time they are made they are merely promises which may or may not be fulfilled. Given that much of a tour operator's brochure consists of promises as to the future, this has caused some difficulties.

Sunair v Dodd 2 All ER 410. A tour operator published a brochure describing the facilities at an hotel as "all twin-bedded rooms with private bath, shower, WC and terrace". Clients who read the brochure in January 1969 and made a booking on the basis of the brochure description discovered, when they arrived at the hotesl in the summer, that their rooms did not have balconies. At the time the brochure had been published the tour operator had a contract with the hotel for rooms with twin beds and balconies.

It was held by the Divisional Court that what the brochure statement meant was that the tour operator was offering to supply rooms with twin beds and balconies and as this was a statement as to future intention it could not be classified as a false statement when it was published. The tour operator was therefore not guilty.

Note, however, that the situation would have been very different if the tour operator had had no contract with the hotel for the rooms described and no intention of providing such rooms. In that case there would have been a false statement—as to the state of mind of the tour operator.

The statement must have been made knowingly or recklessly: To secure a conviction, the prosecution must establish that the statement was made knowingly or recklessly, that is, they must prove a state of mind. In legal terms, they must prove *mens rea* – a guilty mind. Case law, however, has developed to a stage where it can be said that the offence approaches strict liability, that is, liability without fault.

Wings v Ellis AC 272 A tour operator published a brochure which described an hotel as having air-conditioning. This was false but, at the time the brochure was published, the tour operator did not know this. As soon as they discovered the false description, they issued errata to all existing clients and told all sales staff to bring the false description to the attention of new clients when they booked. Despite these precautions, a client managed to book a holiday without being informed that the hotel had no air-conditioning.

Thus, the position was that the tour operator knew that the statement was false but it did not know that the statement was being made. If they had done so, they would have seen to is that the statement was corrected. On appeal to the House of Lords, it was held that *wings* a were tightly convicted. The offence in section 14(1)(a) is to make a statement which we he knows to be false, and this is what *wings* had done. Thus *wings* were convicted even though it might be said that they were not at fault – they were doing their best at the time to avoid committing the offence.

Wings was case under s. 14(1)(a) involving knowledge. The following case, which is not a travel case but where the principles are the same, involves a s.14(1)(b) offence which requires recklessness. Again, it shows that the case law imposes a liability much stricter than one would suspect when first reading the statute.

MFI Warehouses Ltd. v Nattrass 1 All ER 762. The defendants published an advertisement which contained a false statement. The advertisement had been drafted by a director and approved by the chairman. The latter had considered the advertisement for about 5-10 minutes but had not specifically considered whether it contained any false statements. On appeal to the Divisional Court, it was held that the defendants had recklessly made a false statement. Recklessness is actually defined in the Act in the following terms "a statement made regardless of whether it is true or false shall be deemed to be made recklessly..." Literally this meant not having regard to the truth of the statement, which is what had happened. The chairman had not thought about the falsity of the statement.

Who must make the statement? An offence under the TDA requires the prosecution to prove a state of mind – knowledge or recklessness. However, most defendants will be companies who have neither minds nor bodies. The laws solves this problem by requiring the prosecution to establish that one of the 'directing minds' of the company, for example, a director or managing director or company secretary, had the requisite state of mind.

Airtours v Shipley Divisional Ct. Unreported. The defendants had published a brochure which stated that a hotel had a pool when it didn't. They were found not guilty on appeal because they demonstrated that the 'directing minds' of the company had not acted recklessly. They had established a 'due diligence' system which established that they had had regard to the truth or falsity of the statement in the brochure.

(b) *The Consumer Protection Act 1987*

The Consumer Protection Act is concerned with misleading prices. Section 20 creates two offences: giving a misleading price indication (s.20(1)); and giving a price indication which subsequently becomes misleading (s.20(2)).

Section 20(1) Provides

20(1) Subject to the following provisions of this part, a person shall be guilty of an offence if, in the course of any business of his, he gives (by any means whatever) to any consumers an indication which is misleading as to the price at which any goods, services, accommodation or facilities are available (whether generally or from particular persons).

Section 20(2) Provides

20(2) *Subject as aforesaid, a person shall be guilty of an offence if—*

(*a*) in the course of any business of his, he has given an indication to any consumers which, after it was given, has become misleading as mentioned in subsection (1) above; and

(*b*) some or all of those consumers might reasonably be expected to rely on the indication at a time after it has become misleading; and

(*c*) he fails to take all such steps as are reasonable to prevent those consumers from relying on the indication.

Thus, for the prosecution to succeed under s.20(1), they must show that :

- a person in a course of a business of his,
- has given a misleading indication,
- about the price, or
- the method of calculating the price,
- of goods, services, accommodation or facilities,
- to a consumer.

And, under s.20(2), the prosecution must show that

- a person in the course of a business of his,
- has given an indication of the price or its method of calculation,
- which has subsequently become misleading, and
- some consumers might still be relying upon the original indication, and
- he has not taken reasonable steps to correct the indication.

A person in the course of a business of his: as with the TDA, the CPA is only aimed at offences committed in the course of a business. The difference between the two is that, under the CPA, the offence can only be committed by someone acting in the course of a business *of his*. The importance of this is that employees cannot be prosecuted under the CPA whereas they can be under the TDA.

Misleading indication: this is defined very widely in s.21(1) and s.21(2). It would include, for instance, not making it clear that supplements and tax had to be added to the price in the pricing panel; not explaining that prices were based upon two sharing a room; not making clear that under-occupancy supplements were payable; and, not making it clear that insurance was a compulsory extra.

Consumer: this term is defined in s.20(6) as being any person who might wish to be provided with the services otherwise than for the purposes of a business of his. Thus, purchasers of business travel would not be protected but ordinary members of the public would. Note that no purchase has to be made - it covers any private individual *who might wish* to purchase the services.

(c) *The Package Travel Regulations 1992*

The PTR contain a number of criminal offences but the most important is to be found in Reg. 5. It covers both misleading descriptions and misleading prices. It provides:

5(1) Subject to paragraph (4) below, no organiser shall make available a brochure to a possible consumer unless it indicates in a legible, comprehensible and accurate manner the price and adequate information about the matters specified in Schedule 1 to these Regulations in respect of the packages offered for sale in the brochure to the extent that those matters are relevant to the packages so offered.

5(2) Subject to paragraph (4) below, no retailer shall make available to a possible consumer a brochure which he knows or has reasonable cause to believe does not comply with the requirements of paragraph (1).

The prosecution must, therefore, establish in relation to tour operators that

- an organiser,
- has made available a brochure,
- to a possible consumer,
- which does not indicate adequately, accurately, legibly or comprehensibly,
- information listed in Schedule 1.

In relation to travels agents, the prosecution must establish, in addition, that the travel agent knew or had reasonable cause to believe that the brochure did not comply.

Schedule 1 to the Regulations lists the following information:

1. The destination and the means, characteristics and categories of transport used.
2. The type of accommodation, its location, category or degree of comfort and its main features and, where the accommodation is to be provided in a member State, its approval or tourist classification under the rules of that member State.
3. The meals which are included in the package.
4. The itinerary.
5. General information about passport and visa requirements which apply for British citizens and health formalities required for the journey and the stay.
6. Either the monetary amount or the percentage of the price which is to be paid on account and the timeable for payment of the balance.
7. Whether a minimum number of persons is required for the package to take place and, if so, the deadline for informing the consumer in the event of cancellation.
8. The arrangements (if any) which apply if consumers are delayed at the outward or homeward points of departure.
9. The arrangements for security for money paid over and for the repatriation of the consumer in the event of insolvency.

The effect of Reg. 5, taken in conjunction with Schedule 1, is to ensure that *if* a tour operator publishes a brochure, then it must contain certain information that relates to the most important elements of a package holiday. Note that there is no requirement that a tour operator must publish a brochure.

A possible consumer: as with the CPA, there is no need for the prosecution to show that a purchase had been made by a consumer, simply that a brochure had been made available. Thus, simply displaying an inaccurate brochure would be sufficient. Note that the definition of consumer in the PTR is different from that in the CPA. 'Consumer' in the PTR covers anyone who agrees to take the package and, thus, it extends to packages bought in the course of a business.

Adequately, accurately, legibly, comprehensibly: legibly presumably means that if the print cannot be read by someone with good eyesight, then it does not comply with the Regulation. Comprehensible means that it can be understood, thus obscure and overly legalistic language will be penalised. Accurate is a word that is currently causing problems to tour operators who have adopted a practice called 'fluid pricing' (i.e., where they print a price in a brochure which is a maximum price but then indicate that discounts are available for early bookers). It is argued that the price is not accurate because a consumer cannot ascertain in advance from the brochure what price he will pay. Adequate means that there must be enough information on which the consumer can make an informed choice.

Knowledge or reasonable cause: a travel agent is in a different to a tour operator. For a tour operator, the offence is one of strict liability; that is, the prosecution do not have to prove fault to prove their case, However, with travel agents the offence, as with the TDA offences, requires *mens rea,* a 'guilty mind'.

(d) *Defences*

All the offences we have looked at, under the TDA, the CPA and the PTR, have defences. Some are specialised and only apply to the particular legislation, but there is one which is of general application. This is known as the 'due diligence' defence. It appears in slightly different terms in each piece of legislation but essentially it has the same effect whatever the legislation. Reg. 24 of the PTR provides:

24(1) Subject to the following provisions of this regulation, in proceedings against any person for an offence under regulation 5,7,8,16, or 22 of these Regulations, it shall be a defence for that person to show that he took all reasonable steps and exercised all due diligence to avoid committing the offence.

The corresponding provision in the TDA is found in s.24 and in the CPA at s.39. The essence of the defence is that tour operators will escape conviction if they can establish that they were not at fault, because they took all reasonable precautions and exercised all due diligence to avoid commit-ting the offence. Note that the burden of proof is on the tour operator rather than the prosecution and that the burden is difficult to discharge, as illustrated by the following case.

Buckinghamshire CC v Crystal Holiday Ltd (1993) Div. Ct. Unreported. The defendants published a brochure in which they stated that there was a golf course at a particular resort. In fact when the borchure was originally published the golf course was only in the course of construction but everyone confidently believed that the course would be open by the time the season started. Unfortunately because of bad whether the golf course did not open on time. The defendants were prosecuted under the TDA for making a false trade description. Their defence failed because the prosecution pointed out they could have prevented the commission of the offence simply by changing the wording of the brochure to say that they expected the golf course to be open at the beginning of the season. The judge said, "... it seems to me that once one is able to identify a precaution which one can properly be described as a reasonable precaution which was not taken, such as the different wording ... being put in the brochure in this case, then that really is the end of the case so far as (the defence) is concerned."

Nowadays, most tour operators have adopted 'due diligence' systems to ensure that the information in their brochures is thoroughly checked before it is published. In the *Airtours v Shipley* case referred to above, this is what saved them from conviction. Note, however, that the due diligence system was used in that case to prove that Airtours had not acted recklessly under s.14(1)(b) rather than as a due diligence defence under s.24 of the TDA. Technically there is a difference but the effect was the same.

Protection against Insolvency

Expenditure on the average family holiday usually ranks as one of the two or three largest items of expenditure in the family's annual budget. In the vast majority of cases, the money has to be paid in advance to the tour operator. The obvious danger with this is that, if the tour operator becomes insolvent, consumers will lose their money. The problem is exacerbated if the clients happen to be abroad at the time. Prior to 1992, there were various voluntary and statutory schemes in place to protect consumers if this happened. Thus, if a consumer booked an air package holiday they were protected by the Air Travel Organisers' Licensing (ATOL) scheme which required air package tour operators to take out a bond to be paid out to clients in the event of the tour operator's insolvency. ABTA also operated a scheme whereby their members whether air package operators or not, were also required to have bonds to protect their clients. However, the protection was not universal and it was possible for a client to book a holiday with a non-bonded operator and lose their money. Many bus tour operators fell into this category.

Now, the PTR requires all tour operators to be able to provide evidence of security for the return of pre-payments and for repatriation. The Regulations provide that this can be done in a number of ways:

- by bonding,
- by insurance,
- by establishing a trust fund.

If a tour operator chooses to protect his clients by bonding, then the level of the bond is determined by whether or not the tour operator is a member of an 'approved body' which has reserve fund or not. The bonding level is higher for approved bodies with no reserve fund to make up the shortfall if the bond is insufficient. Approved bodies are organisations such as ABTA and AITO. Arrangements falling within the ATOL scheme are automatically covered by the new requirements.

Because bonds and insurance are relatively expensive to acquire many smaller, particularly domestic tour operators, are attracted by the possibility of trust funds. These work by having the pre-payments paid into a trust fund and only paid out again once the holiday has been completed. The arrangements for policing these schemes are weak and there is a real possibility of fraud associated with them.

5

Tourism Marketing Administration

Meaning and Definition

Almost every marketing textbook has a different definition of the term "marketing." The American Marketing Association (AMA) uses the following: "The process of planning and executing the conception, pricing, promotion, and distribution of ideas, goods, and services to create exchanges that satisfy individual and organizational objectives." From this definition, we see that:

- Marketing involves an ongoing process. The environment is "dynamic." This means that the market tends to change-what customers want today is not necessarily what they want tomorrow. For example, sales of beef are declining in the United States because consumers have become health oriented. Similarly, Tupperware parties are less popular today than they once were because there are fewer housewives who do not work outside the home.
- This process involves both planning and implementing (executing) the plan.
- Some of the main issues involved include:
  - o Marketers help design products, finding out what customers want and what can practically be made available given technology and price constraints.
  - o Marketers distribute products-there must be some efficient way to get the products from the factory to the end-consumer.

- o Marketers also promote products, and this is perhaps what we tend to think of first when we think of marketing. Promotion involves advertising-and much more. Other tools to promote products include trade promotion (store sales, coupons, and rebates), obtaining favorable and visible shelf-space, and obtaining favorable press coverage.
- o Marketers also price products to "move" them. We know from economics that, in most cases, sales correlate negatively with price-the higher the price, the lower the quantity demanded. In some cases, however, price may provide the customer with a "signal" of quality. Thus, the marketer needs to price the product to (1) maximize profit and (2) communicate a desired image of the product.
- o Marketing is applicable to services and ideas as well as to tangible products. For example, accountants may need to market their tax preparation services to consumers.

Reasons for studying marketing. There are several good reasons for studying marketing. First of all, marketing issues are important in all areas of the organization-customers are the reasons why businesses exist! In fact, marketing efforts (including such services as promotion and distribution) often account for more than half of the price of a product. As an added benefit, studying marketing often helps us become more savvy consumers. We will learn, for instance, that the per unit price of a bigger package is frequently higher than that of a smaller one, and that more expensive products are frequently not better in quality.

Criteria that must be met for marketing to occur. Several criteria must be met for marketing to occur:

- There must be two parties, each with unsatisfied needs or wants. This want, of course, could be money for the seller.
- Each must have something to offer. Marketing involves voluntary "exchange" relationships where both sides must be willing parties. Thus, a consumer who buys a soft drink in a vending machine for 60¢ must value the soft drink, available at that time and place, more than the money. Conversely, the vendor must value the money more. (It

is interesting to note that money is, strictly speaking, not necessary for this exchange to take place. It is possible, albeit a bit cumbersome, to exchange two ducks for a pair of shoes.)

- The parties must be able to communicate. This could be through a display in a store, an infomercial, or a posting one Bay.

The marketing vs. the selling concept. Two approaches to marketing exist. The traditional selling concept emphasizes selling existing products. The philosophy here is that if a product is not selling, more aggressive measures must be taken to sell it-e.g., cutting price, advertising more, or hiring more aggressive (and obnoxious) sales-people.

When the railroads started to lose business due to the advent of more effective trucks that could deliver goods right to the customer's door, the railroads cut prices instead of recognizing that the customers ultimately wanted transportation of goods, not necessarily railroad transportation. Smith Corona, a manufacturer of typewriters, was too slow to realize that consumers wanted the ability to process documents and not typewriters per se. The marketing concept, in contrast, focuses on getting consumers what they seek, regardless of whether this entails coming up with entirely new products.

The 4 Ps-product, place (distribution), promotion, and price-represent the variables that are within the control of the firm (at least in the medium to long run). In contrast, the firm is faced with uncertainty from the environment.

Marketing Environment

Elements of the Environment: The marketing environment involves factors that, for the most part, are beyond the control of the company. Thus, the company must adapt to these factors. It is important to observe how the environment changes so that a firm can adapt its strategies appropriately. Consider these environmental forces:

- *Competition:* Competitors often "creep" in and threaten to take away markets from firms. For example, Japanese auto manufacturers became a serious threat to American car makers in the late 1970s and early 1980s. Similarly, the

Lotus Corporation, maker of one of the first commercially successful spreadsheets, soon faced competition from other software firms. Note that while competition may be frustrating for the firm, it is good for consumers. (In fact, we will come back to this point when we consider the legal environment). Note that competition today is increasingly global in scope.

- ***Economics:*** Some firms in particular are extremely vulnerable to changes in the economy. Consumers tend to put off buying a new car, going out to eat, or building new homes in bad times. In contrast, in good times, firms serving those needs may have difficulty keeping up with demand.
- ***Political:*** Businesses are very vulnerable to changes in the political situation. For example, because consumer groups lobbied Congress, more stringent rules were made on the terms of car leases. The tobacco industry is currently the target of much negative attention from government and public interest groups. Currently, the desire to avoid aiding the enemy may result in laws that make it more difficult for American firms to export goods to other countries.
- ***Legal:*** Firms are very vulnerable to changing laws and changing interpretations by the courts. Firms in the U.S. are very vulnerable to lawsuits. McDonald's, for example, is currently being sued by people who claim that eating the chain's hamburgers caused them to get fat. Some impacts of the legal environment:
- Firms are significantly limited in what they can do by various laws-some laws, for example, require that disclosures be made to consumers on the effective interest rates they pay on products bought on installment. A particularly interesting group of laws relate to antitrust. These laws basically exist to promote fair competition among firms. Some principles involved here include:
    - o ***Collusion:*** Firms may not "conspire" to fix prices (agree that they will not sell below an agreed upon price) or reduce services.
    - o ***Predation:*** Firms may not sell their products below their cost of production for the purpose of driving

competitors out of business so that they, themselves, can raise prices when competition is reduced.

- o *Market Share:* Firms which have an unacceptably large market share may be "broken" up by court order so that many smaller firms will be around to compete. (This is what happened to AT&T, and at times, IBM has been worried about this prospect).
- o *Tying:* A firm that controls a valuable product may not require the consumer to buy a more commonplace one to get the scarce product. For example, Intel controls many of the newest microprocessors (e.g., Pentium IV). Intel also makes motherboards for computers; however, motherboards are made by a lot of firms. Intel would be thought to abuse its effective monopoly power if it required consumers to buy a motherboard in order to get its newest chips.

- *Technological:* Changes in technology may significantly influence the demand for a product. For example, the advent of the fax machine was bad news for Federal Express. The Internet is a major threat to travel agents.
- *Social:* Changes in customs or demographics greatly influence firms. Fewer babies today are being born, resulting in a decreased demand for baby foods. More women work outside the home today, so there is a greater demand for prepared foods. There are more unmarried singles today. This provides opportunities for some firms (e.g., fast food restaurants) but creates problems for others (e.g., manufacturers of high quality furniture that many people put off buying until marriage). Today, there are more "blended" families that result as parents remarry after divorce. These families are often strapped for money but may require "duplicate" items for children at each parent's residence.

Environmental scanning helps the firm understand developments in the market. Such developments may involve changes in the market place due to social trends (e.g., Gerber, a manufacturer of baby products, faces a serious challenge with declining U.S. birth rates), technology (e.g., VCR makers are threatened by DVD players), or new or potential competitors (e.g.,

Internet service providers are being threatened by increasing marketing efforts from MSN). Note that environmental scanning must be performed continuously, since environmental change does not cease.

Economic Cycles

The economy goes through cycles. In the late 1990s, the U.S. economy was quite strong, and many luxury goods were sold. Currently, the economy is somewhat weak, and many firms are facing the results.

Car makers, for example, have seen declining profit margins (and even losses) as they have had to cut prices and offer low interest rates on financing. Generally, in good economic times, there is a great deal of demand, but this introduces a fear of possible inflation. In the U.S., the Federal Reserve will then try to prevent the economy from "overheating." This is usually done by raising interest rates. This makes businesses less willing to invest, and as a result, people tend to make less money. During a recession, unemployment tends to rise, causing consumers to spend less.

This may result in a "bad circle," with more people losing their jobs due to lowered demands. Some businesses, however, may take this opportunity to invest in growth now that things can be bought more cheaply.

Strategic Planning and the Marketing Process

Plans and planning. Plans are needed to clarify what kinds of strategic objectives an organization would like to achieve and how this is to be done. Such plans must consider the amount of resources available. One critical resource is capital. Microsoft keeps a great deal of cash on hand to be able to "jump" on opportunities that come about. Small startup software firms, on the other hand, may have limited cash on hand. This means that they may have to forego what would have been a good investment because they do not have the cash to invest and cannot find a way to raise the capital. Other resources that affect what a firm may be able to achieve include Trademarks/brand names: It would be very difficult to compete factors such as: Patents: It would be difficult to against Coke and Pepsi in the cola market. compete against Intel and AMD in the microprocessor market since both these People: firms have a number of patents that it is difficult to get around. Even with all of Microsoft's money available, it could not immediately hire the Distribution: Stores have space people needed to manufacture computer chips. for only a fraction of the products they are offered, so they must turn many away. A firm that does not have an established relationship with stores will be at a disadvantage in trying to introduce a new product.

Plans are subject to the choices and policies that the organization has made. Some firms have goals of social responsibility, for example. Some firms are willing to take a greater risk, which may result in a very large payoff but also involve the risk of a large loss, than others.

Strategic marketing is best seen as an ongoing and never-ending process. Typically:

- The organization will identify the objectives it wishes to achieve. This could involve profitability directly, but often profitability is a long term goal that may require some intermediate steps. The firm may seek to increase market share, achieve distribution in more outlets, have sales grow by a certain percentage, or have consumers evaluate the product more favorably. Some organizations have objectives that are not focused on monetary profit-e.g., promoting literacy or preventing breast cancer.
- An analysis is made, taking into consideration issues such as organizational resources, competitors, the competitors' strengths, different types of customers, changes in the market, or the impact of new technology.
- Based on this analysis, a plan is made based on tradeoffs between the advantages and disadvantages of different options available.
- This strategy is then carried out. The firm may design new products, revamp its advertising strategy, invest in getting more stores to carry the product, or decide to focus on a new customer segment.
- After implementation, the results or outcome are evaluated. If results are not as desired, a change may have to be made to the strategy. Even if results are satisfactory, the firm still needs to monitor the environment for changes.

Levels of Planning and Strategies

Plans for a firm can be made at several different levels. At the corporate level, the management considers the objectives of the firm as a whole. For example, Microsoft may want seek to grow by providing high quality software, hardware, and services to consumers. To achieve this goal, the firm may be willing to invest aggressively.

Plans can also be made at the business unit level. For example, although Microsoft is best known for its operating systems and applications software, the firm also provides Internet access and makes video games. Different managers will have responsibilities for different areas, and goals may best be made by those closest to the business area being considered. It is also more practical to hold managers accountable for performance if the plan is being made at a more specific level. Boeing has both commercial aircraft and defense divisions. Each is run by different managers, although there is some overlap in technology between the two. Therefore, plans are needed both at the corporate and at the business levels.

Occasionally, plans will be made at the functional level, to allow managers to specialize and to increase managerial accountability. Marketing, for example, may be charged with increasing awareness of Microsoft game consoles to 55% of the U.S. population or to increase the number of units of Microsoft Office sold. Finance may be charged with raising a given amount of capital at a given cost. Manufacturing may be charged with decreasing production costs by 5%.

The firm needs to identify the business it is in. Here, a balance must be made so that the firm's scope is not defined too narrowly or too broadly. A firm may define its goal very narrowly and then miss opportunities in the market place. For example, if Dell were to define itself only as a computer company, it might miss an opportunity to branch into PDAs or Internet service. Thus, they might instead define themselves as a provider of "information solutions."

A company should not define itself too broadly, however, since this may result in loss of focus. For example, a manufacturer of baking soda should probably not see itself as a manufacturer of all types of chemicals. Sometimes, companies can define themselves in terms of a customer need. For example, 3M sees itself as being in the business of making products whose surfaces are bonded together. This accounts for both Post-It notes and computer disks.

A firm's mission should generally include a discussion of the customers served (e.g., Wal-Mart and Nordstrom's serve different groups), the kind of technology involved, and the markets served.

Several issues are involved in selecting target customers. We will consider these in more detail within the context of segmentation, but for now, the firm needs to consider issues such as:

- The size of various market segments;
- How well these segments are being served by existing firms;
- Changes in the market-e.g., growth of segments or change in technology;
- How the firm should be positioned, or seen by customers. For example, Wal-Mart positions itself as providing value in retailing, while Nordstrom's defines itself more in terms of high levels of customer service.

The Boston Consulting Group (BCG) matrix provides a firm an opportunity to assess how well its business units work together. Each business unit is evaluated in terms of two factors: market share and the growth prospects in the market. Generally, the larger a firm's share, the stronger its position, and the greater the growth in a market, the better future possibilities. Four combinations emerge:

- A star represents a business unit that has a high share in a growing market. For example, Motorola has a large share in the rapidly growing market for cellular phones.
- A question mark results when a unit has a small share in a rapidly growing market. The firm's position, then, is not as strong as it would have been had its market share been greater, but there is an opportunity to grow. For example, Hewlett-Packard has a small share of the digital camera market, but this is a very rapidly growing market.
- A cash cow results when a firm has a large share in a market that is not growing, and may even be shrinking. Brother has a large share of the typewriter market.

- A dog results when a business unit has a small share in a market that is not growing. This is generally a somewhat unattractive situation, although dogs can still be profitable in the short run. For example, Smith Corona how has a small share of the typewriter market.

Firms are usually best of with a portfolio that has a balance of firms in each category. The cash cows tend to generate cash but require little future investment. On the other hand, stars generate some cash, but even more cash is needed to invest in the future-for research and development, marketing campaigns, and building new manufacturing facilities. Therefore, a firm may take excess cash from the cash cow and divert it to the star. For example, Brother could "harvest" its profits from typewriters and invest this in the unit making color laser printers, which will need the cash to grow. If a firm has cash cows that generate a lot of cash, this may be used to try to improve the market share of a question mark. A firm that has a number of promising stars in its portfolio may be in serious trouble if it does not have any cash cows to support it. If it is about to run out of cash-regardless of how profitable it is-is becomes vulnerable as a takeover target from a firm that has the cash to continue running it.

A SWOT ("Strengths, Opportunities, Weaknesses, and Threats") analysis is used to help the firm identify effective strategies. Successful firms such as Microsoft have certain strengths. Microsoft, for example, has a great deal of technology, a huge staff of very talented engineers, a great deal of experience in designing software, a very large market share, a well respected brand name, and a great deal of cash. Microsoft also has some weaknesses, however: The game console and MSN units are currently running at a loss, and MSN has been unable to achieve desired levels of growth. Firms may face opportunities in the current market. Microsoft, for example, may have the opportunity to take advantage of its brand name to enter into the hardware market. Microsoft may also become a trusted source of consumer services. Microsoft currently faces several threats, including the weak economy. Because fewer new computers are bough during a recession, fewer operating systems and software packages.

Rather than merely listing strengths, weaknesses, opportunities, and threats, a SWOT analysis should suggest how the firm may use its strengths and opportunities to overcome weaknesses and threats. Decisions should also be made as to how resources should be allocated. For example, Microsoft could either decide to put more resources into MSN or to abandon this unit entirely. Microsoft has a great deal of cash ready to spend, so the option to put resources toward MSN is available. Microsoft will also need to see how threats can be addressed. The firm can earn political good will by engaging in charitable acts, which it has money available to fund. For example, Microsoft has donated software and computers to schools. It can forego temporary profits by reducing prices temporarily to increase demand, or can "hold out" by maintaining current prices while not selling as many units.

Criteria for effective marketing plans. Marketing plans should meet several criteria:

- The plan must be specific enough so that it can be implemented and communicated to people in the firm. "Improving profitability" is usually too vague, but increasing net profits by 5%, increasing market share by 10%, gaining distribution in 2,000 more stores, and reducing manufacturing costs by 2% are all specific.
- The plan must be measurable so that one can see if it has been achieved. The above plans involve specific numbers.
- The goal must be achievable or realistic. Plans that are unrealistic may result in poor use of resources or lowered morale within the firm.
- The goals must be consistent. For example, a firm cannot ordinarily simultaneously plan improve product features, increase profits, and reduce prices.

Consumer Behaviour

Consumer behavior involves the psychological processes that consumers go through in recognizing needs, finding ways to solve these needs, making purchase decisions (e.g., whether or not to purchase a product and, if so, which brand and where), interpret information, make plans, and implement these plans (e.g., by engaging in comparison shopping or actually purchasing a product).

Sources of influence on the consumer. The consumer faces numerous sources of influence. Often, we take cultural influences for granted, but they are significant. An American will usually not bargain with a store owner. This, however, is a common practice in much of the World. Physical factors also influence our behavior. We are more likely to buy a soft drink when we are thirsty, for example, and food manufacturers have found that it is more effective to advertise their products on the radio in the late afternoon when people are getting hungry. A person's self-image will also tend to influence what he or she will buy-an upwardly mobile manager may buy a flashy car to project an image of success. Social factors also influence what the consumers buy-often, consumers seek to imitate others whom they admire, and may buy the same brands. The social environment can include both the mainstream culture (e.g., Americans are more likely to have corn flakes or ham and eggs for breakfast than to have rice, which is preferred in many Asian countries) and a subculture (e.g., rap music often appeals to a segment within the population that seeks to distinguish itself from the mainstream population). Thus, sneaker manufacturers are eager to have their products worn by admired athletes. Finally, consumer behavior is influenced by learning-you try a hamburger and learn that it satisfies your hunger and tastes good, and the next time you are hungry, you may consider another hamburger.

Consumer choices are often influenced dramatically by values. Some consumers, for example, seek to "fit in with the crowd" and would like to own a car as similar as possible to that of the neighbor. Others, on the other hand, want to stand out. In the consumption context, then, a consumer may choose to spend a great deal of money on buying and maintaining neat and professional attire, not because he or she is particularly interested in that appearance for its own sake, but rather because this will help the consumer be successful in his or her career.

Subculture often significantly influences the consumer. There are several potential ways that a society can be divided up. Some consumers are highly influenced by their ethnic origin. In some areas in Los Angeles, shopkeepers may transact all their business in a language of the predominant immigration patterns into the neighborhood-e.g., Spanish or Korean in some parts of downtown and Chinese in parts of the San Gabriel Valley. Virtual pets at first spread in the U.S. through Asian-American teenagers. Only after a while did the product diffuse into other ethnic groups.

Occasionally, religious groups will influence consumers' behavior, usually because a religion may set certain standards-e.g., some religions do not allow the consumption of alcohol, while others may disapprove of charging interest. The fact that many Americans spend a great deal of time with members of their religious groups in churches, synagogues, and mosques implies that members have a great deal of influence on each other. People in similar age groups also tend to have more influence on each other. This is particularly evident in the spread of fashion. Social status may also have some influence, as people may tend to emulate others in similar occupations or neighborhoods.

One way to look at social influence is though "reference groups"-people against which one compares oneself. Thus, a consumer may notice that all his friends are wearing a special kind of jeans and may expect to be ostracized if he or she chooses to wear a different brand. Interestingly, however, one may also hold dissociative reference groups-people that one would not want to be compared to. For example, Cadillac has an image problem in being associated with older consumers, who are not considered "hip" enough by younger, upwardly mobile consumers that the firm would like to target. Thus, Cadillac ran the campaign "It's not your father's car."

Family may influence the consumer's choices a great deal. Research has shown, for example, that there is a tendency for adult children to use the same brands that their parents used over time. In many cases, these brand choices are made without much conscious thought.

In marketing jargon, a consumer problem refers to a "discrepancy" between the "ideal" situation and reality. Thus, problems can range greatly in severity. One problem, for example, is that you are hungry. The problem is easily solved by eating. Other problems can be significantly more severe-for example, a consumer is scared that he will be rejected by his wife because he is growing bald. Note that problems can be solved in more than one way. Baldness could be addressed by obtaining a wig, medical treatment, buying a fancy car (as an alternative way to achieve attractiveness), or some other creative way.

One model of consumer decision making involves several steps. The first one is problem recognition-you realize that something is not as it should be. Perhaps, for example, your car is getting more difficult to start and is not accelerating well. The second step is information search-what are some alternative ways of solving the problem? You might buy a new car, buy a used car, take your car in for repair, ride the bus, ride a taxi, or ride a skateboard to work. The third step involves evaluation of alternatives. A skateboard is inexpensive, but may be ill-suited for long distances and for rainy days. Finally, we have the purchase stage, and sometimes a post-purchase stage (e.g., you return a product to the store because you did not find it satisfactory). In reality, people may go back and forth between the stages.

For example, a person may resume alternative identification during while evaluating already known alternatives. Consumer involvement will tend to vary dramatically depending on the type of product. In general, consumer involvement will be higher for products that are very expensive (e.g., a home, a car) or are highly significant in the consumer's life in some other way (e.g., a word processing program or acne medication).

It is important to consider the consumer's motivation for buying products. To achieve this goal, we can use the Means-End chain, wherein we consider a logical progression of consequences of product use that eventually lead to desired end benefit. Thus, for example, a consumer may see that a car has a large engine, leading to fast acceleration, leading to a feeling of performance, leading to a feeling of power, which ultimately improves the consumer's self-esteem. A handgun may aim bullets with precision, which enables the user to kill an intruder, which means that the intruder will not be able to harm the consumer's family, which achieves the desired end-state of security. In advertising, it is important to portray the desired end-states. Focusing on the large motor will do less good than portraying a successful person driving the car.

Information search and decision making. Consumers engage in both internal and external information search. Internal search involves the consumer identifying alternatives from his or her memory. For certain low involvement products, it is very important that marketing programs achieve "top of mind" awareness. For example, few people will search the Yellow Pages for fast food restaurants; thus, the consumer must be able to retrieve one's restaurant from memory before it will be considered. For high involvement products, consumers are more likely to use an external search. Before buying a car, for example, the consumer may ask friends' opinions, read reviews in Consumer Reports, consult several web sites, and visit several dealerships. Thus, firms that make products that are selected predominantly through external search must invest in having information available to the consumer in need-e.g., through brochures, web sites, or news coverage.

A compensatory decision involves the consumer "trading off" good and bad attributes of a product. For example, a car may have a low price and good gas mileage but slow acceleration. If the price is sufficiently inexpensive and gas efficient, the consumer may then select it over a car with better acceleration that costs more and uses more gas. Occasionally, a decision will involve a non-compensatory strategy. For example, a parent may reject all soft drinks that contain artificial sweeteners. Here, other good features such as taste and low calories cannot overcome this one "non-negotiable" attribute.

The amount of effort a consumer puts into searching depends on a number of factors such as the market (how many competitors are there, and how great are differences between brands expected to be?), product characteristics (how important is this product? How complex is the product? How obvious are indications of quality?), consumer characteristics (how interested is a consumer, generally, in analyzing product characteristics and making the best possible deal?), and situational characteristics (as previously discussed).

Two interesting issues in decisions are:

- Variety seeking (where consumers seek to try new brands not because these brands are expected to be "better" in any way, but rather because the consumer wants a "change of pace," and
- "Impulse" purchases-unplanned buys. This represents a somewhat "fuzzy" group. For example, a shopper may plan to buy vegetables but only decide in the store to actually buy broccoli and corn. Alternatively, a person may buy an item which is currently on sale, or one that he or she remembers that is needed only once inside the store.

A number of factors involve consumer choices. In some cases, consumers will be more motivated. For example, one may be more careful choosing a gift for an in-law than when buying the same thing for one self. Some consumers are also more motivated to comparison shop for the best prices, while others are more convenience oriented. Personality impacts decisions. Some like variety more than others, and some are more receptive to stimulation and excitement in trying new stores. Perception influences decisions. Some people, for example, can taste the difference between generic and name brand foods while many cannot. Selective perception occurs when a person is paying attention only to information of interest. For example, when looking for a new car, the consumer may pay more attention to car ads than when this is not in the horizon. Some consumers are put off by perceived risk.

Thus, many marketers offer a money back guarantee. Consumers will tend to change their behavior through learning-e.g., they will avoid restaurants they have found to be crowded and will settle on brands that best meet their tastes. Consumers differ in the values they hold (e.g., some people are more committed to recycling than others who will not want to go through the hassle). We will consider the issue of lifestyle under segmentation.

Attitudes. Consumer attitudes are a composite of a consumer's (1) beliefs about, (2) feelings about, (3) and behavioral intentions toward some "object"-within the context of marketing, usually a brand, product category, or retail store. These components are viewed together since they are highly interdependent and together represent forces that influence how the consumer will react to the object.

Beliefs. The first component is beliefs. A consumer may hold both positive beliefs toward an object (e.g., coffee tastes good) as well as negative beliefs (e.g., coffee is easily spilled and stains papers). In addition, some beliefs may be neutral (coffee is black), and some may be differ in valance depending on the person or the situation (e.g., coffee is hot and stimulates--good on a cold morning, but not good on a hot summer evening when one wants to sleep). Note also that the beliefs that consumers hold need not be accurate (e.g., that pork contains little fat), and some beliefs may, upon closer examination, be contradictory.

Affect. Consumers also hold certain feelings toward brands or other objects. Sometimes these feelings are based on the beliefs (e.g., a person feels nauseated when thinking about a hamburger because of the tremendous amount of fat it contains), but there may also be feelings which are relatively independent of beliefs.

For example, an extreme environmentalist may believe that cutting down trees is morally wrong, but may have positive affect toward Christmas trees because he or she unconsciously associates these trees with the experience that he or she had at Christmas as a child.

Behavioral intention. The behavioral intention is what the consumer plans to do with respect to the object (e.g., buy or not buy the brand). As with affect, this is sometimes a logical consequence of beliefs (or affect), but may sometimes reflect other circumstances--e.g., although a consumer does not really like a restaurant, he or she will go there because it is a hangout for his or her friends.

Changing attitudes is generally very difficult, particularly when consumers suspect that the marketer has a self-serving "agenda" in bringing about this change (e.g., to get the consumer to buy more or to switch brands). Here are some possible methods:

- ***Changing Affect:*** One approach is to try to change affect, which may or may not involve getting consumers to change their beliefs. One strategy uses the approach of classical conditioning try to "pair" the product with a liked stimulus. For example, we "pair" a car with a beautiful woman. Alternatively, we can try to get people to like the advertisement and hope that this liking will "spill over" into the purchase of a product. For example, the Pillsbury Doughboy does not really emphasize the conveyance of much information to the consumer; instead, it attempts to create a warm, "fuzzy" image. Although Energizer Bunny ads try to get people to believe that their batteries last longer, the main emphasis is on the likeable bunny. Finally, products which are better known, through the mere exposure effect, tend to be better liked-that is, the more a product is advertised and seen in stores, the more it will generally be liked, even if consumers to do not develop any specific beliefs about the product.

- *Changing Behavior:* People like to believe that their behavior is rational; thus, once they use our products, chances are that they will continue unless someone is able to get them to switch. One way to get people to switch to our brand is to use temporary price discounts and coupons; however, when consumers buy a product on deal, they may justify the purchase based on that deal (i.e., the low price) and may then switch to other brands on deal later. A better way to get people to switch to our brand is to at least temporarily obtain better shelf space so that the product is more convenient. Consumers are less likely to use this availability as a rationale for their purchase and may continue to buy the product even when the product is less conveniently located.
- *Changing Beliefs:* Although attempting to change beliefs is the obvious way to attempt attitude change, particularly when consumers hold unfavorable or inaccurate ones, this is often difficult to achieve because consumers tend to resist. Several approaches to belief change exist:
    - o *Change Currently held Beliefs:* It is generally very difficult to attempt to change beliefs that people hold, particularly those that are strongly held, even if they are inaccurate. For example, the petroleum industry advertised for a long time that its profits were lower than were commonly believed, and provided extensive factual evidence in its advertising to support this reality. Consumers were suspicious and rejected this information, however.
    - o *Change the Importance of Beliefs:* Although the sugar manufacturers would undoubtedly like to decrease the importance of healthy teeth, it is usually not feasible to make beliefs less important--consumers are likely to reason, why, then, would you bother bringing them up in the first place? However, it may be possible to strengthen beliefs that favor us--e.g., a vitamin supplement manufacturer may advertise that it is extremely important for women to replace iron lost through menstruation. Most Add consumers already agree with this, but the belief can be made stronger.

beliefs. Consumers are less likely to resist the addition of beliefs so long as they do not conflict with existing beliefs. Thus, the beef industry has added beliefs that beef (1) is convenient and (2) can be used to make a number of creative dishes. Vitamin manufacturers attempt to add the belief that stress causes vitamin depletion, which sounds quite plausible to most people.

- *Change the Ideal:* It usually difficult, and very risky, to attempt to change ideals, and only few firms succeed. For example, Hard Candy may have attempted to change the ideal away from traditional beauty toward more unique self expression.

One-sided vs. two-sided appeals. Attitude research has shown that consumers often tend to react more favorably to advertisements which either (1) admit something negative about the sponsoring brand (e.g., the Volvo is a clumsy car, but very safe) or (2) admits something positive about a competing brand (e.g., a competing supermarket has slightly lower prices, but offers less service and selection). Two-sided appeals must, contain overriding arguments why the sponsoring brand is ultimately superior-that is, in the above examples, the "but" part must be emphasized.

Reference Groups: A useful framework of analysis of group influence on the individual is the so called reference group-the term comes about because an individual uses a relevant group as a standard of "reference" against which oneself is compared. Reference groups come in several different forms.

The aspirational reference group refers to those others against whom one would like to compare oneself. For example, many firms use athletes as spokespeople, and these represent what many people would ideally like to be. Associative reference groups include people who more realistically represent the individuals' current equals or near-equals-e.g., coworkers, neighbors, or members of churches, clubs, and organizations. Finally, the dissociative reference group includes people that the individual would not like to be like.

For example, the store literally named The Gap came about because many younger people wanted to actively dissociate from parents and other older and "uncool" people. The Quality Paperback

Book specifically suggests in its advertising that its members are "a breed apart" from conventional readers of popular books.

The Family Life Cycle. Individuals and families tend to go through a "life cycle." The simple life cycle goes from:

child/teenager – young single – young couple – full nest – empty nest – widow(er).

In real life, this situation is, of course, a bit more complicated. For example, many couples undergo divorce. Then we have the scenario:

full nest – single parent

This situation can result either from divorce or from the death of one parent. Divorce usually entails a significant change in the relative wealth of spouses. In some cases, the non-custodial parent (usually the father) will not pay the required child support, and even if he or she does, that still may not leave the custodial parent and children as well off as they were during the marriage. On the other hand, in some cases, some non-custodial parents will be called on to pay a large part of their income in child support. This is particularly a problem when the non-custodial parent remarries and has additional children in the second (or subsequent marriages). In any event, divorce often results in a large demand for:

- low cost furniture and household items
- time-saving goods and services.

Divorced parents frequently remarry, or become involved in other non-marital relationships; thus, we may see

full nest – single parent – blended family

Another variation involves

young single – single parent

Here, the single parent who assumes responsibility for one or more children may not form a relationship with the other parent of the child.

Generally, there are two main themes in the Family Life Cycle, subject to significant exceptions:

- As a person gets older, he or she tends to advance in his or her career and tends to get greater income (exceptions: maternity leave, divorce, retirement).

- Unfortunately, obligations also tend to increase with time (at least until one's mortgage has been paid off). Children and paying for one's house are two of the greatest expenses.

Note that although a single person may have a lower income than a married couple, the single may be able to buy more discretionary items since he or she has fewer current obligations. This will change when a house is bought or children come along.

Family Decision Making: Individual members of families often serve different roles in decisions that ultimately draw on shared family resources. Some individuals are information gatherers/holders, who seek out information about products of relevance. These individuals often have a great deal of power because they may selectively pass on information that favors their chosen alternatives. Influencers do not ultimately have the power decide between alternatives, but they may make their wishes known by asking for specific products or causing embarrassing situations if their demands are not met. The decision maker(s) have the power to determine issues such as:

- Whether to buy;
- Which product to buy (pick-up or passenger car?);
- Which brand to buy;
- Where to buy it; and
- When to buy.

Note, however, that the role of the decision maker is separate from that of the purchaser. From the point of view of the marketer, this introduces some problems since the purchaser can be targeted by point-of-purchase (POP) marketing efforts that cannot be aimed at the decision maker. Also note that the distinction between the purchaser and decision maker may be somewhat blurred:

- The decision maker may specify what kind of product to buy, but not which brand;
- The purchaser may have to make a substitution if the desired brand is not in stock;
- The purchaser may disregard instructions (by error or deliberately).

It should be noted that family decisions are often subject to a great deal of conflict. The reality is that few families are wealthy enough to avoid a strong tension between demands on the family's resources. Conflicting pressures are especially likely in families with children and/or when only one spouse works outside the home. Note that many decisions inherently come down to values, and that there is frequently no "objective" way to arbitrate differences. One spouse may believe that it is important to save for the children's future; the other may value spending now (on private schools and computer equipment) to help prepare the children for the future. Who is right? There is no clear answer here. The situation becomes even more complex when more parties-such as children or other relatives-are involved. Culture is part of the external influences that impact the consumer. That is, culture represents influences that are imposed on the consumer by other individuals.

The United States has undergone some changes in its predominant culture over the last several decades. Again, however, it should be kept in mind that there are great variations within the culture. For example, on the average, Americans have become less materialistic and have sought more leisure; on the other hand, the percentage of people working extremely long hours has also increased.

Significant changes have occurred in gender roles in American society. One of the reasons for this is that more women work outside the home than before. However, women still perform a disproportionate amount of housework, and men who participate in this activity tend to do so reluctantly. In general, commercials tend to lag somewhat behind reality-e.g., few men are seen doing housework, and few women are seen as buyers and decision makers on automobile purchases.

Regional influence, both in the United States and other areas, is significant. Many food manufacturers offer different product variations for different regions. Joel Girardeau, in his book The Nine Nations of North America, proposed nine distinct regional subcultures that cut across state lines. Although significant regional differences undoubtedly exist, research has failed to support Garreau's specific characterizations/

Consumer behavior is frequently affected by the situation. For example, people may buy different products when shopping for others than they would for themselves. We tend to make quicker but less elaborate decisions when facing time pressure. There are also influences of mood. For example, people who are unhappy tend to make more rational and more critical decisions.

The Means-End Chain: Consumers often buy products not because of their attributes per se but rather because of the ultimate benefits that these attributes provide, in turn leading to the satisfaction of ultimate values. For example, a consumer may not be particularly interested in the chemistry of plastic roses, but might reason as follows:

Highly reliable synthetic content of roses — Roses will stay in original condition for a long time — Significant other will appreciate the roses longer — Significant other will continue to love one — Self esteem.

The important thing in a means-end chain is to start with an attribute, a concrete characteristic of the product, and then logically progress to a series of consequences (which tend to become progressively more abstract) that end with a value being satisfied. Thus, each chain must start with an attribute and end with a value. An important implication of means-end chains is that it is usually most effective in advertising to focus on higher level items. For example, in the flower example above, an individual giving the flowers to the significant other might better be portrayed than the flowers alone.

***Organizational Buyers*:** A large portion of the market for goods and services is attributable to organizational, as opposed to individual, buyers. In general, organizational buyers, who make buying decisions for their companies for a living, tend to be somewhat more sophisticated than ordinary consumers. However, these organizational buyers are also often more risk averse. There is a risk in going with a new, possibly better (lower price or higher quality) supplier whose product is unproven and may turn out to be problematic. Often the fear of running this risk is greater than the potential rewards for getting a better deal. In the old days, it used to be said that "You can't get fired for buying IBM." This attitude is beginning to soften a bit today as firms face increasing pressures to cut costs.

Organizational Buyers Come in Several Forms: Resellers involve either wholesalers or retailers that buy from one organization and resell to some other entity. For example, large grocery chains sometimes buy products directly from the manufacturer and resell them to end-consumers. Wholesalers may sell to retailers who in turn sell to consumers. Producers also buy products from sub-manufacturers to create a finished product. For example, rather than manufacturing the parts themselves, computer manufacturers often buy hard drives, motherboards, cases, monitors, keyboards, and other components from manufacturers and put them together to create a finished product. Governments buy a great deal of things. For example, the military needs an incredible amount of supplies to feed and equip troops. Finally, large institutions buy products in huge quantities. For example, UCR probably buys thousands of reams of paper every month.

Organizational buying usually involves more people than individual buying. Often, many people are involved in making decisions as to (a) whether to buy, (b) what to buy, (c) at what quantity, and (d) from whom. An engineer may make a specification as to what is needed, which may be approved by a manager, with the final purchase being made by a purchase specialist who spends all his or her time finding the best deal on the goods that the organization needs. Often, such long purchase processes can cause long delays. In the government, rules are often especially stringent-e.g., vendors of fruit cake have to meet fourteen pages of specifications put out by the General Services Administration. In many cases, government buyers are also heavily bound to go with the lowest price. Even if it is obvious that a higher priced vendor will offer a superior product, it may be difficult to accept that bid.

International Marketing

Protectionism: Although trade generally benefits a country as a whole, powerful interests within countries frequently put obstacles-i.e., they seek to inhibit free trade. There are several ways this can be done:

- ***Tariff Barriers:*** A duty, or tax or fee, is put on products imported. This is usually a percentage of the cost of the good.
- ***Quotas:*** A country can export only a certain number of goods to the importing country. For example, Mexico can export only a certain quantity of tomatoes to the United

States, and Asian countries can send only a certain quota of textiles here.

- *"Voluntary" Export Restraints:* These are not official quotas, but involve agreements made by countries to limit the amount of goods they export to an importing country. Such restraints are typically motivated by the desire to avoid more stringent restrictions if the exporters do not agree to limit themselves. For example, Japanese car manufacturers have agreed to limit the number of automobiles they export to the United States.
- *Subsidies to Domestic Products:* If the government supports domestic producers of a product, these may end up with a cost advantage relative to foreign producers who do not get this subsidy. U.S. honey manufacturers receive such subsidies.
- Non-tariff barriers, such as differential standards in testing foreign and domestic products for safety, disclosure of less information to foreign manufacturers needed to get products approved, slow processing of imports at ports of entry, or arbitrary laws which favor domestic manufacturers.

Cultural Lessons: We considered several cultural lessons in class; the important thing here is the big picture. For example, within the Muslim tradition, the dog is considered a "dirty" animal, so portraying it as "man's best friend" in an advertisement is counter-productive. Packaging, seen as a reflection of the quality of the "real" product, is considerably more important in Asia than in the U.S., where there is a tendency to focus on the contents which "really count." Many cultures observe significantly greater levels of formality than that typical in the U.S., and Japanese negotiator tend to observe long silent pauses as a speaker's point is considered.

Product Need Satisfaction: We often take for granted the "obvious" need that products seem to fill in our own culture; however, functions served may be very different in others-for example, while cars have a large transportation role in the U.S., they are impractical to drive in Japan, and thus cars there serve more of a role of being a status symbol or providing for individual indulgence. In the U.S., fast food and instant drinks such as Tang are intended for convenience; elsewhere, they may represent more of a treat. Thus, it is important to examine through marketing research consumers' true motives, desires, and expectations in buying a product.

Approaches to Product Introduction: Firms face a choice of alternatives in marketing their products across markets. An extreme strategy involves customization, whereby the firm introduces a unique product in each country, usually with the belief tastes differ so much between countries that it is necessary more or less to start from "scratch" in creating a product for each market. On the other extreme, standardization involves making one global product in the belief the same product can be sold across markets without significant modification-e.g., Intel microprocessors are the same regardless of the country in which they are sold. Finally, in most cases firms will resort to some kind of adaptation, whereby a common product is modified to some extent when moved between some markets-e.g., in the United States, where fuel is relatively less expensive, many cars have larger engines than their comparable models in Europe and Asia; however, much of the design is similar or identical, so some economies are achieved. Similarly, while Kentucky Fried Chicken serves much the same chicken with the eleven herbs and spices in Japan, a lesser amount of sugar is used in the potato salad, and fries are substituted for mashed potatoes.

There are certain benefits to standardization. Firms that produce a global product can obtain economies of scale in manufacturing, and higher quantities produced also lead to a faster advancement along the experience curve. Further, it is more feasible to establish a global brand as less confusion will occur when consumers travel across countries and see the same product. On the down side, there may be significant differences in desires between cultures and physical environments-e.g., software sold in the U.S. and Europe will often utter a "beep" to alert the user when a mistake has been made; however, in Asia, where office workers are often seated closely together, this could cause embarrassment.

Adaptations Come in Several Forms: Mandatory adaptations involve changes that have to be made before the product can be used-e.g., appliances made for the U.S. and Europe must run on different voltages, and a major problem was experienced in the

European Union when hoses for restaurant frying machines could not simultaneously meet the legal requirements of different countries. "Discretionary" changes are changes that do not have to be made before a product can be introduced (e.g., there is nothing to prevent an American firm from introducing an overly sweet soft drink into the Japanese market), although products may face poor sales if such changes are not made. Discretionary changes may also involve cultural adaptations-e.g., in Sesame Street, the Big Bird became the Big Camel in Saudi Arabia.

Another distinction involves physical product vs. communication adaptations. In order for gasoline to be effective in high altitude regions, its octane must be higher, but it can be promoted much the same way. On the other hand, while the same bicycle might be sold in China and the U.S., it might be positioned as a serious means of transportation in the former and as a recreational tool in the latter. In some cases, products may not need to be adapted in either way (e.g., industrial equipment), while in other cases, it might have to be adapted in both (e.g., greeting cards, where the both occasions, language, and motivations for sending differ). Finally, a market may exist abroad for a product which has no analogue at home-e.g., hand-powered washing machines. Measuring country wealth.

Economics: There are two ways to measure the wealth of a country. The nominal per capita gross domestic product (GDP) refers to the value of goods and services produced per person in a country if this value in local currency were to be exchanged into dollars. Suppose, for example, that the per capita GDP of Japan is 3,500,000 yen and the dollar exchanges for 100 yen, so that the per capita GDP is (3,500,000/100)=$35,000. However, that $35,000 will not buy as much in Japan-food and housing are much more expensive there. Therefore, we introduce the idea of purchase parity adjusted per capita GDP, which reflects what this money can buy in the country. This is typically based on the relative costs of a weighted "basket" of goods in a country (e.g., 35% of the cost of housing, 40% the cost of food, 10% the cost of clothing, and 15% cost of other items). If it turns out that this measure of cost of living is 30% higher in Japan, the purchase parity adjusted GPD in Japan would then be ($35,000/(130%) = $26,923. (The Gross Domestic Product (GPD) and Gross National Product (GNP) are almost identical figures. The GNP, for example, includes income made by citizens working abroad, and does not include the income of foreigners working in the country. Traditionally, the GNP was more prevalent; today the GPD is more commonly used-in practice, the two measures fall within a few percent of each other.)

In general, the nominal per capita GPD is more useful for determining local consumers' ability to buy imported goods, the cost of which are determined in large measure by the costs in the home market, while the purchase parity adjusted measure is more useful when products are produced, at local costs, in the country of purchase. For example, the ability of Argentineans to purchase micro computer chips, which are produced mostly in the U.S. and Japan, is better predicted by nominal income, while the ability to purchase toothpaste made by a U.S. firm in a factory in Argentina is better predicted by purchase parity adjusted income.

It should be noted that, in some countries, income is quite unevenly distributed so that these average measures may not be very meaningful. In Brazil, for example, there is a very large underclass making significantly less than the national average, and thus, the national figure is not a good indicator of the purchase power of the mass market. Similarly, great regional differences exist within some countries-income is much higher in northern Germany than it is in the former East Germany, and income in southern Italy is much lower than in northern Italy.

Methods of Entry: With rare exceptions, products just don't emerge in foreign markets overnight-a firm has to build up a market over time. Several strategies, which differ in aggressiveness, risk, and the amount of control that the firm is able to maintain, are available:

- Exporting is a relatively low risk strategy in which few investments are made in the new country. A drawback is that, because the firm makes few if any marketing investments in the new country, market share may be below potential. Further, the firm, by not operating in the country, learns less about the market (What do consumers really want? Which kinds of advertising campaigns are most successful? What are the most effective methods of distribution?) If an importer is willing to do a good job of marketing, this arrangement may represent a "win-win" situation, but it may be more difficult for the firm to enter on its own later if it decides that larger profits can be made within the country.

- Licensing and franchising are also low exposure methods of entry-you allow someone else to use your trademarks and accumulated expertise. Your partner puts up the money and assumes the risk. Problems here involve the fact that you are training a potential competitor and that you have little control over how the business is operated. For example, American fast food restaurants have found that foreign franchisers often fail to maintain American standards of cleanliness. Similarly, a foreign manufacturer may use lower quality ingredients in manufacturing a brand based on premium contents in the home country.
- ***Joint Venture:*** Here, a firm partners up with a firm already in the country. Each partner contributes. Usually, the host country partner contributes expertise about the country and possibly some manufacturing facilities. The "guest" partner usually contributes technology and/or financial resources. This reduces risk and investment to some extent, but also reduces the control since agreements must now be made to satisfy the partner.
- Direct entry strategies, where the firm either acquires a firm or builds operations "from scratch" involve the highest exposure, but also the greatest opportunities for profits. The firm gains more knowledge about the local market and maintains greater control, but now has a huge investment. In some countries, the government may expropriate assets without compensation, so direct investment entails an additional risk. A variation involves a joint venture, where a local firm puts up some of the money and knowledge about the local market.

U.S. laws of particular interest to firms doing business abroad.

- ***Anti-trust:*** U.S. antitrust laws are generally enforced in U.S. courts even if the alleged transgression occurred outside U.S. jurisdiction. For example, if two Japanese firms collude to limit the World supply of VCRs, they may be sued by the U.S. government (or injured third parties) in U.S. courts, and may have their U.S. assets seized.

- The Foreign Corrupt Influences Act came about as Congress was upset with U.S. firms' bribery of foreign officials. Although most if not all countries ban the payment of bribes, such laws are widely flaunted in many countries, and it is often useful to pay a bribe to get foreign government officials to act favorably. Firms engaging in this behavior, even if it takes place entirely outside the U.S., can be prosecuted in U.S. courts, and many executives have served long prison sentences for giving in to temptation. In contrast, in the past some European firms could actually deduct the cost of foreign bribes from their taxes! There are some gray areas here-it may be legal to pay certain "tips"-known as "facilitating payments"-to low level government workers in some countries who rely on such payments as part of their salary so long as these payments are intended only to speed up actions that would be taken anyway. For example, it may be acceptable to give a reasonable (not large) facilitating payment to get customs workers to process a shipment faster, but it would not be legal to pay these individuals to change the classification of a product into one that carries a lower tariff.
- *Anti-boycott Laws:* Many Arab countries maintain a boycott of Israel, and foreigners that want to do business with them may be asked to join in this boycott by stopping any deals they do with Israel and certifying that they do not trade with that country. It is illegal for U.S. firms to make this certification even if they have not dropped any actual deals with Israel to get a deal with boycotters.
- *Trading with the Enemy:* It is illegal for U.S. firms to trade with certain countries that are viewed to be hostile to the U.S.-e.g., Libya and Iraq.

Marketing Research

Marketing research is often needed to ensure that we produce what customers really want and not what we think they want.

Primary vs. secondary research methods. There are two main approaches to marketing. Secondary research involves using information that others have already put together. For example, if you are thinking about starting a business making clothes for tall people, you don't need to question people about how tall they are to find out how many tall people exist-that information has already been published by the U.S. Government. Primary research, in contrast, is research that you design and conduct yourself. For example, you may need to find out whether consumers would prefer that your soft drinks be sweater or tarter.

Research will often help us reduce risks associated with a new product, but it cannot take the risk away entirely. It is also important to ascertain whether the research has been complete. For example, Coca Cola did a great deal of research prior to releasing the New Coke, and consumers seemed to prefer the taste. However, consumers were not prepared to have this drink replace traditional Coke.

Several tools are available to the market researcher-e.g., mail questionnaires, phone surveys, observation, and focus groups. Please see the chart for advantages and disadvantages of each.

Surveys are useful for getting a great deal of specific information. Surveys can contain open-ended questions (e.g., "In which city and state were you born? ____________") or closed-ended, where the respondent is asked to select answers from a brief list (e.g., "__Male ___ Female." Open ended questions have the advantage that the respondent is not limited to the options listed, and that the respondent is not being influenced by seeing a list of responses. However, open-ended questions are often skipped by respondents, and coding them can be quite a challenge. In general, for surveys to yield meaningful responses, sample sizes of over 100 are usually required because precision is essential. For example, if a market share of twenty percent would result in a loss while thirty percent would be profitable, a confidence interval of 20-35% is too wide to be useful.

Surveys come in several different forms. Mail surveys are relatively inexpensive, but response rates are typically quite low-typically from 5-20%. Phone-surveys get somewhat higher response rates, but not many questions can be asked because many answer options have to be repeated and few people are willing to stay on the phone for more than five minutes. Mall intercepts are a convenient way to reach consumers, but respondents may be reluctant to discuss anything sensitive face-to-face with an interviewer.

Surveys, as any kind of research, are vulnerable to bias. The wording of a question can influence the outcome a great deal. For example, more people answered no to the question "Should speeches against democracy be allowed?" than answered yes to "Should speeches against democracy be forbidden?" For face-to-face interviews, interviewer bias is a danger, too. Interviewer bias occurs when the interviewer influences the way the respondent answers. For example, unconsciously an interviewer that works for the firm manufacturing the product in question may smile a little when something good is being said about the product and frown a little when something negative is being said. The respondent may catch on and say something more positive than his or her real opinion. Finally, a response bias may occur-if only part of the sample responds to a survey, the respondents' answers may not be representative of the population.

Focus groups are useful when the marketer wants to launch a new product or modify an existing one. A focus group usually involves having some 8-12 people come together in a room to discuss their consumption preferences and experiences. The group is usually led by a moderator, who will start out talking broadly about topics related broadly to the product without mentioning the product itself. For example, a focus group aimed at sugar-free cookies might first address consumers' snacking preferences, only gradually moving toward the specific product of sugar-free cookies. By not mentioning the product up front, we avoid biasing the participants into thinking only in terms of the specific product brought out. Thus, instead of having consumers think primarily in terms of what might be good or bad about the product, we can ask them to discuss more broadly the ultimate benefits they really seek.

For example, instead of having consumers merely discuss what they think about some sugar-free cookies that we are considering releasing to the market, we can have consumers speak about their motivations for using snacks and what general kinds of benefits they seek. Such a discussion might reveal a concern about healthfulness and a desire for wholesome foods. Probing on the meaning of wholesomeness, consumers might indicate a desire to avoid artificial ingredients. This would be an important concern in the marketing of sugar-free cookies, but might not have come up if consumers were asked to comment directly on the product where the use of artificial ingredients is, by virtue of the nature of the product, necessary.

Focus groups are well suited for some purposes, but poorly suited for others. In general, focus groups are very good for getting breadth-i.e., finding out what kinds of issues are important for consumers in a given product category. Here, it is helpful that focus groups are completely "open-ended:" The consumer mentions his or her preferences and opinions, and the focus group moderator can ask the consumer to elaborate. In a questionnaire, if one did not think to ask about something, chances are that few consumers would take the time to write out an elaborate answer. Focus groups also have some drawbacks, for example: They represent small sample sizes. Because of the cost of running focus groups, only a few groups can be run. Suppose you run four focus groups with ten members each. This will result in an n of 4(10)=40, which is too small to generalize from. Therefore, focus groups cannot give us a good idea of: What proportion of the population is likely to buy the product. What price consumers are willing to pay. The groups are inherently social. This means that: Consumers will often say things that may make them look good (i.e., they watch public television rather than soap operas or cook fresh meals for their families daily) even if that is not true. Consumers may be reluctant to speak about embarrassing issues (e.g., weight control, birth control).

Personal interviews involve in-depth questioning of an individual about his or her interest in or experiences with a product. The benefit here is that we can get really into depth (when the respondent says something interesting, we can ask him or her to elaborate), but this method of research is costly and can be extremely vulnerable to interviewer bias.

Projective techniques are used when a consumer may feel embarrassed to admit to certain opinions, feelings, or preferences. For example, many older executives may not be comfortable admitting to being intimidated by computers. It has been found that in such cases, people will tend to respond more openly about "someone else." Thus, we may ask them to explain reasons why a friend has not yet bought a computer, or to tell a story about a person in a picture who is or is not using a product. The main problem with this method is that it is difficult to analyze responses.

Observation of consumers is often a powerful tool. Looking at how consumers select products may yield insights into how they make decisions and what they look for. For example, some American manufacturers were concerned about low sales of their products in Japan.

Observing Japanese consumers, it was found that many of these Japanese consumers scrutinized packages looking for a name of a major manufacturer-the product specific-brands that are common in the U.S. (e.g., Tide) were not impressive to the Japanese, who wanted a name of a major firm like Mitsubishi or Proctor & Gamble. Observation may help us determine how much time consumers spend comparing prices, or whether nutritional labels are being consulted.

Physiological measures are occasionally used to examine consumer response. For example, advertisers may want to measure a consumer's level of arousal during various parts of an advertisement.

Some cautions should be heeded in marketing research. First, in general, research should only be commissioned when it is worth the cost. Thus, research should normally be useful in making specific decisions (what size should the product be? Should the product be launched? Should we charge $1.75 or $2.25?)

Secondly, marketing research can be, and often is, abused. Managers frequently have their own "agendas" (e.g., they either would like a product to be launched or would prefer that it not be launched so that the firm will have more resources left over to tackle their favorite products). Often, a way to get your way is to demonstrate through "objective" research that your opinions make economic sense. One example of misleading research, which was reported nationwide in the media, involved the case of "The Pentagon Declares War on Rush Limbaugh."

The Pentagon, within a year of the election of Democrat Bill Clinton, reported that only 4.2% of soldiers listening to the Armed Forces Network wanted to hear Rush Limbaugh. However, although this finding was reported without question in the media, it was later found that the conclusion was based on the question "What single thing can we do to improve programming?" If you did not write in something like "Carry Rush Limbaugh," you were counted as not wanting to hear him.

Segmentation, Targeting and Positioning

Segmentation, targeting, and positioning together comprise a three stage process. We first (1) determine which kinds of customers exist, then (2) select which ones we are best off trying to serve and, finally, (3) implement our segmentation by optimizing our products/services for that segment and communicating that we have made the choice to distinguish ourselves that way.

Segmentation involves finding out what kinds of consumers with different needs exist. In the auto market, for example, some consumers demand speed and performance, while others are much more concerned about roominess and safety. In general, it holds true that "You can't be all things to all people," and experience has demonstrated that firms that specialize in meeting the needs of one group of consumers over another tend to be more profitable.

Generally, there are three approaches to marketing:

- In the undifferentiated strategy, all consumers are treated as the same, with firms not making any specific efforts to satisfy particular groups. This may work when the product is a standard one where one competitor really can't offer much that another one can't. Usually, this is the case only for commodities.
- In the concentrated strategy, one firm chooses to focus on one of several segments that exist while leaving other segments to competitors. For example, Southwest Airlines focuses on price sensitive consumers who will forego meals and assigned seating for low prices.
- In contrast, most airlines follow the differentiated strategy: They offer high priced tickets to those who are inflexible in that they cannot tell in advance when they need to fly and find it impractical to stay over a Saturday. These travelers-usually business travelers-pay high fares but can only fill the planes up partially. The same airlines then sell some of the remaining seats to more price sensitive customers who can buy two weeks in advance and stay over.

Note that segmentation calls for some tough choices. There may be a large number of variables that can be used to differentiate consumers of a given product category; yet, in practice, it becomes impossibly cumbersome to work with more than a few at a time. Thus, we need to determine which variables will be most useful in distinguishing different groups of consumers. We might thus decide, for example, that the variables that are most relevant in separating different kinds of soft drink consumers are (1) preference for taste vs. low calories, (2) preference for Cola vs. non-cola taste, (3) price sensitivity-willingness to pay for brand names; and (4) heavy vs. light consumers. We now put these variables together to arrive at various combinations. Several different kinds of variables can be used for segmentation.

Demographic variables essentially refer to personal statistics such as income, gender, education, location (rural vs. urban, East vs. West), ethnicity, and family size. Campbell's soup, for instance, has found that Western U.S. consumers on the average prefer spicier soups-thus, you get a different product in the same cans at the East and West coasts. Facing flat sales of guns in the traditional male dominated market, a manufacturer came out with the Lady Remmington, a more compact, handier gun more attractive to women.

Taking this a step farther, it is also possible to segment on lifestyle and values. Some consumers want to be seen as similar to others, while a different segment wants to stand apart from the crowd. Another basis for segmentation is behavior. Some consumers are "brand loyal"-i.e., they tend to stick with their preferred brands even when a competing one is on sale. Some consumers are "heavy" users while others are "light" users. For example, research conducted by the wine industry shows that some 80% of the product is consumed by 20% of the consumers-presumably a rather intoxicated group.

One can also segment on benefits sought, essentially bypassing demographic explanatory variables. Some consumers, for example, like scented soap (a segment likely to be attracted to brands such as Irish Spring), while others prefer the "clean" feeling of unscented soap (the "Ivory" segment). Some consumers use toothpaste primarily to promote oral health, while another segment is more interested in breath freshening. In the next step, we decide to target one or more segments. Our choice should generally depend on several factors. First, how well are existing segments served by other manufacturers? It will be more difficult to appeal to a segment that is already well served than to one whose needs are not currently being served well. Secondly, how large is the segment, and how can we expect it to grow? (Note that a downside to a large, rapidly growing segment is that it tends to attract competition). Thirdly, do we have strengths as a company that will help us appeal particularly to one group of consumers? Firms may already have an established reputation. While McDonald's has a great reputation for fast, consistent quality, family friendly food, it would be difficult to convince consumers that McDonald's now offers gourmet food. Thus, McD's would probably be better off targeting families in search of consistent quality food in nice, clean restaurants.

Positioning involves implementing our targeting. For example, Apple Computer has chosen to position itself as a maker of user-friendly computers. Thus, Apple has done a lot through its advertising to promote itself, through its unintimidating icons, as a computer for "non-geeks." The Visual C software programming language, in contrast, is aimed a "techies."

Repositioning involves an attempt to change consumer perceptions of a brand, usually because the existing position that the brand holds has become less attractive. Sears, for example, attempted to reposition itself from a place that offered great sales but unattractive prices the rest of the time to a store that consistently offered "everyday low prices." Repositioning in practice is very difficult to accomplish. A great deal of money is often needed for advertising and other promotional efforts, and in many cases, the repositioning fails.

Product Mix

Products come in several forms. Consumer products can be categorized as convenience goods, for which consumers are willing to invest very limited shopping efforts. Thus, it is essential to have these products readily available and have the brand name well known. Shopping goods, in contrast, are goods in which the consumer is willing to invest a great deal of time and effort. For example, consumers will spend a great deal of time looking for a new car or a medical procedure. Speciality goods are those that are of interest only to a narrow segment of the population-e.g., drilling machines. Industrial goods can also be broken down into subgroups, depending on their uses. It should also be noted that, within the context of marketing decisions, the term product refers to more than tangible goods-a service can be a product, too.

A firm's product line or lines refers to the assortment of similar things that the firm holds. Brother, for example, has both a line of laser printers and one of typewriters. In contrast, the firm's product mix describes the combination of different product lines that the firm holds. Boeing, for example, has both a commercial aircraft and a defense line of products that each take advantage of some of the same core competencies and technologies of the firm. Some firms have one very focused or narrow product line (e.g., KFC does only chicken right) while others maintain numerous lines that hopefully all have some common theme. This represents a wide product mix 3M, for example, makes a large assortment of goods that are thought to be related in the sense that they use the firm's ability to bond surfaces together. Depth refers to the variety that is offered within each product line. Maybeline offers a great deal of depth in lipsticks with subtle differences in shades while Morton Salt offers few varieties of its product.

Products may be differentiated in several ways. Some may be represented as being of superior quality (e.g., Maytag), or they may differ in more arbitrary ways in terms of styles-some people like one style better than another, while there is no real consensus on which one is the superior one. Finally, products can be differentiated in terms of offering different levels of service-for example, Volvo offers a guarantee of free, reliable towing anywhere should the vehicle break down. American Express offers services not offered by many other charge cards.

New product development tends to happen in stages. Although firms often go back and forth between these idealized stages, the following sequence is illustrative of the development of a new product:

- ***New Product Strategy Development:*** Different firms will have different strategies on how to approach new products. Some firms have stockholders who want to minimize risk and avoid investing in too many new innovations. Some firms can only survive if they innovate frequently and have stockholders who are willing to take this risk. For example, Hewlett-Packard has to constantly invent new products since competitors learn to work around its patents and will be able to manufacture the products at a lower cost.

- *Idea Generation:* Firms solicit ideas as to new products it can make. Ideas might come from customers, employees, consultants, or engineers. Many firms receive a large number of ideas each year and can only invest in some of them.
- *Screening and Evaluation:* Some products that after some analysis are clearly not feasible or are not consistent with the core competencies of the firm are eliminated.
- *Business Analysis:* Ideas are now exposed to more rigorous analysis. Profit projections, risks, market size, and competitive response are considered. If promising, market research may be done.
- *Development:* The product is designed and manufacturing facilities are planned.
- *Market Testing:* Frequently, firms will try to "test" a product in one region to see if it will sell in reality before it is released nationally and internationally. There is a lesser risk if the firm only commits money to advertising and other marketing efforts in one region. Retailers will also be more receptive in other parts of the country and world if it has been demonstrated that the product sold well in one region. The firm may also experiment with different prices for the product.
- *Commercialization:* Facilities to manufacture the product on a larger scale are now put into operation and the firm starts a national marketing campaign and distribution effort.

Products often go through a life cycle. Initially, a product is introduced. Since the product is not well known and is usually expensive (e.g., as microwave ovens were in the late 1970s), sales are usually limited. Eventually, however, many products reach a growth phase-sales increase dramatically. More firms enter with their models of the product. Frequently, unfortunately, the product will reach a maturity stage where little growth will be seen. For example, in the United States, almost every household has at least one color TV set. Some products may also reach a decline stage, usually because the product category is being replaced by something better. For example, typewriters experienced declining sales as more consumers switched to computers or other word processing equipment. The product life cycle is tied to the phenomenon of diffusion of innovation. When a new product comes out, it is likely to first be adopted by consumers who are more innovative than others-they are willing to pay a premium price for the new product and take a risk on unproven technology. It is important to be on the good side of innovators since many other later adopters will tend to rely for advice on the innovators who are thought to be more knowledgeable about new products for advice.

At later phases of the PLC, the firm may need to modify its market strategy. For example, facing a saturated market for baking soda in its traditional use, Arm & Hammer launched a major campaign to get consumers to use the product to deodorize refrigerators. Deodorizing powders to be used before vacuuming were also created.

It is sometimes useful to think of products as being either new or existing. Many firms today rely increasingly on new products for a large part of their sales. New products can be new in several ways. They can be new to the market-no one else ever made a product like this before. For example, Chrysler invented the minivan. Products can also be new to the firm-another firm invented the product, but the firm is now making its own version. For example, IBM did not invent the personal computer, but entered after other firms showed the market to have a high potential. Products can be new to the segment-e.g., cellular phones and pagers were first aimed at physicians and other price-insensitive segments. Later, firms decided to target the more price-sensitive mass market. A product can be new for legal purposes. Because consumers tend to be attracted to "new and improved" products, the Federal Trade Commission (FTC) only allows firms to put that label on reformulated products for six months after a significant change has been made.

The diffusion of innovation refers to the tendency of new products, practices, or ideas to spread among people. Usually, when new products or ideas come about, they are initially only adopted by a small group of people. Later, many innovations spread to other people. The bell shaped curve frequently illustrates the rate of adoption of a new product. Cumulative adoptions are reflected by the S-shaped curve. The saturation point is the maximum proportion of consumers likely to adopt a product. In the case of refrigerators in the U.S., the saturation level is nearly one hundred percent of households. The figure will almost certainly be well below that for video games that, even when spread out to a large part of the population, will be of interest to far from everyone.

Several specific product categories have case histories that illustrate important issues in adoption. Until some time in the 1800s, few physicians bothered to scrub prior to surgery, even though new scientific theories predicted that small microbes not visible to the naked eye could cause infection. Younger and more progressive physicians began scrubbing early on, but they lacked the stature to make their older colleagues follow.

ATM cards spread relatively quickly. Since the cards were used in public, others who did not yet hold the cards could see how convenient they were. Although some people were concerned about security, the convenience factors seemed to be a decisive factor in the "tug-of-war" for and against adoption.

The case of credit cards was a bit more complicated and involved a "chicken-and-egg" paradox. Accepting credit cards was not a particularly attractive option for retailers until they were carried by a large enough number of consumers. Consumers, in contrast, were not particularly interested in cards that were not accepted by a large number of retailers. Thus, it was necessary to "jump start" the process, signing up large corporate accounts, under favorable terms, early in the cycle, after which the cards became worthwhile for retailers to accept.

Rap music initially spread quickly among urban youths in large part because of the low costs of recording. Later, rap music became popular among a very different segment, suburban youths, because of its apparently authentic depiction of an exotic urban lifestyle.

Hybrid corn was adopted only slowly among many farmers. Although hybrid corn provided yields of about 20% more than traditional corn, many farmers had difficulty believing that this smaller seed could provide a superior harvest. They were usually reluctant to try it because a failed harvest could have serious economic consequences, including a possible loss of the farm. Agricultural extension agents then sought out the most progressive farmers to try hybrid corn, also aiming for farmers who were most respected and most likely to be imitated by others. Few farmers switched to hybrid corn outright from year to year. Instead, many started out with a fraction of their land, and gradually switched to 100% hybrid corn when this innovation had proven itself useful.

Several forces often work against innovation. One is risk, which can be either social or financial. For example, early buyers of the CD player risked that few CDs would be recorded before the CD player went the way of the 8 track player. Another risk is being perceived by others as being weird for trying a "fringe" product or idea. For example, Barbara Mandrell sings the song "I Was Country When Country Wasn't Cool."

Other sources of resistance include the initial effort needed to learn to use new products (e.g., it takes time to learn to meditate or to learn how to use a computer) and concerns about compatibility with the existing culture or technology. For example, birth control is incompatible with religious beliefs that predominate in some areas, and a computer database is incompatible with a large, established card file.

Innovations come in different degrees. A continuous innovation includes slight improvements over time. Very little usually changes from year to year in automobiles, and even automobiles of the 1990s are driven much the same way that automobiles of the 1950 were driven. A dynamically continuous innovation involves some change in technology, although the product is used much the same way that its predecessors were used-e.g., jet vs. propeller aircraft. A discontinous innovation involves a product that fundamentally changes the way that things are done-e.g., the fax and photocopiers. In general, discontinuous innovations are more difficult to market since greater changes are required in the way things are done, but the rewards are also often significant.

Several factors influence the speed with which an innovation spreads. One issue is relative advantage (i.e., the ratio of risk or cost to benefits). Some products, such as cellular phones, fax machines, and ATM cards, have a strong relative advantage. Other products, such as automobile satellite navigation systems, entail some advantages, but the cost ratio is high. Lower priced products often spread more quickly, and the extent to which the product is trialable (farmers did not have to plant all their land with hybrid corn at once, while one usually has to buy a cellular phone to try it out) influence the speed of diffusion. Finally, the extent of switching difficulties influences speed-many offices were slow to adopt computers because users had to learn how to use them.

Some cultures tend to adopt new products more Modernity: The extent to which quickly than others, based on several factors: the culture is receptive to new things. In some countries, such as Britain and Saudi Arabia, tradition is greatly valued-thus, new products often don't fare Homophily: too well. The United States, in contrast, tends to value progress. The more similar to each other that members of a culture are, the more likely an innovation is to spread-people are more likely to imitate similar than different models. The two most rapidly adopting countries in the World are the U.S. and Japan. While the U.S. interestingly scores very low, Japan scores high. Physical distance: The greater the distance between people, the less likely Opinion leadership: The more opinion leaders are innovation is to spread valued and respected, the more likely an innovation is to spread. The style of opinion leaders moderates this influence, however. In less innovative countries, opinion leaders tend to be more conservative, i.e., to reflect the local norms of resistance.

It should be noted that innovation is not always an unqualifiedly good thing. Some innovations, such as infant formula adopted in developing countries, may do more harm than good. Individuals may also become dependent on the innovations. For example, travel agents who get used to booking online may be unable to process manual reservations.

Sometimes innovations are disadopted. For example, many individuals disadopt cellular phones if they find out that they don't end up using them much.

Branding: An essential issue in product management is branding. Different firms have different policies on the branding on their products. While 3M puts its brand name on a great diversity of products, Proctor & Gamble, on the opposite extreme, maintains a separate brand name for each product. In general, the use of brand extensions should be evaluated on the basis of the compatibility of various products-can the same brand name represent different products without conflict or confusion? Coca Cola for many years resisted putting its coveted brand name on a diet soft drink. In the old days, available sweeteners such as saccharin added an undesirable aftertaste, implying a clear sacrifice in taste for the reduction in calories. Thus, to avoid damaging the brand name Coca Cola, Coke instead named its diet cola Tab. Only after Nutrasweet was introduced was the brand extension allowed. Research shows that consumers are more receptive to brand extensions when (1) the company appears to have the expertise to make the product [McDonald's was not thought as credible as a photo-finishing service], (2) the products are congruent (compatible), and (3) the brand extension is not seen as being exploitative of a high quality brand name [e.g., one should not use a premium brand name like Heineken to make a trivially easy product like popcorn].

Co-branding involves firms using two or more brands together to maximize appeal to consumers. Some ice cream makers, for example, use their own brand name in addition to naming the brands of ingredients contained. Sometimes, this strategy may help one brand at the expense of the other. It is widely believed, for example, that the "Intel inside" messages, which Intel paid computer makers to put on their products and packaging, reduced the value of the computer makers' brand names because the emphasis was now put on the Intel component. Certain "peripheral" characteristics of products may "signal" quality or other value to consumers. For some products, packaging accounts for a large part of the total product manufacturing cost. Long warranties often signal to consumers that the product is of good quality since the manufacturer is willing to take responsibility for its functioning.

There is no clear distinction between a "pure" tangible product and a service. Most products contain some of both. A computer, for example, is a tangible product, but it often comes with a warranty and software updates.

Distribution System of Products

Distribution (also known as the place variable in the marketing mix, or the 4 Ps) involves getting the product from the manufacturer to the ultimate consumer. Distribution is often a much underestimated factor in marketing. Many marketers fall for the trap that if you make a better product, consumers will buy it. The problem is that retailers may not be willing to devote shelf-space to new products. Retailers would often rather use that shelf-space for existing products have that proven records of selling.

Although many firms advertise that they save the consumer money by selling direct and "eliminating the middleman," this is a dubious claim. The truth is that intermediaries, such as retailers and wholesalers, tend to add efficiency because they can do specialized tasks better than the consumer or the manufacturer. Because wholesalers and retailers exist, the consumer can buy one pen at a time in a store located conveniently rather than having to order it from a distant factory. Thus, distributors add efficiency by:

- Breaking bulk-the consumer can buy small quantities at a time. Modest scale retailers (e.g., a college bookstore) can buy modest quantities.
- Distributing. The consumers can buy at a neighborhood store, which in turn can buy from a regional warehouse.
- Carrying inventory
- Financing

Channel structures vary somewhat by the nature of the product. Jet aircraft are custom made and shipped directly to the airline. Automobiles, because they are difficult to move, are shipped directly to a dealer. Other products are shipped through a wholesaler who can more efficiently handle, and combine, products from many different suppliers. Several layers of wholesalers may exist, depending on the product. Occasionally, agents may also be involved. Agents usually do not handle products, but instead take care of the business aspect of negotiating with distributors, which manufacturers may feel uncomfortable or ill prepared for doing themselves.

Manufacturers of different kinds of products have different interests with respect to the availability of their products. For convenience products such as soft drinks, it is essential that your product be available widely. Chances are that if a store does not have a consumer's preferred brand of soft drinks, the consumer will settle for another brand rather than taking the trouble to go to another store. Occasionally, however, manufacturers will prefer selective distribution since they prefer to have their products available only in upscale stores.

Parallel distribution structures refer to the fact that products may reach consumers in different ways. Most products flow through the traditional manufacturer--> retailer--> consumer channel. Certain large chains may, however, demand to buy directly from the manufacturer since they believe they can provide the distribution services at a lower cost themselves. In turn, of course, they want lower prices, which may anger the traditional retailers who feel that this represents unfair competition. Firms may also choose to utilize factory outlet stores. To allay concerns held by conventional stores, however, these factory outlet stores are usually located in areas where they are not easily accessible.

We must consider what is realistically available to each firm. A small manufacturer of potato chips would like to be available in grocery stores nationally, but this may not be realistic. We need to consider, then, both who will be willing to carry our products and whom we would actually like to carry them. In general, for convenience products, intense distribution is desirable, but only brands that have a certain amount of power-e.g., an established brand name-can hope to gain national intense distribution.

Note that for convenience goods, intense distribution is less likely to harm the brand image-it is not a problem, for example, for Haagen Dazs to be available in a convenience store along with bargain brands-it is expected that people will not travel much for these products, so they should be available anywhere the consumer demands them. However, in the category of shopping goods, having Rolex watches sold in discount stores would be undesirable-here, consumers do travel, and goods are evaluated by customers to some extent based on the surrounding merchandise.

In general, a brand can expect lesser distribution in its early stages-fewer retailers are motivated to carry it. Similarly, when a product category is new, it will be available in fewer stores-e.g., in the early days, computer disks were available only in specialty stores, but now they can be found in supermarkets and convenience stores as well. Certain products that are not well established may have to get their start on "infomercials," only slowly getting entry into other types out outlets. Different parties involved in the marketing of products tend to have different, and often conflicting, interests:

- Full service retailers tend dislike intensive distribution.
- Low service channel members can "free ride" on full service sellers.
- Manufacturers may be tempted toward intensive distribution-appropriate only for some; may be profitable in the short run.

Market balance suggests a need for diversity in product categories where intensive distribution is appropriate. Service requirements also differ by product category.

Diversion occurs when merchandise intended for one market is bought up by a distributor that then ships it to a different market. Sometimes, a manufacturer will run a promotion in one region but not in another, and speculators will then buy extra quantity in the promoted area and ship it another area. The speculator will then sell it to local retailers or distributors for a price slightly lower than what is being charged through the regular channel but at a price that still allows a nice profit. Certain products sell for different prices in different countries. As we discussed in the unit of international marketing, a gray market occurs when a product is bought in one country and exported to another where the price is generally higher. Both Luis Vuitton suitcases and golf clubs were imported to Japan, depressing prices there.

Integrated Marketing: Communication and Promotion

Integrated Marketing Communication (IMC) involves the idea that a firm's promotional efforts should be coordinated to achieve the best combined effects of the firm's efforts. Resources are allocated to achieve those outcomes that the firm values the most. Promotion involves a number of tools we can use to increase demand for our products.

The most well known component of promotion is advertising, but we can also use tools such as the following:

- Public relations (the firm's staff provides information to the media in the hopes of getting coverage). This strategy has benefits (it is often less expensive and media coverage is usually more credible than advertising) but it also entails a risk in that we can't control what the media will say. Note that this is particularly a useful tool for small and growing businesses-especially those that make a product which is inherently interesting to the audience.

- ***Trade Promotion:*** Here, the firm offers retailers and wholesalers temporary discounts, which may or may not be passed on to the consumer, to stimulate sales.
- ***Sales Promotion:*** Consumers are given either price discounts, coupons, or rebates.
- ***Personal Selling:*** Sales people either make "cold" calls on potential customers and/or respond to inquiries.
- ***In-store Displays:*** Firms often pay a great deal of money to have their goods displayed prominently in the store. More desirable display spaces include: end of an aisle, free-standing displays, and near the check-out counter. Occasionally, a representative may display the product.
- Samples.

Generally, a sequence of events is needed before a consumer will buy a product. This is known as a "hierarchy of effects." The consumer must first be aware that the product exists. He or she must then be motivated to give some attention to the product and what it may provide. In the next stage, the need is for the consumer to evaluate the merits of the product, hopefully giving the product a try. A good experience may lead to continued use. Note that the consumer must go through the earlier phases before the later ones can be accomplished.

Promotional objectives that are appropriate differ across the Product Life Cycle (PLC). Early in the PLC-during the introduction stage-the most important objective is creating awareness among consumers. For example, many consumers currently do not know the Garmin is making auto navigation devices based on the global position satellite (GPS) system and what this system can do for them. A second step is to induce trial-to get consumers to buy the product for the first time. During the growth stage, important needs are persuading the consumer to buy the product and prefer the brand over competing ones. Here, it is also important to persuade retailers to carry the brand, and thus, a large proportion of promotional resources may need to be devoted to retailer incentives. During the maturity stage, the firm may need to focus on maintaining shelf space, distribution channels, and sales.

Different promotional approaches will be appropriate depending on the stage of the consumer's decision process that the marketer wishes to influence. Prior to the purchase, the marketer will want to establish a decision to purchase the product and the specific brand. Here, samples might be used to induce trial.

During the purchase stage, when the consumer is in the retail store, efforts may be made to ensure that the consumer will choose one's specific brands. Paying retailers for preferred shelf space as well as point of purchase (POP) displays and coupons may be appropriate. After the purchase, an appropriate objective may be to induce a repurchase or to influence the consumer to choose the same brand again. Thus, the package may contain a coupon for future purchase.

There are two main approaches to promoting products

- The "push" strategy is closely related to the "selling concept" and involves "hard" sell and aggressive price promotions to sell at this specific purchase occasion.
- In contrast, the "pull" strategy emphasizes creating demand for the brand so that consumers will come to the store with the intention of buying the product. Hallmark, for example, has invested a great deal in creating a preference for its greeting cards among consumers.

There are several ways that a firm can budget for advertising. The strategy used depends on the firm's policy and internal politics. Some of the methods commonly used are:

- *Percentage of Sales:* Here, the firm decides to base its advertising budget on how much has been sold. This appears to be an "objective" way to make the budget decision and to "reward" performing brands and products with resources. However, this method is quite arbitrary. A firm may find it worthwhile to invest heavily in advertising up-front-before the product has begun to sell significantly-so that a promising product can achieve its potential. When a product is performing well, staying with a fixed percentage may also result in spending more than is cost-effective.

- ***Percentage of Profits:*** This is similar to the above, but takes into consideration that some products may have larger margins than others. Thus, a product with lesser sales but high margins may be a better investment than one with high sales but low margins. Still, however, this method is arbitrary and questionable because of the factors listed above.
- ***Competitive Parity:*** This entails setting the budget to match competitors. Note, however, that different brands may have different needs. Coke and Pepsi may be competing "head-on," and competitive parity may be appropriate. In contrast, some firms may be targeting customers who are relatively brand loyal while others target "switchers." The firm that targets loyal customers may be better off spending money on product quality than on promotion.
- ***Affordability:*** This entails budgeting based on the resources that the firm has available. Smaller firms obviously do not have the same resources as larger ones. However, the firm should still evaluate how effective such a budget will be in meeting the brand's needs. A firm may be able to afford to spend more than is appropriate. In contrast, other firms may not be able to spend what is needed to adequately influence consumers. In such cases, it may be more appropriate for the firm to try to sell of this brand rather than fighting a losing battle.
- ***Objective and Task:*** This method sets the budget based on what is needed to achieve what the firm has set out to accomplish. The ultimate budget may then have little relation to the factors discussed above.

There are several types of advertising. In terms of product advertising, the "pioneering" ad seeks to create awareness of a product and brand and to instill an appreciation among consumers for its possibilities.

The competitive or persuasive ad attempts to convince the consumer either of the performance of the product and/or how it is superior in some way to that of others. Comparative advertisements are a prime example of this. For instance, note the ads that show that some trash bags are more durable than others.

Reminder advertising seeks to keep the consumer believing what other ads have already established. For example, Coca Cola ads tend not to provide new information but keep reinforcing what a great drink it is.

Developing an advertising program entails several steps:

- Identifying the target audience. Market reports can be bought that investigate the media habits of consumers of different products and/or the segments that the firm has chosen to target.
- Determining appropriate advertising objectives. As discussed, these objectives might include awareness, trial, repurchase, inducing consumers to switch from another brand, or developing a preference for the brand.
- Settling on an advertising budget.
- Designing the advertisements. Some commonly used approaches:
    - o Information/persuasion. Comparative ads attempt to get consumers to believe that the sponsoring product is better. Although these are frequently disliked by Americans, they tend to be among the most effective ads in the U.S. Comparative advertising is illegal in some countries and is considered very inappropriate culturally in some societies, especially in Asia.
    - o Fear appeals try to motivate consumers by telling them the consequences of not using a product. Mouthwash ads, for example, talk about the how gingivitis and tooth loss can result from poor oral hygiene. It is important, however, that a specific way to avoid the feared stimulus be suggested directly in the ad. Thus, simply by using the mouthwash advertised, these terrible things can be avoided.
    - o Sex appeals are more common-and more explicit-in some cultures than in others. Their effectiveness depends a great deal on how well such ads are designed for the specific product category. In many cases, sex appeal is used more to get the consumer's attention than for actual persuasion. o Humor appeal. The use of humor in advertisements is quite common.

This method tends not to be particularly useful in persuading the consumer. However, more and more advertisers find themselves using humor in order to compete for the consumer's attention. Often, the humor actually draws attention away from the product-people will remember what was funny in the ad but not the product that was advertised. Thus, for ads to be effective, the product advertised should be an integral part of what is funny.

Numerous media are available for the advertiser to choose from. Each medium tends to have advantages and disadvantages.

It is essential to pretest advertisements to see how effective they actually are in influencing consumers. An ad may have to be redesigned if it is found not be to be as effective as targeted. Note that selecting advertisements is often a "numbers game" where a lot of advertisements are created and the ones that "test" best are selected.

The effectiveness of advertising is a highly controversial topic. Research suggests that in many cases advertising leads to a relatively modest increase in sales. One study suggests, for example, that when a firm increases its advertising spending by 1%, sales go up by 0.05%. (The same research found that, in contrast, if prices are lowered by 1%, sales tend to increase by 2%). In general, it appears that advertising is more effective in selling durable goods (e.g., stereo systems, cars, refrigerators, and furniture) than for non-durable goods (e.g., restaurant meals, candy bars, toilet paper, and bottled water). Also, advertising appears to be more effective for new products. This suggests that advertising is probably most effective for providing information (rather than persuading people). Note that many advertising agencies make a large part of their money on commissions on advertising sold. Thus, they have a vested interest in selling as much advertising as possible, and may strongly advise clients to spend excessive amounts on advertising.

Research suggests that advertising effectiveness follows a sort of "S-" shaped curve. Very small amounts of advertising are too small to truly register with consumers. At the medium level, advertising may be effective. However, above a certain level (labeled "saturation point" on the chart), additional adverting appears to have a limited effect. (This is comparable to the notion of "diminishing returns to scale" encountered in economics).

There are several potential ways to measure advertising effectiveness. Two main categories include:

- "Field" based studies. These studies look at what happens with real consumers in real life. Thus, for example, we can examine what happens to sales of a company's products when the firm increases advertising. Unfortunately, this is often a misleading way to measure advertising impact because we live in a "messy" world where other factors influence sales as well. For example, a soft drink firm could conclude that there is very little correlation between advertising and sales because another, much more powerful factor is at work: temperature. That is, the firm may find that although a great deal of advertising is done in the winter, sales are greater in summer months because people drink more soft drinks in hot weather. Note that the choice of brand of soft drink purchased in the summer may very well be influenced by advertising heard at other times.
- Laboratory studies. To get around the confounds imposed by nature, advertising reseachers often use artificial situations to evaluate advertising. This sacrifices the use of real consumers in real settings, but allows the marketer to control sources of influence. An advertising firm may hire people to come in and participate in research. The consumers may come in and be asked to view some television and respond to a questionnaire about the programming later. Half of the subjects can then see a version which includes an ad to be tested (the other half is known as the "control" group, which will serve as a basis for comparison). We can now compare the two groups on factors such as attitude toward the brand, purchase intention, and preference.

A significant objective of advertising is attitude change. A consumer's attitude toward a product refers to his or her beliefs about, feeling toward, and purchase intentions for the product. Beliefs can be both positive (e.g., for McDonald's food: tastes good, is convenient) and negative (is high in fat). In general, it is usually very difficult to change deeply held beliefs. Thus, in most cases, the advertiser may better off trying to add a belief (e.g., beef is convenient) rather than trying to change one (beef is really not very fatty). Consumer receptivity to messages aimed at altering their beliefs will tend to vary a great deal depending on the nature of the product. For unimportant products such as soft drinks, research suggests that consumers are often persuaded by having a large number of arguments with little merit presented (e.g., the soda comes in a neat bottle, the bottle contains five percent more soda than competing ones). In contrast, for high involvement, more important products, consumers tend to scrutinize arguments more closely, and will tend to be persuaded more by high quality arguments.

Celebrity endorsements are believed to follow a similar pattern of effectiveness. For trivial products, a popular endorser is often effective regardless of his or her qualifications to endorse (e.g, Bill Cosby endorses Coca Cola and Jell-O without having particular credentials to do so). On the other hand, for more important products, consumers will often scrutinize the endorser's credentials. For example, a basket ball player may be perceived as knowledgeable about athletic shoes, but not particularly so about life insurance.

Direct Marketing

Direct marketing involves bypassing the retailer in reaching the consumer. Generally, this is not cost-effective, but exceptional situations may make it so. For example, certain customers may buy in very large quantities. Others may be spread over large geographic areas and require specialized products (e.g., beekeepers).

Direct marketing provides exceptional opportunities for segmentation. An excellent tool is the so called "merge-purge" technique. Marketers can buy lists of names and addresses of consumers from numerous sources (e.g., vehicle registrations, college enrollment, magazine subscriptions, catalog purchases). One can then combine different sources (e.g., surfers are likely to live in areas indicated by coastal zip codes, may subscribe to surfing magazines, and may have made purchases from surfing goods catalogs) and eliminate the overlaps (those people who appear on more than one list). Thus, we can target our potential buyers more closely than we could by advertising in newspapers (which are not read by many surfers and also reach a large number of non-surfers who are not interested in our products).

A great deal of interest has arisen in recent years on the potential for marketing on the Internet. While the jury is still out on this medium's ultimate potential, sales so far have been limited, although a large potential may exist. It should be noted that a large segment of the population in the U.S. is still not "connected," with numbers being even lower in even many developed countries. Many consumers are also reluctant to provide credit cards and other personal information on the Net, although attitudes in this area may change with. Note that the Internet may serve purposes other than direct sales. For example, the Internet is a good way to provide information to consumers, and this can be done at a relatively low cost.

Electronic Commerce

Online marketing can serve several purposes:

- *Promotion/advertising:* Customers can be quite effectively targeted in many situations because of the context that they, themselves, have sought out. For example, when a consumer searches for a specific term in a search engine, a "banner" or link to a firm selling products in that area can be displayed. Print and television advertisements can also feature the firm's web address, thus inexpensively drawing in those who would like additional information.
- *Customer Service:* The site may contain information for those who no longer have their manuals handy and, for electronic products, provide updated drivers and software patches.
- *Market Research:* Data can be collected relatively inexpensively on the Net. However, the response rates are likely to be very unrepresentative and recent research shows that it is very difficult to get consumers to read instructions. This is one of the reasons why the quality of data collected online is often suspect.

There are many obstacles to the growth of e-commerce:

- *Reach:* Although the majority of U.S. households now have computers connected to the Internet, a very large minority does not, and penetration rates are considerably lower in some countries. In foreign countries, even those households that have computers may be reluctant to spend time online due to the per minute charges, which discourage the more leisurely "browsing" American style.

- *Concerns about Privacy:* A number of consumers are concerned about giving up information to marketers that can easily be collected electronically. Naturally, few consumers would like information about their medical status widely collected by firms, but many consumers are even reluctant to have marketers know the ages of their children and past book purchase records.
- *Reputational Issues:* Although not as much of a problem as before, firms operating online or through direct mail have often been viewed with suspicion since consumers may question whether they will be around if they do not deliver satisfactorily.
- *Costs:* During the "boom," Internet firms were not expected to be efficient and thus developed bad habits. Although shipping and handling charges can help cover costs of shipping and administration, these often take away the attractiveness of Internet shopping. The most successful e-commerce firms turn out to be the ones that have been successful doing other kinds of direct marketing (e.g., catalog sales) before and have developed the discipline and efficiency required there. For products that have relatively high absolute margins-e.g., computers-there is more money to cover administrative costs.
- *Language:* Since the Internet reaches around the world, it is often difficult to match viewers with their preferred languages. Because U.S. firms and individuals tended to predominate among those first to occupy the Web, most sites are in U.S. English. British speakers of English generally do not perceive American English as American-they tend to perceive spelling such as "color" rather than their "colour" as misspellings. French consumers do not like to have to click to get from an English language to a French language site. It is estimated that by the year

2007, the majority of web surfers will not be comfortable in English and will want sites in their own languages.

- *Government Regulations:* In the U.S., the government has tried to keep its hands off the Net as much as possible to foster its growth as a trade area, and a recently expired moratorium on new sales taxes was even instituted to make Internet shopping more attractive. However, governments in many other countries are more forceful in their regulations. In countries such as China, where sites can be used to spread "subversive" ideas, there is a great deal of government scrutiny and suspicion.
- *Cultural Obstacles:* The whole purpose of the web is to make information readily available. In countries where information is closely guarded, that is a frightening idea. There is often also a desire for personal interaction, which may be required to establish the trust needed to secure a deal.
- *Payment Issues:* U.S. consumers exposed to credit card fraud have very limited liabilities, but these protections do not exist to the same extent in Europe or Asia. In China, much of the purpose of the Internet is defeated with some 80% of transactions being completed off-line, usually with funding instruments other than credit cards.

There are a number of problems in running and developing web sites. First of all, the desired domain name may not be available-e.g., American Airlines could not get "American.com" and had to settle for "AmericanAir.com."

There is also a question having your site identified to potential users. Research has found that most search engines have a great deal of "false hits" (sites irrelevant that are identified in a search-e.g., information about computer languages when the user searches for foreign language instruction) and "misses" (sites that would have been relevant but are not identified). It is crucial for a firm to have its site indexed favorably in major search engines such as Yahoo, AOLFind, and Google.

However, there is often a constant struggle between web site operators and the search engines to outguess each other, with the web promoters trying to "spam" the search engines with repeated usage of terms and "meta tags." The fact that many computer users employ different web browsers raises questions about compatibility.

A major problem is that many of the more recent, fancier web sites rely on "java script" to provide animation and various other impressive features. These animations have proven very unreliable. Sites may "crash" on the user or prove unreliable, and many consumers have found themselves unable to complete their transactions.

There are a number of legal issues associated with the Internet:

- ***Reach Across Borders:*** Web sites transcend country lines and thus, a firm may be subjected to legal standards of different countries. It may be difficult to create advertising that simultaneously complies with rules for each country.
- ***Taxation:*** There is a great deal of ambiguity as to which state and local governments may collect taxes on merchandise sold on the Internet. There is also a question as to who has the responsibility for making the payment-the seller or the buyer?
- ***Privacy Issues:*** Many foreign governments prohibit the collection of personal information of consumers (as Amazon.com does), which greatly reduces the customization opportunities online.

Web Site Design: The web designer must make various issues into consideration:

- ***Speed vs. Aesthetics:*** As we saw, some of the fancier sites have serious problems functioning practically. Consumers may be impressed by a fancy site, or may lack confidence in a firm that offers a simple one. Yet, fancier sites with extensive graphics take time to download-particularly for users dialing in with a modem as opposed to being "hard" wired-and may result in site crashes.
- ***Keeping users on the Site:*** A large number of "baskets" are abandoned online as consumers fail to complete the "check-out" process for the products they have selected. One problem here is that many consumers are drawn away from a site and then are unlikely to come back. A large number of links may be desirable to consumers, but they tend to draw people away. Taking banner advertisers on

your site from other sites may be profitable, but it may result in customers lost.

- *Information Collection:* An increasing number of consumers resist collection of information about them, and a number of consumers have set up their browsers to disallow "cookies," files that contain information about their computers and shopping habits.

Hotel Tourism Management

Hospitality and Tourism Management (HTM) is a major in a Bachelors of Science in Business Administration.

Graduate students graduate with a Masters of Business Administration, a Masters or Science, or a Doctorate of Philosophy in Hospitality and Tourism Management. It is a focus that is studied by individuals that are intending to work in the Hospitality Industry, examples of which are; Hotels, Resorts, Casinos, and Restaurants.

Within the HTM concentration there is generally:

- Food Management and Operations (Examples: Food Science, Food Selection and Preparation, Food and Beverage Operations)
- Lodging Operations (Examples: Hotel Operations, Lodging Management, Financial Management and Cost Control for Hospitality Organizations)
- Global Tourism (Examples: Travel and Tourism Management, Tourism Analysis, Hospitality and Research Methods)
- Event Management (Examples: Hospitality Sales, Catering Management, Hospitality Marketing Management)

Several large corporations such as Marriot, Hyatt, Wyndham and Hilton Hotels have summer internships/manager in training programs for students majoring in Hospitality and Tourism Management, to help students get valuable work experience.

National University of Management

N.U.M. is the leading university in providing educational training to all people in the areas of Management, Economics, Commerce, IT, Business Law, Tourism, and Foreign languages accompanied by research and development in response to the needs of job market today.

Mission: The mission of N.U.M. is to serve the country through educational training by providing graduates with academic excellence, wisdom, morality, and good responsibility in the society. With the vision above, NUM is trying its best to:

- Train students with their day-to-day work for their job satisfaction.
- Illustrate the reality of conflicts and resolutions in terms of managers entrepreneurs.
- Provide opportunities for all levels of people to improve their knowledge and ability through part-time training.

History: The National University of Management (NUM) was founded in 1983 as the Economics Science Institute (ESI), and until 1991 received assistance from the National Economics University in Hanoi, Vietnam. During this period, students were enrolled in a five-year undergraduate program with the Vietnamese language serving as the main language of instruction. The curriculum, set by the visiting faculty from Hanoi, included major fields in Finance, Commerce, Agriculture, Industry, and Socialist Planning.

With the opening up of Cambodia to the international community during the early 1990's. The ESI was renamed the Faculty of Business (FOB). Initial support for the FOB was provided by the Asia Foundation and later through a three years USAID grant (1994 to 1997) by the Georgetown University and the University of Sanfrancisco.

This support provided teacher training, institutional development, and encouraged transformation of the curriculum along the lines of an international or American style business school. Marketing and Accounting majors were introduced during this period, and the length of the undergraduate program was reduced from five to four years of study. Commercial law course were also added to the curriculum by the University of San Francisco Law school.

This support provided teacher training, institutional development, and encouraged transformation of the curriculum along the lines of an international or American style business school. Marketing and Accounting majors were introduced during this period, and the length of the undergraduate program was reduced from five to four years of study. Commercial law course were also added to the curriculum by the University of San Francisco Law school.

In 2004, the FOB was transformed into the National University of Management (NIM) and program offerings were expanded to include the fields of Tourism and Hospitality Management, Finance & Banking and MIS. NUM also opened the first MBA program in Cambodia in cooperation with the University Utara Malaysia (UUM), which is s State sponsored university located in Northern Malaysia.

NUM also maintains a five year faculty exchange and research program with the University of Antwerp. Belgium and has just recently opened a Center for Entrepreneurship and Development in partnership with Fisk University (Nashville,U.S) and Tennessee State University, sponsored by UNCF/USAID.

Currently, more than 10,000 students attend courses at NUM's main campus in Phnom Penh. NUM also operates a full Bachelor of Business Administration degree program in Battambang with more than 700 students attending courses at NUM 's provincial campus.

According to the World Travel and Tourism Council (1997), the economics of the 21st century will be dominated by three industries: telecommunications, information technology and tourism. The travel and tourism industries have grown by 500% in the last 25 years and it is estimated that by the year 2007 tourists will spend US$884 billion in foreign countries on tourism related activities. Travel and tourism represents a broad range of related industries. The growth of these industries has opened up many new job opportunities for graduates in areas such as:

- hotels
- restaurants
- retailing
- transportation
- travel agencies
- tour companies

- tourist attractions
- leisure, recreation and sport
- cultural industries

It is interesting to realise that in 1997 travel and tourism provides 10.5% of the total world employment, with up to 25% of all employment, in some areas, such as the Caribbean. It has been estimated that, by 2007, more than 100 million people worldwide will be employed in this sector. Because of this, tourism is now seen to be of importance to most countries of the world.

During this time, the nature of tourism has developed in scope and direction, away from traditional activities, such as the sunshine sand and sea holidays to a wide range of new activities such as cultural tourism, adventure tourism, sports and leisure activities and eco-tourism.

Careers in Hospitality and Tourism Management

Given the potential for interesting and rewarding careers in these industries many young people are looking for suitable courses which will help prepare them for careers in management within the tourism and hospitality industries.

The UK higher education system has a well developed range of courses, at all levels from Higher National Diploma, BA or BSc degrees and MA/MSc/MBA Masters courses and using alternative methods of studying, (including full-time, part-time and distance learning). When looking at courses in hospitality and tourism, there can seem to be a bewildering variety of course titles covering the main employment areas of travel, tourism, hotels and restaurants. Typical titles include:

For hotels and restaurant management:

- hospitality management
- international hospitality management
- hotel and catering management

For travel and tourism:

- tourism management
- tourism studies
- travel and tourism

There are also joint degrees where it is possible to study combinations of subjects, such as tourism and hospitality, tourism and leisure, hospitality and marketing. Most undergraduate courses (HND/BSc/BA) will include a period of work experience as part of the course, varying in length from 6 months to one year.

This work experience is seen to be a central part of the course, where the student gets the opportunity to practise what they have learned in college or university. Employers also see great value in this work experience when considering the employment of graduates.

Given the international nature of these industries, another valuable part of any course is the study of languages. Most courses in hospitality and tourism provide access to language courses, either as core components or as options.

Courses at Masters level are becoming increasingly important in tourism and hospitality. These Masters level courses are useful to two groups of people:

- those who have completed a degree course in a subject other than hospitality or tourism but who are looking at ways of getting employment in the industry;
- those who have a degree or sub-degree qualification in hospitality or tourism together with significant management experience within the hospitality or tourism industries and who wish to develop themselves to a higher level or to seek a more senior position in industry. There are many Masters courses in Hospitality Management, Hotel and Catering Management and Tourism Management in universities and colleges in the UK.

In addition to the above courses, there are also more specialised Masters courses in Tourism covering areas such as Cultural Tourism, Tourism Marketing, Tourism Planning, Museum Management, Heritage Management, Cultural Tourism and Sustainable Tourism: these are suitable for people who have an interest in employment in a specific sector of the industry.

Within the UK there are many university and college courses to choose from, but each course will have its own unique characteristics. Before applying, you should think carefully about the type of career you want: if it is in a hotel are you interested in restaurant management or rooms division management? Do you see yourself as a practical hands-on person or someone who is happier to work behind the scenes in a desk based job? Do you aspire to become a general manager of a hotel which is part of one of the major worldwide groups, or do you want to manage your own operation? Are you more interested in one of the functional management areas, such as marketing, human resources, conferences.

6

Importance of Front Desk Management

Managing tourism destinations is an important part of controlling tourism's environmental impacts. Destination management can include land use planning, business permits and zoning controls, environmental and other regulations, business association initiatives, and a host of other techniques to shape the development and daily operation of tourism-related activities. The term "destination" refers broadly to an area where tourism is a relatively important activity and where the economy may be significantly influenced by tourism revenues. Destination management is complicated by the fact that a single, recognizable destination may include several municipalities, provinces, or other government entities-in island environments it may be the entire country. Participating governance structures led by local authorities, with the involvement of local NGOs, community and indigenous representatives, academia, and local chambers of commerce, make up what are known as "Destination Management Organizations" (DMOs). Often DMOs take the form of local tourism boards, councils, or development organizations. The network of local tourism businesses (hotels, attractions, transportation services, service providers such as guides and equipment rentals, restaurants, etc.) are also a significant part of a destination.

Destination Management Approach

The needs, expectations and anticipated benefits of tourism vary greatly from one destination to the next, and there is certainly no "one size fits all" approach to destination management. As local communities living in regions with tourism potential develop a vision for what kind of tourism they want to facilitate, a comprehensive planning framework such as Local Agenda 21 has proved useful and is being used more and more often. Promoting sustainable tourism within Local Agenda 21 processes is a way to strengthen local stewardship of the environment.

Cities and Tourism

Cities to Absorb Growth in World Tourism: International tourist arrivals in 1995 were 563 million and are expected to reach 1.6 billion by the year 2020. These forecasts use a conservative growth rate of 4.3% and 6.7% respectively; less than the current growth rate. They do not include any domestic tourism which can readily be anticipated to equal the international. It is obvious that most of this increase will have to be absorbed by cities.

World Tourism Organisation: The most recent trends and forecasting studies by the World Tourism Organisation indicate that cities will continue to be in high demand by tourists of all sorts, and the problems associated with the handling of these tourists will have to be more systematically tackled by all parties concerned.

Cities face, therefore, a double challenge.

Firstly, they have to be able to respond to the expectations and needs of the growing numbers of tourists who are attracted to their rich and varied array of cultural, business, entertainment, shopping, sports and other attractions; furthermore, they need to continuously renovate and improve such facilities in order to maintain their share in the competitive tourism market and the benefits resulting from it.

Secondly, cities have to ensure that tourism is developed and managed in such a way that it benefits the resident population, does not contribute to the deterioration of the urban environment but rather to its enhancement, and does not become a financial burden to the local authority. Some of the key stakeholders in urban tourism include: Private Sector i.e. airlines, hotel chain operators and owners, tour operators, credit card companies, tourist attraction operators (theme parks, events etc.), real estate agencies;

- Public Sector i.e. city managers (from the historic city to the seaside resort), transportation planners, bus and train operators, information departments, economic development agencies, national parks, national tourist organisations;

- Touristic Institutions i.e. museums, art galleries, historic facilities (e.g. the national trust) and educational organisations.

There are three key dimensions of tourism in cities and urban areas:

- Products-the anticipated changes necessary from tourist attraction providers; theme parks, operators of events (sports, shows, fairs), museums and hotels. What are their plans, how do they respond to the anticipated growth?
- Information-How does a city make itself more tourist friendly? What are the information systems available to tourists? How do tour operators deal with this growing demand? How to accumulate information on customer preferences and requirement, seasonal changes, age groups etc.? How to develop enduring attractions which will provide sustainable development? What information does the city provide in order to attract tourist attraction providers?
- Impacts-economic and development opportunities as well as the impact of tourism growth on sustainable development, transportation, cultural and environmental, social and economic aspects.

Environmental Management System and Eco-Tourism

Since the introduction of Agenda 21, the hospitality sector has adopted numerous strategies, approaches and measures in response to the challenge of sustainable development. These include:

- Environmental management systems and tools
- Education, awareness creation, training and information dissemination
- Voluntary initiatives
- Multi-stakeholder communication and consultation

- Environmental reporting
- Implementation of the Rio principles

The sector has particularly used environmental management systems and tools to demonstrate committment to an environmentally friendly work ethic. Many multinational and independent hotel companies have introduced environmental management practices at the property level. Ideally, the framework for this involves defining an environmental policy and building a management system to measure environmental impacts and compliance with the policy and local regulations, as well as documenting the system's performance for inspection and auditing purposes. Such environmental management systems (EMS) help businesses to evaluate, manage and reduce their negative environmental impacts by providing a methodology to integrate environment management into business operations in a systematic manner.

Common Tourist Destinations

The Republic of India, commonly known as India, is a country in South Asia. It is the seventh-largest country by geographical area, the second most populous country, and the most populous liberal democracy in the world. India has a coastline of over seven thousand kilometres, bounded by the Indian Ocean on the south, the Arabian Sea on the west, and the Bay of Bengal on the east. India borders Pakistan to the west; People's Republic of China, Nepal and Bhutan to the northeast; and Bangladesh and Myanmar to the east. Home to the Indus Valley Civilization and a region of historic trade routes and vast empires, the Indian subcontinent was identified with its commercial and cultural wealth for much of its long history.

Four major world religions, Hinduism, Buddhism, Jainism and Sikhism originated here, while Islam, Christianity, Judaism and Zoroastrianism, arrived in the first millennium CE and shaped India's variegated culture. Gradually annexed by the British East India Company from the early 18th century and colonised by Great Britain starting the mid-19th century, India became a modern nation-state in 1947 after a struggle for independence marked by widespread use of nonviolent resistance as a means of social protest.

With the world's fourth largest economy in purchasing power and the second fastest growing large economy, India has made rapid progress in the last decade, especially in information technology. Although India's standard of living is projected to rise sharply in the next half-century, it currently battles high levels of poverty, persistent malnutrition, and environmental degradation. A multi-lingual, multi-ethnic society, India is also home to a diversity of wildlife in a variety of protected habitats. India is one of the popular tourist destinations in Asia.

Bounded by the Himalayan ranges in the north, and surrounded on three sides by water (the Arabian Sea, Bay of Bengal, and the Indian Ocean), with a long history and diverse culture, India offers a wide array of places to see and things to do. In 2004, foreign tourists visiting India spent 15.4 billion USD-the ninth highest in the world. India is also ranked among the top 3 adventure tourism destinations.

Taj Mahal

Perhaps India's best-known site is the Taj Mahal, one of the world's greatest architectural achievements. It was built between 1631 and 1653 by Emperor Shah Jahan in honor of his wife, Arjumand Banu, more popularly known as Mumtaz Mahal. The Taj Mahal serves as her tomb. Taj Mahal is a 3 hour drive from Delhi.

The Golden Triangle

One of the popular tourist circuits is called the Golden Triangle: the cities Delhi; Agra (site of the Taj Mahal); and Jaipur. Delhi is approximately 200 kilometers away from Agra, and 250 kilometers from Jaipur.

Wildlife Sanctuaries

India also has a large variety of protected wildlife. The country's protected wilderness consists of 75 National parks of India and 421 Sanctuaries, of which 19 fall under the purview of Project Tiger. Its climatic and geographic diversity makes it the home of over 350 mammals and 1200 bird species, many of which are unique to the subcontinent. Some well known national wildlife sanctuaries include Corbett, Kanha, Sariska, Periyar, Ranthambore, and Bharatpur.

Andhra Pradesh

Andhra Pradesh is very good place for tourism. Andhra Pradesh is India's fifth largest state. AP is also known as the "Rice Granary of India". The main languages spoken in Andhra Pradesh are Telugu, Hindi, Urdu and English.

The weather is mostly tropical. June to September are the monsoon months and travel is not advised during this time. November to January are the best time to visit. Andhra Pradesh has a rich cultural heritage. Andhra Pradesh has a variety of attractions including beaches, hills, wildlife, forests and temples.

People coming to Andhra Pradesh visit:

* Hyderabad
* Tirupati
* Vizag
* Nagarjuna sagar
* Vijaywada
* Warangal

Delhi

The capital of the vast, mystic subcontinent that is India. A fine blend of old and new, ancient and modern in every stream of life is the soul of Delhi. A melting pot of cultures and traditions, religions and castes Delhi is true to its democratic nature.

Delhi has ruled... always from the mythological days to the present, the Aravali ridges and the Yamuna river stand a mute witness to it. The rulers left behind their trade marks in the architecture. Tughlakabad fort and the Qutab Minar, the Jama Masjid and the Lotus temple, The Humayun's tomb and the Red Fort, and India Gate and the Magnificent President's house.

Delhi is famous for its wide roads and crisp winters. One of the few places in India where colours of nature changes with the seasons. From Kerala to Kashmir and from Gujarat to Assam all the mouth watering delicacies and shopping goods are found in Delhi.

The cosmopolitan nature of the city has only added to the beauty and glory of it. Big gardens, wide roads, ancient structures, and power of politics is what Delhi is all about.

Goa

Goa is a tiny emerald land on the west coast of India situated between the borders of Maharashtra and Karnataka and is better known to the world as the former Portuguese enclave on Indian soil. With the rule of the Portuguese for over 450 years and the consequential influence of the Latin culture, Goa presents a somewhat different picture to the foreign visitor than any other part of the country.

Not only is the proportion of Christians (almost all of whom are Catholics) in the total population of Goa much higher than that obtaining in most of the other States; the general way of living is also markedly different. Western influence is evident in the dress and food habits, and the general life of the people is quiet and peaceful. A striking feature of Goa is the harmonious relationship between the two principal religious communities, the Hindus and the Catholics, who have lived together peacefully for generations.

The Bom Jesus cathedral is another famous attraction in Goa.

Jammu and Kashmir

Tourist destinations in Jammu and Kashmir include:

* Srinagar
* Jammu
* Leh
* Amarnath
* Vaishno Devi
* Dull Lake

Other cities of interest in Northern India include Gwalior, Khajuraho, Varanasi, Mathura, and Haridwar.

Moving south, many places are a mix of ancient historic sites as well as industrial/technological hubs. Some of these are listed below.

Karnataka

The southern state of Karnataka offers:

* Bangalore, the IT capital of India, is also significant for its history

* Mysore, about 140 km from Bangalore, has palaces, KRS Dam, several temples, a Hindu temple atop Chamundi Hills, Chamundeswari Temple.
* Srirangapatna, where nearby fortresses can be found (Tipu's)
* Hampi the city of ruins (1500s when the Muslim kings destroyed the prosperous Vijayanagar empire)
* The Belur and Halebidu temples are famed for their sculptural beauty.
* Sravanabelagola has a Jain temple dedicated to king Bahubali. The statue is massive and a Maha Masthaka Abhishekham performed one every year, attracts a huge number of pilgrims
* Sringeri, located in the western ghats, has a wonderful temple dedicated to Sarada devi.
* The Western Ghats offer many other places of exceptional beauty like Agumbe, Horanadu etc.
* Madikeri, Kodagu, Talakaveri, Kemmanagundi all places of immense natural beauty.

Kerala

Kerala is an evergreen lush state, tucked away in the southern corner of India. It is one of the most haunted visits of tourists in India. The state has its own tourism brand name-"God's Own Country", which has super-brand status. The state was nicked as one of the "10 paradises of the world" by the National Geographic traveller, the only other Indian place listed being the Taj Mahal.

Kerala is famous for its backwaters and lagoons. There are also several beautiful beaches along the coastline of Kerala. There are also hill stations and tropical rainforests with exquisite flora and fauna including endangared animals like elephant, tiger, nilgiri thar and lion-tailed macaque. Recently, a new brand of tourism was introduced called Monsoon Tourism, aimed at beckoning tourists to enjoy the beauty of the state's hauntigly beautiful rainy season extending from June to September.

Kerala is also known for its Ayurveda, the ancient medicinal system of India. The government of Kerala offers tourism packages related to Ayurvedaand promotes health tourism since treatment charges are low in Kerala. On the cultural front, the several unique and colourful festivals of Kerala like Onam, Thrissur Pooram, the snake boat races etc. provide great attraction to tourists. The classical artforms Kathakali, Mohiniyattam etc. are also a delight. The martial artform Kalaripayattu is the parent form of all famous martial arts like karate and kungfu. The Kerala Cuisine is also world famous. Also Kerala's rich history of maritime trade from ancient times has left a number of interesting historical monuments.

The major attractions in Kerala include:

* Kumarakom, Kuttanad, Kumbalanghi and other backwater locations.
* Vembanad Lake and the housboats of Alappuzha
* Beaches like Kovalam, Marari etc.
* Hill stations at Thekkady and Munnar
* The city of Kochi with its Chinese fishing nets, Bolgatty Palace, Mattanchery Jewish Synagogue, Jew Street, Fort Kochi etc.
* Enchanting waterfalls at Athirappilly and Vazhachal
* Periyar Tiger Reserve, Iravikulam National Park, Thattekad Bird Sanctuary and other forests
* Its historical monuments like Bakel Fort, Edakal cave of Wayanad
* Kerala Kalamandalam, deemed university teaching classical artforms
* Kalady, birthplace of Adi Sankaracharya, Sabarimala Temple, Guruvayur Temple, Malayatoor Church and other pilgirimage centres

Orissa

Orissa has been a preferred destination from ancient days for people having interest in spirituality, religion, culture, art and beauty of the nature. Ancient and medieval architecture, pristine sea beaches, nature at her beautiful best, the classical and ethnic dance forms and a variety of festivals, all in combine attract tourists from far off places to explore this state to a have a divine exposure of love and hospitality. Orissa has kept alive Buddhism and the Buddha in its ancient womb. The spirit of Buddhism still haunts the very air of Orissa. Rock-edicts that have challenged time stand huge and over-powering by the banks of the river Daya. The silent stones sing out songs of peace and non-violence. The torch of Buddhism is still ablaze in the sublime triangle at Udayagiri, Lalitgiri & Ratanagiri, on the banks of river Birupa. The surrounding hills of Langudi and Kayama stand as mute witness to the quirks and twists of history.

Precious fragments of a glorious past come alive in the shape of stupas, rock-cut caves, rock-edicts, excavated monastries, viharas, chaityas and sacred relics in caskets. Rock-edicts of Ashoka are a bonus for your eyes. Orissa is the home for various tribal communities who have contributed uniquely to the multicultural and multilingual character of the state. Their handicrafts, different dance forms, jungle products and their unique life style blended with their healing practices have got world wide attention.

Pondicherry

* Aurobindo Ashram
* Auroville

Rajasthan

Rajasthan has a rich history and culture making it one of the most popular tourist destinations in India. Shown here is the Hawa Mahal in Jaipur, Rajasthan. Rajasthan, the "Land of the Kings", is one of the most attractive tourist destinations in Northern India. The vast sand dunes of the Thar Desert attract millions of tourists from around the globe every year. Major visitor attractions in Rajasthan include:

* Jaipur-The capital of Rajasthan, famous for its rich history and royal architecture
* Jodhpur-fortress-city at the edge of the Thar Desert, famous for its blue homes and architecture
* Jaisalmer-famous for its golden fortress
* Barmer-Barmer and surrounding areas offer perfect picture of typical Rajasthani villages.
* Bikaner-famous for its medieval history as a trade route outpost

* Mount Abu
* Pushkar-It has the only Brahma temple in the world

Sikkim

Originally know as Suk-Hem, which in the local language means "peaceful home", Sikkim was an independent kingdom till the year 1974, when it became a part of the Republic Of India. The capital of Sikkim is Gangtok, located approximately 185 kilometres from New Jalpaiguri, the nearest railway station to Sikkim. Although an airport is under construction at Dekiling in East Sikkim, the nearest airport to Sikkim would be Bagdogra.

Sikkim is the land of Orchids and mystic culture and colourful tradition. Sikkim is well know among trekkers and adventure lovers, as West Sikkim has a lot to give them. Some must-visit places within Sikkim include:

1. NIT (National Institute Of Tibetology)
2. Hanuman and Ganesh Tok
3. Nathula pass
4. Baba Harbajan Mandir
5. Seven View Points
6. Rumtek Monastery
7. Lachen and Lachung
8. Pelling
9. Pemayantzy
10. Uttaray
11. Dzongri
12. Chewa-bhanjang
13. Barsay
14. Legship-Hot water spring
15. Khorong Hotwater spring 16.Samdrupsey at Namchi

Places near Sikkim include Darjeeling also know as the Queen of hills and Kalimpong. Darjeeling, other than its world famous "Darjeeling tea" is also famous for its refined "Prep schools" founded during the British Raj. A few of the top Schools in the District are:

1. St.Paul's School-Known as Eton of the East. It is 190 years old, thus one of the oldest schools in India.
2. Mt.Hermon School.
3. St.Joseph's School-where the H.M of Bhutan and the Late H.M of Nepal did their schooling.
4. Loreto Convent-where Late Mother Teresa served for many years.
5. Dr.Graham's Homes.
6. St.Joseph's Convent.
7. St.Augustine's School. Kalimpong is famous for its Flora cultivation and is home to many internationally known Nurseries.

National Policy on Tourism Development

The National Policy for Tourism development in India is based on a broad action plan including:

- Preservation of natural heritage
- Socio-economic development of the tourism destinations
- Increasing employment opportunities
- Development of domestic tourism
- Development of international tourism and optimisation of foreign exchange earnings
- Diversification of tourism products

All of which together will increase India 's share in world tourism.

In the 1990's, World Tourism Organization projections indicated that global international tourist arrivals would increase at around 4.8% p.a. from around 500 millions in 1993 to 661 millions by the year 2000, and then by 3.6% p.a. to 937 million by the year 2010.

The South Asia region, within which India is located, received 3.2 million international arrivals, i.e. 0.7% of global tourist arrivals in the 90's.

After analysing this scenario, the Government of India concluded that more destinations should be identified for integrated resort development. This was implemented by the

'Special Tourism Area' programme aimed at development and popularisation of 'Beach Tourism' in the country.

'Special Tourism Area' scheme to attract investment in hitherto unknown destinations, which held immense beach tourism potential.

Baikal: A Special Tourism Area

In 1992, the Government of India declared Baikal as a Special Tourism Area. Extremely scenic landscape, extensive beaches, numerous estuaries and backwaters and unspoilt environs qualified Baikal as a potential site for an international standard beach destination.

Baikal is unarguably one of the best potential beach resort destinations in South Asia. India has a very few comparable locations that offer the diversity of attractions to be found in Baikal. Yet, unlike most other existing resort destinations which are close to a major urban centre, and thus already over developed, the Baikal area is still virgin and pristine, offering the opportunity to set up a new planned resort destination.

The basic thrust of the project is sustainable tourism and is considered in terms of the socio-economic and environmental sustainability.

Baikal Project: India 's First Planned Beach Destination

Historical Perspective

Government of India in an effort to develop potential beach locations, which could be developed as international standard beach destinations had the western cost, surveyed in 1990. The survey identified Baikal the village in Kasaragod district in northern most part of Kerala as potential locale for the development of beach resort destination.

In 1992 the Government of India declared Baikal as "Special Tourism Area" for integrated resort development. Thereafter Government of Kerala entrusted a multidisciplinary team consisting of planners, landscape architects, urban and transport specialists, structural consultants and tourism leisure industry experts with the preparation of project of project blue print for the development of Baikal.

In 1995 Baikal Resort Development Corporation was formed for the implementation of Baikal Tourism Project.

The Baikal Project envisages setting up of an integrated beach destination at Baikal, with the objective of developing including social infrastructure in the region. BRDC conducted systematic surveys of the region through CESS (Centre for Earth Science Studies) and has developed 76 hectares (189 acres) of land that is ideal for setting up resorts.

Techno-economic Feasibility Studies

It is prepared by experts in the concerned areas. The following broad issues were examined during the studies, in order to sustain the destination:

- o Environmental issues-an appraisal of the environment, natural forces and ecology of the region and assessment of the impact of tourism on these.
- o Infrastructure-Reconnaissance, inventory preparation and assessment of the existing infrastructure.
- o Socio-cultural issues-Appraisal of cultural background and lifestyle, economic status, possibility of local participation, their relocation implications, measure to sustain socio-economic development.
- o Market potential and cost benefit-Assessment of market potential of the region, possible economic benefits to the region, development costs, fund sourcing and preparation of viable investment plan.

The findings have been translated into a physical plan in which tourism plays a major role in the overall development of the region.

Broad Essentials

- o Minimize shift in Agricultural land use-Minimize loss of existing agricultural land and to strengthen the resource base for traditional sectors like fishing and agriculture
- o Provide employment to the locals.
- o Resorts and protect the bio-diversity of the area, and safeguard the interests of fishermen and farmers
- o Keep a check on the commercialization of cultural values and art forms

Project Features

Land Development

Necessary development works have been carried out on the land. These include fencing, approach road construction, provision of HT lines. Water supply lines are being provided.

Landscape Policy

The landscape policy for Baikal aims at:-

- Conserving and strengthening the existing natural systems
- Enhancing the scenic properties of the region

Areas of concern include landform/topography and hydrogeology.

Modification of terrain should be in tune with the natural drainage patterns. Topsoil conservation through protection of existing vegetation and provision of new vegetative cover on fallow land. Protection of watersheds and catchments areas to maintain the ecological balance. Storm water drainage systems should minimise erosion and maximise both percolation and ground water recharge.

Basic Infrastructure

The basic infrastructure of the land includes power, water supply, communication, road networks, street lighting, public amenities and tourist attraction facilities.

Some of the work completed include:

- Roads, with the participation of the concerned Panchayats
- Access roads to resort sites
- Road junction improvements
- Studies and surveys like master plan etc
- Extension of HT Electric Line to Resorts
- 7 mld water supply scheme which is nearing completion

Further infrastructure developments taken up and proposed include:

- Development and improvement of further roads and junctions
- Sanitation facilities

- o Public wayside amenities
- o Street lighting

Facilities to Tourists

To offer varied experience to tourists within a short distance and time, attractive tourist spots have been developed nearby. Facilities include:

- o Thanal Vishrama Kendram (tourist facility near Baikal Fort)
- o Beautification of the surrounding areas of the Baikal Fort
- o Seaside pathway along the Baikal Fort
- o Erection of display and signboards in Kasargod district
- o Public beach at Pallikkara near Baikal Fort
- o Aqua Park and Chandragiri Boat Club
- o House boating cruise in Tejaswini backwaters in Valiyaparamba
- o Backwater Tourism-Houseboat
- o Children's parks at Baikal Fort and Thanal Vishrama Kendram
- o Trekking and adventure tourism

Plan for Future Activities

- o Heritage tourism projects for conservation and development of 8 Forts around Baikal.
- o Development of Valiyaoaramba as a Backwater destination of north Kerala.
- o Development of Baikal Fort Beach
- o Setting up of Eco lodges and other tourism products.
- o International standard water sports centre
- o Theme Parks
- o Augmenting facilities for tourists visiting Baikal

Baikal Fort

Over three and a half centuries old, Baikal Fort looms large against the backdrop of the Arabian Sea, rising dramatically from amidst the tall grass. Easily one of the best-preserved forts in the State, Baikal shows little signs of the many aeons that have passed by. And standing on a 35-acre headland, 130 feet above sea level, the fort is the largest in the State. Soaring observation towers, once cannon emplacements, lend Baikal Fort a majesty quite becoming of its former role as a military station.

These will be your vantage points to take in the splendours of the sea that spread to the north, south and west and the rich naturescapes to the east. A water reservoir with a long flight of steps and a magazine for storing ammunition add to the mystery of the place. Folklore has it that there are several secret underground passages here, once used for military purposes. With two of them now open to the public, you can as well take a walk down the corridors of time. Baikal is the most famous of the forts of Kasaragod, renowned as the land of forts; the others being Kumbala, Kasaragod, Kundankuzhi, Bandadukka and Povval.

Chandragiri Fort

Six km away, perched beside the Chandragiri River, is the Chandragiri Fort. Built during the 17th century by Sivappa Naik of Bedanore, who is said to have built the Baikal Fort too, Chandragiri's western rampart is an ideal place to watch sunsets.

Hosdurg Fort

Further down, 15 km away from Baikal is the Hosdurg Fort-a chain of forts built by Somasekhara Nayak of the Ikkeri dynasty. Today Hosdurg's historic aura has a spiritual touch to it, thanks to the Nityanand Ashram located there.

Untouched Pictures of Serenity

Valiyaparamba

Perhaps the most beautiful backwater stretch of Kerala, Valiyaparamba is 19 km from Baikal. Four rivers give shape to this network of waterways that lazily snake through the land, between palm groves and paddy fields. Hire a Kettuvallam-the traditional houseboat of Kerala-for an unmatched experience of the backwaters. Nothing lets you take in the rustic beauty of Kasaragod; the refreshing glimpses of life around the waterways, as does a houseboat cruise. What makes this goods carrier turned leisure boat much sought after by tourists are the luxuries on offer-one /two bedrooms, an attached toilet / bath, a kitchenette plus a crew comprising a cook, oarsmen and guide. And, as you glide past little thatched houses, past the clusters of green; past fleets of ducks you'll finally discover that serenity has a name. A visit to the turtle hatchery centre nearby will provide the perfect finale.

Chandragiri

Unveil more frames of tranquility at Chandragiri River. Flowing beside the famous fort by the same name, boat trips are available from here to nearby islands and palm groves.

Untainted Portraits of Beauty (Beaches)

Baikal Beach

An unmatched experience of the sun, sea and the sand is this shallow beach, that offers, apart from the charm of unexplored nature, spectacular views of the Baikal Fort nearby. Adding more charm to the spectacular landscape are the swaying palm trees that border the beach.

Kappil Beach

Five km away is Kappil Beach. Vast, remote and secluded, it is refreshingly different from popular beach destinations in its inspiring settings and ambience. Nearby is the Kodi Cliff that looks as if it sprang straight out of the sea. Take in one of the most panoramic views of the sea from here.

Kanwatheertha Beach

Located 3 km from Manjeswaram, what makes this beach special is a large swimming-pool like formation of the sea on the vast beach.

Azhithala Beach

Serene, secluded and punctuated with casuarinas trees, Azhithala Beach, located 25 km to the south of Baikal, is the ideal setting for long walks and out-of-this-world moments.

Unexplored Areas

Ranipuram

Shola woods, monsoon forests and grasslands ..... Ranipuram, 58 km from Baikal is a stunning landscape in every shade of green.

Situated at a cool 750 m above sea level, it is popular not just as a natural haven, but also as an adventure hotspot. For hidden beneath the evergreen canopy are delightful trekking trails that nature enthusiasts are slowly discovering.

Formerly known as Madathumala, Ranipuram's extensive forests merge with those of the nearby State of Karnataka. While the varied vegetation will make this place a favourite with nature lovers, the wild elephants that wander the mountains will offer the experience of a lifetime for wildlife enthusiasts.

Kottancherry

Visitors can have more of adventure at Kottancherry which resembles the famous hill station of Kodaikanal in its scenic beauty. The rainforests near Konnakkad present excellent options for trekking.

Possadigumpe

Ideal for an enchanting one-day tour is Possadigumpe, located on a hillock 323 m above sea level and 18 km east of Mangalpady in Dharmathadka. The delightfully cool environs of this place make it just the right place for a picnic.

Artistic Forms

Perhaps the most enduring image of Kasaragod is the Theyyam, the oldest ritualistic temple art form of India and one of the most spectacular in artistry and symbolism. Watch a grand display of this unique ritual art at the numerous Kaliyattoms held here from October to May every year. Two other art forms that are performed in Kasaragod are Kalaripayattu, the martial art form of Kerala and Yakshagana, the art form that has its roots in Karnataka.

Places of Worship

Kasaragod has the rare distinction of housing some of the historically and religiously important places of worship in India. Foremost among them is the Malik Dinar Juma Masjid-believed to have been built by Malik Ibn Dinar-at Thalankara. Equally significant is the 9th century Ananthapuram Lake Temple, said to be the original abode of Ananthapadmanabha, the presiding deity of Kerala's most famous place of worship, Sree Padmanabhaswamy

Temple. Situated 30 km from Baikal, this is the only lake temple in Kerala.

Other prominent pilgrim centres include Madiyankulam Durge Temple at Kanhangad, famous for the Bhutha dance held during the annual festival, the Sree Mahalingeswara Temple at Adoor on the banks of River Payaswini, the Madhur Temple with its rich architecture and copper plate roofing and Manjeswaram, home to 15 mosques and two Jain temples. Anandashram is an internationally renowned spiritual centre, 15 km form Baikal.

Gateways

Aralam Wildlife Sanctuary (120 km from Baikal): Elephants, sloth, bears, sambars, mousedeer etc. can be found in this 55 sq.km sanctuary.

Muzhappilangad (105 km from Baikal): Kerala's only drive-in beach; 4 km long; a swimmer's paradise.

Parassinikadavu (68 km from Baikal): Famed for the Muthappan Temple, where Muthappan Theyyams are performed every morning and evening.

Wayanad (150 km from Baikal): Known for its picturesque hill stations, spice plantations, luxuriant forests; attractions include the Pookot Lake, Wayanad Wildlife Sanctuary and Edakkal Caves.

Kappad Beach (165 km from Baikal): Historic beach where Vasco da Gama landed on the 27 th of May, 1498.

Coorg (120 km from Baikal): Hill station famous for rolling hills, forests, coffee plantations.

Nagarhole Wildlife Sanctuary: 643 sq. km of rich and varied flora and fauna.

Kabini: 65 km form Nagarhole Wildlife Sanctuary; famous for the Kabini River Lodge, formerly a Maharajah's hunting lodge.

Sringeri: Famed as the Southern seat of the orthodox Hindu hierarchy.

Mookambika (210 km from Baikal): Famous for the Mookambika Temple, an important pilgrim centre of South India.

Gokarna: A Centre of Sanskrit learning; boasts of a beach.

Dharmasthala: Home to the famous Manjunatha Temple

Udupi (126 km from Baikal): Important Vaishnavite town.

The Culture and Tradition

At the broadest level, the natural and cultural heritage belongs to all people. We each have a right and responsibility to understand, appreciate and conserve its universal values.

Heritage is a broad concept and includes the natural as well as the cultural environment. It encompasses landscapes, historic places, sites and built environments, as well as bio-diversity, collections, past and continuing cultural practices, knowledge and living experiences. It records and expresses the long processes of historic development, forming the essence of diverse national, regional, indigenous and local identities and is an integral part of modern life. It is a dynamic reference point and positive instrument for growth and change. The particular heritage and collective memory of each locality or community is irreplaceable and an important foundation for development, both now and into the future.

At a time of increasing globalisation, the protection, conservation, interpretation and presentation of the heritage and cultural diversity of any particular place or region is an important challenge for people everywhere. However, management of that heritage, within a framework of internationally recognised and appropriately applied standards, is usually the responsibility of the particular community or custodian group.

A primary objective for managing heritage is to communicate its significance and need for its conservation to its host community and to visitors. Reasonable and well managed physical, intellectual and/or emotive access to heritage and cultural development is both a right and a privilege. It brings with it a duty of respect for the heritage values, interests and equity of the present-day host community, indigenous custodians or owners of historic property and for the landscapes and cultures from which that heritage evolved.

Dynamic Interaction

Domestic and international tourism continues to be among the foremost vehicles for cultural exchange, providing a personal experience, not only of that which has survived from the past, but of the contemporary life and society of others. It is increasingly appreciated as a positive force for natural and cultural conservation.

Tourism can capture the economic characteristics of the heritage and harness these for conservation by generating funding, educating the community and influencing policy. It is an essential part of many national and regional economies and can be an important factor in development, when managed successfully.

Tourism itself has become an increasingly complex phenomenon, with political, economic, social, cultural, educational, bio-physical, ecological and aesthetic dimensions. The achievement of a beneficial inter-action between the potentially conflicting expectations and aspirations of visitors and host or local communities, presents many challenges and opportunities.

The natural and cultural heritage, diversities and living cultures are major tourism attractions. Excessive or poorly-managed tourism and tourism related development can threaten their physical nature, integrity and significant characteristics. The ecological setting, culture and lifestyles of host communities may also be degraded, along with the visitor's experience of the place.

Tourism should bring benefits to host communities and provide an important means and motivation for them to care for and maintain their heritage and cultural practices. The involvement and cooperation of local and/or indigenous community representatives, conservationists, tourism operators, property owners, policy makers, those preparing national development plans and site managers is necessary to achieve a sustainable tourism industry and enhance the protection of heritage resources for future generations.

ICOMOS, the International Council on Monuments and Sites, as the author of this Charter, other international organisations and the tourism industry, are dedicated to this challenge.

Main Objectives of the Charter

The Objectives of the International Cultural Tourism Charter are:

* To facilitate and encourage those involved with heritage conservation and management to make the significance of that heritage accessible to the host community and visitors.
* To facilitate and encourage the tourism industry to promote and manage tourism in ways that respect and enhance the heritage and living cultures of host communities.

* To facilitate and encourage a dialogue between conservation interests and the tourism industry about the importance and fragile nature of heritage places, collections and living cultures, including the need to achieve a sustainable future for them.
* To encourage those formulating plans and policies to develop detailed, measurable goals and strategies relating to the presentation and interpretation of heritage places and cultural activities, in the context of their preservation and conservation.

In addition:

* The Charter supports wider initiatives by ICOMOS, other international bodies and the tourism industry in maintaining the integrity of heritage management and conservation.
* The Charter encourages the involvement of all those with relevant or at times conflicting interests, responsibilities and obligations to join in achieving its objectives.
* The Charter encourages the formulation of detailed guidelines by interested parties, facilitating the implementation of the Principles to their specific circumstances or the requirements of particular organisations and communities.

Principles of the Cultural Tourism Charter

First Principle

Since domestic and international tourism is among the foremost vehicles for cultural exchange, conservation should provide responsible and well managed opportunities for members of the host community and visitors to experience and understand that community's heritage and culture at first hand.

The natural and cultural heritage is a material and spiritual resource, providing a narrative of historical development. It has an important role in modern life and should be made physically, intellectually and/or emotively accessible to the general public. Programmes for the protection and conservation of the physical attributes, intangible aspects, contemporary cultural expressions and broad context, should facilitate an understanding and appreciation of the heritage significance by the host community and the visitor, in an equitable and affordable manner.

Individual aspects of natural and cultural heritage have differing levels of significance, some with universal values, others of national, regional or local importance. Interpretation programmes should present that significance in a relevant and accessible manner to the host community and the visitor, with appropriate, stimulating and contemporary forms of education, media, technology and personal explanation of historical, environmental and cultural information.

Interpretation and presentation programmes should facilitate and encourage the high level of public awareness and support necessary for the long term survival of the natural and cultural heritage.

Interpretation programmes should present the significance of heritage places, traditions and cultural practices within the past experience and present diversities of the area and the host community, including that of minority cultural or linguistic groups. The visitor should always be informed of the differing cultural values that may be ascribed to a particular heritage resource.

Second Principle

The relationship between Heritage Places and Tourism is dynamic and may involve conflicting values. It should be managed in a sustainable way for present and future generations. Places of heritage significance have an intrinsic value for all people as an important basis for cultural diversity and social development. The long term protection and conservation of living cultures, heritage places, collections, their physical and ecological integrity and their environmental context, should be an essential component of social, economic, political, legislative, cultural and tourism development policies.

The interaction between heritage resources or values and tourism is dynamic and ever changing, generating both opportunities and challenges, as well as potential conflicts. Tourism projects, activities and developments should achieve positive outcomes and minimise adverse impacts on the heritage and lifestyles of the host community, while responding to the needs and aspirations of the visitor. Conservation, interpretation and tourism development programmes should be based on a comprehensive understanding of the specific, but often complex or conflicting aspects of heritage significance of the particular place. Continuing research and consultation are important to furthering the evolving understanding and appreciation of that significance.

The retention of the authenticity of heritage places and collections is important. It is an essential element of their cultural significance, as expressed in the physical material, collected memory and intangible traditions that remain from the past. Programmes should present and interpret the authenticity of places and cultural experiences to enhance the appreciation and understanding of that cultural heritage.

Tourism development and infrastructure projects should take account of the aesthetic, social and cultural dimensions, natural and cultural landscapes, bio-diversity characteristics and the broader visual context of heritage places. Preference should be given to using local materials and take account of local architectural styles or vernacular traditions.

Before heritage places are promoted or developed for increased tourism, management plans should assess the natural and cultural values of the resource. They should then establish appropriate limits of acceptable change, particularly in relation to the impact of visitor numbers on the physical characteristics, integrity, ecology and biodiversity of the place, local access and transportation systems and the social, economic and cultural well being of the host community. If the likely level of change is unacceptable the development proposal should be modified.

There should be on-going programmes of evaluation to assess the progressive impacts of tourism activities and development on the particular place or community.

Third Principle

Conservation and Tourism Planning for Heritage Places should ensure that the Visitor Experience will be worthwhile, satisfying and enjoyable. Conservation and tourism programmes should present high quality information to optimise the visitor's understanding of the significant heritage characteristics and of the need for their protection, enabling the visitor to enjoy the place in an appropriate manner.

Visitors should be able to experience the heritage place at their own pace, if they so choose. Specific circulation routes may be necessary to minimise impacts on the integrity and physical fabric of a place, its natural and cultural characteristics.

Respect for the sanctity of spiritual places, practices and traditions is an important consideration for site managers, visitors, policy makers, planners and tourism operators. Visitors should be encouraged to behave as welcomed guests, respecting the values and lifestyles of the host community, rejecting possible theft or illicit trade in cultural property and conducting themselves in a responsible manner which would generate a renewed welcome, should they return. Planning for tourism activities should provide appropriate facilities for the comfort, safety and well-being of the visitor, that enhance the enjoyment of the visit but do not adversely impact on the significant features or ecological characteristics.

Fourth Principle

Host communities and indigenous peoples should be involved in planning for conservation and tourism.

The rights and interests of the host community, at regional and local levels, property owners and relevant indigenous peoples who may exercise traditional rights or responsibilities over their own land and its significant sites, should be respected. They should be involved in establishing goals, strategies, policies and protocols for the identification, conservation, management, presentation and interpretation of their heritage resources, cultural practices and contemporary cultural expressions, in the tourism context. While the heritage of any specific place or region may have a universal dimension, the needs and wishes of some communities or indigenous peoples to restrict or manage physical, spiritual or intellectual access to certain cultural practices, knowledge, beliefs, activities, artefacts or sites should be respected.

Fifth Principle

Tourism and conservation activities should benefit the host community. Policy makers should promote measures for the equitable distribution of the benefits of tourism to be shared across countries or regions, improving the levels of socio-economic development and contributing where necessary to poverty alleviation. Conservation management and tourism activities should provide equitable economic, social and cultural benefits to the men and women of the host or local community, at all levels, through education, training and the creation of full-time employment opportunities.

A significant proportion of the revenue specifically derived from tourism programmes to heritage places should be allotted to the protection, conservation and presentation of those places, including their natural and cultural contexts. Where possible, visitors should be advised of this revenue allocation. Tourism programmes should encourage the training and employment of guides and site interpreters from the host community to enhance the skills of local people in the presentation and interpretation of their cultural values. Heritage interpretation and education programmes among the people of the host community should encourage the involvement of local site interpreters. The programmes should promote a knowledge and respect for their heritage, encouraging the local people to take a direct interest in its care and conservation.

Conservation management and tourism programmes should include education and training opportunities for policy makers, planners, researchers, designers, architects, interpreters, conservators and tourism operators. Participants should be encouraged to understand and help resolve the at times conflicting issues, opportunities and problems encountered by their colleagues.

Sixth Principle

Tourism promotion programmes should protect and enhance Natural and Cultural Heritage characteristics. Tourism promotion programmes should create realistic expectations and responsibly inform potential visitors of the specific heritage characteristics of a place or host community, thereby encouraging them to behave appropriately.

Places and collections of heritage significance should be promoted and managed in ways which protect their authenticity and enhance the visitor experience by minimising fluctuations in arrivals and avoiding excessive numbers of visitors at any one time. Tourism promotion programmes should provide a wider distribution of benefits and relieve the pressures on more popular places by encouraging visitors to experience the wider cultural and natural heritage characteristics of the region or locality.

The promotion, distribution and sale of local crafts and other products should provide a reasonable social and economic return to the host community, while ensuring that their cultural integrity is not degraded.

Career in Tour and Tourism

Tourism and its related business activities belong to the most important sectors of the economies worldwide. Surprisingly this is widely underestimated because the complexity of tourism does not allow its quantitative perception and its real economic relevance. For this reason it has not been realized thoroughly that the tourism industry is the biggest employer in the world, and will continue to be despite the actual recession due to terrorism and other turbulences that have disturbed the peaceful environment of travellers.

Universities and training institutions recognized the needs of the prosperous tourism industry and have been developing qualification programmes on different levels and differentiations of focus. But they have been followers of the industry's demand rather than strategic planners aiming at an anticipated goal of management competence.

How to Support the Industry

Today it is necessary for universities and other institutions involved to be more entrepreneurial and more strategy orientated. They have to assess the actual tourism industry with its needs and demands for management excellence to enable themselves to design and implement curricula for programmes which guarantee the output of appropriate graduates.

The Growing Needs: In cooperation with the industry, universities must look ahead and try to get an imagination of the prospective development. Management skills are changing permanently, refreshing them is a continuous necessity. Tourism management is no exception. The industry is becoming more and more global. Global players are dominating the market while local partners depend on them, on their strategies and preferences. Management and operations for all people involved have become more sophisticated and challenging over the years.

Competition between tour operators, hotel chains, destinations, airlines, agencies etc. is fierce. At this stage industry needs excellent management competence, but where to recruit this excellence?

Negligence and Ignorance of Academics: The underestimation of the tourism business has been shared by universities for long. Similar to the century-long fight of business administration and management for recognition by the academic community, tourism management in many cases is not recognized as a serious subject. This irrational perception of tourism business with its relation to leisure and travel is still influencing the choice made by students today in the programmes provided by universities and other institutes.

Such programmes don't appeal to male students because they don't consider tourism as a reasonable career opportunity. They prefer courses in general business administration and management, however for the tight labour market they cannot avoid the tourism industry as an employer later on. What they lack in this case is a sound qualification in tourism management. This can only partly be compensated by learning on the job, what does not fulfill the career expectations of young managers and does not meet the requirements for differentiation of human resource departments as well. Additional qualification is a must. Is this qualification provided by an MBA?

Additional Qualification

An MBA is not an appropriate means for compensating the lack of compentence as long as the MBA is merely seen as an introduction to general management. Graduates of business studies got this introduction and much more in their four years degree course. Such an introduction is appropriate for those whose first academic degree was engineering, informatics, architecture etc., but not for graduates of business studies. For them the core subject of an additional qualification must be related to the specific industry or to the management function they are in respectively they want to acquire.

An elective focused on their speciality, as it is offered in many MBA programmes, does in no way fulfill the requirements. They must get the opportunity to dig deeper into their core skills (e.g. marketing or HRM) but now related to their business (e.g. global marketing in tourism) respectively to their function (e.g.

staffing of subsidiaries abroad). A master of science is not the right answer to the respective demand because it is not regarded as an award of excellence in management but rather as a sign of academic excellence and a step to the PhD.

The Specialist MBA: Only a Specialist MBA is the adequate solution, an MBA in tourism or in international tourism management. Such a specialized programme would overcome the problem and results in multiple demand. Are there constraints to the implementation of a specialist tourism MBA?

A Contradiction in Terms?: In the traditional academic perspective, the MBA is by definition a broad qualification in general management. Specialities can only be electives, which should never dodge the breadth of business orientation intended. From this point of view the Specialist MBA is a contradiction in terms. But this traditional perspective to an MBA is being pushed back by the market forces. And it is not reasonable to withstand this development. Further specialisation has to be achieved by Specialist MBA programmes.

Higher Management Career: Since the MBA became the brand of highest academic award of managers it cannot be denied that this award is appreciated not only by managers whose first academic education was different to business administration and management. Should the MBA shop be closed for those who got their first degree in business administration and management and who covered almost all the subjects of the MBA syllabus so that they cannot be motivated to get an MBA in terms of a mere general introduction to business and management? Should they waive on an MBA degree, the highest appropriate practice orientated academic award for their career?

The MBA became a mark of distinction for academics in business. Therefore it must be accessible for all who want to add a specialized qualification to their first academic degree. For graduates in business administration this can only be something apart from general business management: it has to be a Specialist MBA. In such a case the entry requirement for all should be equal, a degree in a business related subject.

A Pragmatic Solution: It has to be acknowledged that the additional skills which an engineer gains by an MBA course (Type 1) deserves the same award like the additional qualification of a business graduate who gets an MBA with the specialization in international marketing or information systems (Type 2). The quality and the rating of the two types of MBAs achieve the same levels, only the qualifications differ.

Universities should not assume that the business world would not be able to identify the difference between the variety of MBAs. The Specialist MBA is improving the possibility to differentiate and to select the candidates who are fitting best into the needs of the employers.

Specialist MBA in Tourism Management

Taking all those factors into account it is only a logical consequence to create Specialist MBAs focusing on tourism management, to equip the tourism industry with highly skilled management staff. But how to dot hat? The tourism business is known for its complexity and its international dimension. An MBA specialised on tourism or international tourism cannot cover everything. Therefore even the design of this industry related Specialist MBA remains general, covering the most important basic skills required by the tourism industry.

What Tourism Management Means: The touristic product is a bundle of offered components. Many industries are brought together in a system of relationships. Their capability of interaction and cooperation in the respective environments determines the economic success of each of them. Management of the different elements in various scopes of tourism needs highly developed skills to cope with the challenges of a business which is volatile and constantly influenced by the changes of travel motivations of tourists and the trends in society or by natural disasters and political developments.

Managers in the tourism business need-more than in other scopes of business-the awareness of the complexity of interrelationships of the players and a sensibility for changes in demands and environments. They need the skills to adjust the business to these respective changes. That requires strategic thinking, creativity, intercultural competence, skills of communication and leadership, the capability of self-learning and the stimulation of organizational learning as well as knowledge management.

Specialist MBA in International Tourism Management: An MBA in international tourism management with about 600 hours of class presence therefore should include the following subjects of different weight:

- The phenomenon of tourism and its systems
- Economics of tourism and its industries
- Environments of tourism
- Tourism demand
- International and global tourism management
- Culture and cross-cultural management
- Tourism marketing
- Marketing research in tourism
- Strategic planning in tourism
- Business policy and ethics
- Specific management functions in tourism (e.g. HRM, financial management, operations management, strategic quality management)
- Management of international projects
- E-tourism
- Communication and negotiation

An MBA in international tourism management is inevitably a real necessity. This need is pushed by the industry that is constantly affected not only by the economic changes but also by other phenomena surrounding them. It is therefore a rational move to be taken by the learning institutions to develop such a programme to accommodate this need-rather than to reject this demand.

The market requires Specialist MBAs. It is the logic of the general trends of more specialization driven by the concentration process in particular. Universities have to design qualification programmes which support these requirements as far as academic responsibility allows. By offering Specialist MBAs universities don't loose their virtues. Their interest should only be to secure transparency of what is offered and which award is delivered. It is possible to avoid confusion by clear information on the respective type of MBA. So universities are contributing to the needs of employers and ambitious young managers by the differentiation of awards, which are not differing in quality but only in its specific qualification.

The Specialist MBA in international tourism management will provide the prospective candidates with the competitive advantage of securing a career in the respective industry.

7

Management of Indian Best Hotels

Taj Hotels

Taj Hotels Resorts and Palaces is the largest Indian luxury hotel chain. A wholly owned subsidiary of the Tata Group, Taj Hotels Resort and Palaces comprises 57 hotels in 39 locations across India with an additional 18 international hotels in the Maldives, Mauritius, Malaysia, Seychelles, United Kingdom, United States of America, Bhutan, Sri Lanka, Africa, the Middle East and Australia. Their first and most well known property is the Taj Mahal Palace & Tower in Colaba, Mumbai. The Taj Mahal Palace & Tower, Mumbai was opened on December 16, 1903, by the founder of the Tata Group, Jamshetji Nusserwanji Tata. Taj President-a business hotel and Taj Land's End-an ultimate luxury boarding are also located in Mumbai. It operates TajAir, a luxury private jet operation with state-of-the-art Falcon 2000 aircraft designed by Dassault Aviation, France; and Taj Yachts, two 3-bedroom luxury yachts which can be used by guests in Mumbai and Kochi.

Falaknuma Palace

Falaknuma Palace is situated on a hill 650 meters in height, in the Old City of Hyderabad, India. It was built by Nawab Vikar-ul-Umra. It was purchased by the then Nizam VI during 1897 for use as a royal guest house. The palace provides a good view of Hyderabad. The palace is spread out in a scorpion shape with two pincers spread out as wings on the north. The middle part occupies the main building. The Harem quarters and the kitchen stretch towards the south.

The palace was designed by an Italian architect. The palace boasts of lavishly decorated interiors made of the Italian marble, and follows a western architectural style. It took almost nine years to complete. This famous palace houses a large collection of rare treasures, paintings, statues, furniture, manuscripts and books collected by the Nizam. The jade collection displayed here is considered to be unique in the world. Some old models of artillery are also exhibited in the front.

The Palace is being converted into a heritage hotel by the Taj Hotels group.

Hotel Organization in Future

No hotel company operating today can be unaware of the swift pace of global change and its impact on every facet of the hospitality industry. With just five years left in this century, we can expect change to be the only constant. New business practices are evolving virtually as fast as our technologies, while resistance to change has become one of the primary causes of business failure.

The specter of constant change raises fundamental questions as to the creation of shareholder wealth in a capital-constrained, highly competitive environment. How will hotel organizations build shareholder wealth, and what key drivers will result in success? What future products and services will be essential in a technology-driven, global environment marked by rising customer expectations? Moreover, what alternative approaches and skills must organizations develop to ensure market success?

The future success of hotel organizations will be driven in large part by the ability to foresee--and capitalize--on change. Beyond this truism, however, there is an urgent need to identify what will be required in the competitive environment of the future with its intense focus on serving customer needs. The hospitality industry–as is the case with business generally--is subject to deep currents of change set in motion as economic and social systems shaped in the industrial era evolve to a knowledge-based era driven by technology advances.

In this period of global transition, it behooves hotel organizations to examine the key factors that will not only define success, but the ability to survive in coming years. Many of these issues were spotlighted in a global study undertaken by the Economist Intelligence Unit and co-sponsored by Arthur Andersen. The Successful Corporation of the Year 2000 surveyed more than 600 senior executives around the world. Its mission was to identify the characteristics needed to lead successful businesses in the next century. These executives offer a number of compelling messages regarding the key success factors of the future.

Customers will have the strongest influence on the corporation in the year 2000. Indeed, these executives believe that the customer will be "king" in the new century. Exceptional leadership was by far the attribute most frequently cited by CEOs and senior executives; the consensus appears to be that successful companies in the year 2000 will be led by corporate visionaries. A strategic planning focus is not only essential, but must embody a concept of planning for the future that anticipates change, rather than being based exclusively on historical models. In structuring organizations for the future, companies must build management capabilities to deal with one of the most critical challenges–diversity in the marketplace. Employing information technology to drive business success in this information-driven era is not only the path of least resistance, but vital to virtually every aspect of operations.

The study's top-line results create an excellent backdrop to address key issues confronting the hotel industry, and what factors will lead to membership–rather than rejection–in the elite club of the world's corporate success stories in the year 2000.

From an Asset to Customer Focus

Recognizing that the hotel industry has a somewhat split personality reflecting the inherent conflicts between its real estate and operational aspects, it is important to understand the industry's real estate origins and how they are shaping the challenges ahead. The origins of the industry's real estate persona are embodied in the classic theory of location-"if we build it, they will come." As a result of this "building" complex, the industry has tended to have a real estate and asset orientation, rather than a customer focus. From the hotel company perspective–especially that of the brand-oriented "chain"–the varied interests of a diffused property ownership group can be quite different than the singular interest of the chain that operates and markets the properties.

Even when the ownership of geographically dispersed hotel properties is controlled by a single hotel organization, the financial structuring tends to be property-specific. Corporate financial strategies are frequently subjugated to the needs of the last property deal brought into the company's fold. Each property in a so-called "chain," is frequently the subject of a unique and distinctive ownership and financial structure. This phenomenon–quite common in the real estate sector, but unusual for business enterprises generally–makes for elusive economies of scale in the structuring and financing of property-driven expansion.

Collectively, these factors have produced low comparative returns in real estate, although criticism levelled at commercial real estate returns is somewhat less germane to the hotel industry, where management and franchise fees can produce high returns for those companies where property ownership is held by third parties. Nevertheless, average returns in the real estate industry in the United States, for example, are just over 10 percent, compared to small company stock returns at almost 20 percent and large company stocks at an average of about 15 percent.

While hotel chains have adopted traditional corporate frameworks, there are a number of predominantly real estate-driven, family-owned businesses in the hotel sector that continue to operate as relatively unstructured organizations. In meeting the future, these businesses will need plans, people and processes in order to establish viable corporate forms that can compete in tomorrow's marketplace and capitalize upon its opportunities.

In today's changed environment, the hotel organization must deal with a number of new realities. Investors in our industry are no longer satisfied with long-term capital appreciation and psychic income that heretofore were often the justification for otherwise seemingly uneconomic investments in hotel property or, indeed, hotel chains. The first reality is that there is a very specific and identifiable relationship between bottom line performance and value. Improvements in business operations raises values. It is not surprising, therefore, that the new owners attracted to this industry in recent years have new sets of demands. This transformation from an old-guard group of investors and owners to income and return-driven newcomers has meant that the once "quiet enjoyment" of operators in their management of hotels for third parties is being disturbed, interrupted and overturned.

These challenges all take place in an environment where capital has become extremely selective in markets that have little stability. A global shortage of capital will not remain a short-term problem, and future hotel organizations must have a stronger alignment to capital providers–a critical "customer" group. Hotel companies will need to compete by offering better returns and performance than in the past. Hotel chains have found their development timetables quashed in recent years, making it difficult to achieve goals of critical mass often required to improve performance. These factors are driving consolidation in the brand "sweepstakes." Capital markets, therefore, continue to favour well-established companies, a reality that must drive entrepreneurial organizations to meet the future now by planning for an evolving corporate context in which to operate.

Key Success Factors-The Future

Within this broad context, hotel developers, owners and management companies will all need to develop new strategies, skills and processes that look forward to the competitive demands of the future. These ultimately must address issues related to vision and planning, as well as organizational skill sets and processes to attract and retain customers. To stake a claim in the future, current business practices should be examined in light of what can be expected to be the key success factors in the year 2000.

Embrace a global change orientation. As the information age produces greater worldwide integration of business activities, a global knowledge base will become invaluable. Success in local and regional hotel markets will be shaped decisively by a global business environment that defines capital movement, customer expectations and applications of new technologies.

Focus on the Customer

If the customer is "king" in the 21st century, hotel organizations will be best served by focusing less on their hotel assets as measures of success, and more on their customers. This involves a fundamental shift in viewing the real estate asset as the wealth creator--to the customer as the key to building shareholder wealth. A customer focus must imbue business decisions at all levels of developing and operating a hotel organization. Pursuing such a course will inevitably impact shareholder wealth. To accomplish this, however, customers need to participate in the product development process.

Fully realizing a customer focus in the industry poses a significant challenge. The hotel industry must confront problems due to conflicts between operational needs and real estate goals. Quite simply, an operator must remain customer-focused, but the short-term strategies to meet these needs may be inconsistent with the long-term objectives of property owners. Balancing those goals will be essential. A customer focus implies a significant shift in what drives hotel development--placing primary emphasis on the customer with the locations to follow. Nevertheless, a hotel organization with its large investment in fixed assets--the real estate--can never be as nimble as a consumer products company in adjusting products and services to match rapid shifts in the marketplace.

The Japanese taught us that the concept of "zero defects" in products and services can yield tremendous benefits. But today an even more rigorous standard dominates--quality that surprises. In practical terms, the hotel industry finds it extremely difficult to meet the standard of zero defects in service. Hotel services are based primarily on people, not computers or other equipment. Quality that surprises takes the concept of zero defects a step further. Yesterday's surprising product or service is today's status quo. Twenty years ago, a business executive did not expect a consistent and predictable level of service wherever he or she travelled in the world. Today that is a standard--not the exception--as is the expectation for sophisticated technology in hotel rooms to support business needs. With customer discrimination so acute, it is not surprising that brand loyalty is a diminishing "commodity" in the hotel industry.

Find the Ingredients for Visionary Leadership

Today's hotel organizations need to recognize the need for

visionary leadership. The ability to forecast the future--to anticipate change rather than react to it--will be one of the single greatest determinants of market dominance in the years ahead. The old "command and control" model of leadership is giving way to a focus on leadership in ideas, information, inspiration, vision and teamwork. Warren Bennis, an authority on leadership in the U.S., puts it this way--"For the most part, failing organizations tend to be over-managed and under-led. The leader sets the tone for the moral character, the vision, the corporate culture and the fiber of the institution."

While visionary leadership is essential, it must be linked to business operations and foster a risk bias, rather than a procedural bias. This will allow the organization to stretch and, in turn, change. And it must be shared by empowered professionals and staff throughout the organization, including those who meet the customer.

Overcoming the resistance to change can be a daunting task, particularly in large hotel organizations in which diversions from the status quo may threaten established management lines. It suggests that a culture based on conformance may need to be replaced by an emphasis on flexibility, learning and cooperation. Management competencies will need to be aligned in order to achieve the desired result. For many organizations, this may mean a shift from traditional hierarchies typical of companies in an industrial era to a flatter organization with a more transparent interface between leadership, organizational functions and employees.

Create a defensible position through corporate strategy. For many of the industry's leaders, vision is driven by the strategic planning process, a function which has become critical for success.

Strategic planning, however, has at times been a step-child in the hotel industry, and it is often the first to be cut when organizations are downsized. It is clearly in transition. There also has been a tendency to decentralize and simplify this function--both actions of potential benefit. Strategic planning must be led by the top people in the organization--the CEO and COO. On the other hand, it should be close enough to the customer to ensure that planners can "listen" to and be influenced by customer needs.

Empower Management

Beyond the ability to envision the future, core management capabilities will make the difference--they are essential. A clear vision without the management skills to support it cannot be a recipe for success. First and foremost, hotel management must have strategic development skills and the ability to integrate complex factors affecting success. Market volatility has become the norm, in part caused by the rapidly changing tastes of customers. Customers are increasingly approaching the hotel industry with widely different social, economic and political backgrounds, to say nothing of employees. Being able to deal with these diversities in a positive and constructive fashion that capitalizes on the differences, rather than working to find ways to mitigate them, is the clear path for successful management in the future.

The organization will also need to be imbued with a sense of entrepreneurship that reacts proactively to the market's diversity. Traditional organizations that follow well-documented rules must give way to leaders who can balance a sense of discipline with that of flexibility. Talent and resources must be marshalled and leveraged. In an industry with high fixed costs and labour intensity, the concept of leverage in the hotel business is an all-important one. Improving labour productivity through technology must be a goal for today's forward-looking hotel organization. Management must also be able to narrow the gap between the employer and the employee, forcing a flatter organization in the process. This will put management closer to the customer and speed the two-way communication process up and down the organization.

Be in the Information Fast Lane

The traditional role of information technology (IT) as a back office support for accounting and bookkeeping has clearly moved front and centre stage. IT today influences all aspects of business from corporate strategies to organizational structure--and from the very business processes it is designed to support to performance measurement. In a world where the customer is "king," IT must also deliver in two critical areas: sales and marketing and customer service.

Technology was once viewed as a way to reduce costs by replacing people. That attitude has been firmly supplanted by one that seeks IT support for the creative work that all organizations must pursue. IT must allow organizations to react more speedily to market needs and, of course, produce the fulfilment of customer demands both quickly and accurately. To do this IT must operate on a decentralized basis. IT delivers, but it has to be the right information to the right people, and it needs to be done on a timely basis.

Improving the Management Project

Improving Management of NGO and Privately Owned Nature Reserves and High Biodiversity Islands in Seychelles Project funded by the Global Environment Facility through the World Bank

The Seychelles is known world wide as a storehouse of rare biodiversity. Historically, most of the islands and ecosystems have been severely impacted by human activities. Nevertheless, a few examples of whole island ecosystems have been protected and restored. These islands are Cousin, Cousine, Aride, Fregate and Aldabra, all managed, surprisingly, by civil society organisations. Nevertheless, there are significant barriers to sustainability of conservation efforts by these organisations.

The focus of the project is two islands, Cousin and Cousine, which are host to numerous rare and endemic species, and immense biodiversity. These include shared resources such as 10 species of breeding seabirds, 5 species of endemic land birds, rare floral species, 8 species of reptiles and hundreds species of invertebrates, the most important population of hawksbill turtles in the Western Indian Ocean and the highest biomass of reef fish in the granitic islands of Seychelles. The project is to ensure the islands' function as a reserve for the preservation of globally important biodiversity through understanding processes and changes in sites, species and habitats in the islands for better management and decision-making on activities to preserve this globally important biodiversity.

Cousin and Cousine are adjacent to Praslin-the second most populous island of the Seychelles. Cousin was purchased in the 1960's through a world wide appeal at a time when unique biodiversity in Seychelles was in jeopardy. An international NGO held the title to the island because land tenureship was the only method of securing the island for perpetuity and thereby restoring the ecosystems. This NGOs also assisted the previous owners of Cousine in the early years to conserve its biodiversity. This proved to be a very wise move because the islands are remarkable in that unlike other granitic islands of Seychelles, endemic and globally important fauna and flora have been saved.

They have been protected by NGO/private resources and management, and at least for Cousin, through national legislation and policy. The ownership and management regimes by civil society organisations and the relative remoteness, which are the main reasons why biodiversity has been saved, are now proving to be constraints for not only continuing with established activities but also for initiating new programs; the civil society organisations cannot source adequate resources from the local private sector, governmental or international sources. In addition, anthropogenic impacts and lack of knowledge of ecosystem-level changes, all mean that science and conservation action on each of them cannot move beyond present capacity and limits.

The project assumption is that conservation of island biodiversity can be sustained and at the same time greatly improved through an inter-island integrated and collaborative approach geared to clear management outcomes and also to the development of public education and community buy-in. The project recognises the importance of developing financial sustainability to maintain these conservation programs. The project intends to build long-term capacity for sustainable conservation and use of island biodiversity through program and capacity building, infrastructure acquisition and installation, co-management, and education and advocacy. The two islands are small, close to each other, and share similar and sensitive ecosystems, associated conservation activities and problems. They are both focused on biodiversity conservation, chiefly concerning globally threatened endemic land birds and internationally important colonies of breeding seabirds. Each island also hosts similar important reptile, botanical and invertebrate species. Both islands have a distinguished conservation history and offer a slightly different model and philosophy for biodiversity conservation. Cousin Island is owned by an international NGO but managed by an independent, locally registered, not-for-profit Association. Cousine Island is owned and managed by a private limited company registered in Seychelles. Management of the islands are supposed to be undertaken with in-country resources.

Project Vision

The project will remove barriers that currently prevent civil society organisations from augmenting and enhancing their capacity to conserve and restore species, sites and habitats.

The project will aims to create partnerships between neighbouring islands which have shared globally important biodiversity and similar environmental issues. This will be done through a substantial number of new and improved linked programs, the creation of a common resource and management center, institutional strengthening and capacity building, and public education and advocacy. The ultimate aim of this model partnership is to catalyze further collaboration and public buy-in, to remove other barriers and to mitigate negative ecosystem changes. The process set in motion by the project will improve the management of high biodiversity islands as well as increase the number of managed conservation sites in Seychelles. This project will thus have global biodiversity benefits, lead to greater sustainability of biodiversity and permit the sharing of these benefits to be directed principally at local levels. The vision mirrors the three principal objectives of the 1992 Convention of Biological Diversity.

Overall Goal of the Project

The Goal of the project is to improve management of biodiversity-rich islands by installing a shared multi-pronged programme framework and infrastructure for enhanced and sustainable conservation, financing and use of biodiversity.

The project vision and overall goal will be delivered through two principal components namely Small Island Ecosystem Management, and Public Education and Advocacy.:.

Component 1: Small Island Ecosystem Management

A. Improved management of terrestrial and marine habitats and important species.

B. Establish collaborative management and resource center on Praslin

C. Institutional strengthening
D. Capacity building and training

Component 2: Public Education and Advocacy

A. Develop biodiversity awareness and advocacy programs
B. Establish community outreach, partnerships and stakeholder participation programs

Project Partners

Nature Seychelles, formerly known as BirdLife Seychelles, is a local not-for-profit association registered in Seychelles. It is currently the largest independent environment organisation in Seychelles. The association is involved in a suite of activities including species and habit conservation, monitoring, research, island restoration, eco-tourism, education and awareness and advocacy.

Nature Seychelles manages Cousin Island Special Reserve and has a presence on several other islands. It has a multi-stakeholder and result-oriented approach through its programs such as the Seychelles Magpie-robin Recovery Team (SMART) and the Seychelles Seabird Group (SSG) as well with other organisations such as the WildLife Clubs of Seychelles, Ministry of Environment and Ministry of Education.

Its donors and partners include the World Bank/GEF and the Royal Society for Protection of Birds. It is a member of the BirdLife International network, WIOMSA, the African Bird Club and IUCN, works in close collaboration with WWF, the Mauritian WildLife Foundation and many others.

Cousine Island LTD (Owner and Manger of Cousine Island): is a private limited company registered in the Seychelles. The company has built a very small and ecologically friendly luxury hotel. The island is not legally protected and the owner is not obliged to conserve its biodiversity. The company has voluntarily put in a system for biodiversity conservation using its own resources. It delegates management responsibility for the island to a Conservation Warden. The Warden works in close collaboration with the hotel manager. The purpose of setting up the small hotel is to bring in sufficient revenues to maintain the conservation and research programs on the island and to maintain it as a high biodiversity area. The company supports other conservation programs in Seychelles, for example the Magpie Robin Recovery Program and the Seychelles Rare Birds Committee.

Landmarks Achievements

Hotel Association of India, established on 24th October 1996, within a short span of less than a decade of its inception, has successfully provided an integrated hospitality platform produced ground breaking results and recorded several notable 'firsts' for the hospitality industry described in the ensuing pages:-

Export House Status for Tourism and Hospitality Industry

Among the path breaking industry 'first' initiatives of Hotel Association of India is the unique recognition secured for tourism and hospitality sectors in India as 'export industries'. This was an unparelled achievement of the Association which undertook the entire groundwork and created consensus in support of according export status for hospitality industries.

HAI organized series of inter-active meetings with the concerned Ministries of the Government of India, culminating in a high level Conclave presided over by Shri Ramakrishna Hegde, then Hon'ble Minister of Commerce, Government of India, on 16th July 1998 at the Oberoi Hotel, New Delhi which cleared the decks for the action plan blue-printed by HAI receiving the official seal of approval of the Government of India manifested in the a Gazette Notification of November 26th, 1998 declaring Hotels and Tourism Units eligible for the benefits of Service Export House/ International Service Export House/International Star Service Export House/International Super Star Service Export House categories on the basis of their quantum of foreign exchange earnings. This extraordinary recognition placed hotels and tourism units on par with industries engaged in export of products for imports of projects and products against their foreign exchange entitlements and facilitated hotels in acquiring competitive edge vis-à-vis hotels overseas in providing world class facilities.

Tourism Export Promotion Council

Another notable first for hospitality and tourism industries, synchronizing with the grant of Export House Status, was notched by the Hotel Association of India by formulating the Constitution of the Tourism Export Promotion Council (TEPC) on 20th November 1998. The approval of the Company Law Board was also secured for the new body under Section 25 of the Companies Act 1956. TEPC represented an unique experiment in bringing together for the first time all constituents of the tourism sector-hotels, travel agents, tour operators, transporters, airlines, tourism finance companies-under a single umbrella on a common platform.

Establishment of SAARC Hotel Association

HAI reached beyond the national boundaries to provide regional co-operation aiming hotels in South Asia and became the prime mover in the formation of the SAARC Hotel Association. This was achieved by developing close synergy between the hospitality industry organizations of Bangladesh, Bhutan, India, Maldives, Nepal, Pakistan and Sri Lanka. The SAARC Hotel Association was formally launched at Mumbai on 7th April 1999 with Nepal being assigned the responsibility of hosting the SAARC body for its initial two years and later by rotation by other member countries.

International Code of Conduct to Govern Relations Between Hoteliers, Travel Agents and Tour Operators

For the first time in the history of travel trade in India on 28.4.2000, HAI successfully evolved consensus among the Travel Agents Association of India (TAAI) and the Indian Association of Tour Operators (IATO) and the Hotel Association of India (HAl) resulting in the signing of the International Code of Practice governing the relations between Hoteliers, Travel Agents and Tour Operators.

The code represents a watershed for the tourism and travel industry in India, as protracted negotiations for adopting a code of practice for over three decades had not yielded any results till HAl took the lead and crafted consensus in favour of adopting the global practice. It's signing by the three national bodies signalled to the international travel fraternity and business travellers that India had opted for internationally approved policies of hotel bookings, cancellations, refunds, claims etc.

Legal 'First' For Hotel Industry

The Hotel Association of India took the lead in invoking the intervention of the High Court of Delhi in protecting the interests of hospitality industry in India on a matter of vital importance to the hotels as well as to the foreign and domestic tourist staying in hotels. Hotel Association of India filed a writ in the High Court Delhi against an arbitrary and ad'hoc administrative directive requiring the hotels in approved categories, classified by the Ministry of Tourism, to follow a Single Tariff system. The directive would have proved detrimental and counter productive to national tourism interests. The industry perspective presented by HAI was accepted by the High Court of Delhi which granted a Stay in favour of hotel industry, signifying an unique legal validation of hospitality industry system of operation across the country.

Seeking Repeal of Anti-women Legislation

The Punjab Excise Act enacted during the British rule in India in 1914 contains an archaic and anti-women provision prohibiting the employment of women in licenced premises, i.e., bars and restaurants in hotels. The Hotel Association of India challenged the validity of this ancient legislation before the Hon'ble High Court to protect the interest of women. The HAI's Writ against the constitutional validity of the provisions of the Punjab Excise Act, 1914

Media Centric Initiatives

The large number of foreign correspondents stationed in India, representing powerful and popular foreign publications, newspapers, journals, T. V. Channels, Broadcasters play a major role in making or marring the image of India as a peaceful tourists destination country through their news reports and dispatches. HAI took the lead in organizing the first ever hospitality industry meeting with the foreign correspondent stationed in New Delhi. The event was organized with the objective to discuss adverse the impact of Travel Advisories issued by foreign Governments on the State of Indian hospitality and tourism industry and correct their perspective to restore consumer confidence in travel, tourism and hospitality sectors adversely affected by global events of preceding years. Because of the unique nature of the special event and its potential for future tourists arrivals in India, the Ministry of Tourism fully associated with HAI.

Survey on the Impact of Travel Advisories in Hospitality Industry

Foreign Embassies and Missions are often instrumental in advising their respective countries to issue "Travel Advisories" to caution their citizens from undertaking visits to specific countries owing to adverse conditions of safety and security. Travel Advisories against visiting India were issued by several countries following global events like the terrorist attacks on 9/11 in USA and 13/12 in New Delhi, War in Afghanistan and tension on Indo-Pak borders etc. The adverse travel advisories affected tourists arrivals to India over a prolonged period.

The Hotel Association of India stepped in by organizing an innovative Survey among foreign tourists staying in hotels to obtain their reactions to such advisories issued by the foreign governments. The HAI Survey brought out that a preponderant majority of tourists declared India as a safe and peaceful destination and foreign travellers viewed the travel advisories and warnings as "coloured by political considerations" and based on "inadequate knowledge of ground realities". Some of them opined that they found New Delhi "safer than Manhattan". HAI Survey facilitated the Governments of the respective countries in reviewing and withdrawing the adverse travel advisories and re-assured tourists of their safety and security in India.

Setting Up of Confederation of Indian Travel and Tourism Industry

Another first initiative mooted by the Association related to the need for creating a Confederation of Indian Travel and Tourism Industry (CITTI) as an umbrella organization to represent all components of the Travel & Travel industry in India. Unlike other industries, there has never been an umbrella organization in the tourism industry. To fill this gap, HAI proposed the setting up of CITTI which would address the policy issues and concerns of the industry. The Constitution of the proposed new body has been drawn up and made available to all sectoral associations to facilitate its establishment in the future.

Study of Tariff System in Hotels

The first ever 'While Paper' on Tariff Systems in Hotels in India, produced by a Central Government Autonomous Organisation the National Institute of Public Finance and Policy (NIPFP), was undertaken at the behest of the Hotel Association of India. The NIPFP headed by eminent economists of the standing of Dr. Raja J Chelliah, former Chief Economic Advisor of the Government of India and Dr. C. Rangarajan, former Governor of the Reserve Bank of India, provided the Indian hospitality industry with its most appropriate perspective and authentic study of tariff systems.

First Afro-Asian Infotech Hotels Expo

HAI-led initiative resulted in Afro-Asian Region's first Conference-cum-Exposition on Information Technology being institutionalized as 'an annual event in New Delhi for countries in the South Asian Region.

The first Conference-cum-Expo organized by HAl on April 10-11, 2000 at the ITC Maurya Sheraton Hotel, New Delhi received support from the United Nations Economic and Social Commission for Asia and the Pacific, and the SAARC Tourism Council. The Ministries of Tourism and Information Technology, Government of India, extended official support to HAl as Co-sponsors of the event.

Second Afro-Asian Infotech-hotels Expo

The Second Conference-cum-Exposition on Information Technology in Hotels was organized on March 15-16, 2001 at the Taj Palace Hotel, New Delhi.

This Afro-Asian conference was supported by United Nation Economic and Social Commission for Asia and like the front conference the Pacific (UN-ESCAP); Ministry of Tourism, Ministry of Information Technology, Government of India, SAARC Tourism Council and SAARC Hotel Association, Pacific Asia Travel Association (PATA) and International Hotel & Restaurant Association (IH&RA).

Creating a National Network of HAI Chapters

The Hotel Association of India, established in April 1997,

enlisted co-operation on a voluntary basis of professional hoteliers in twenty five State and fifty three cities to monitor hospitality related developments to enable the Association to address the concerns of the hospitality industry at the grass-roots level.

Going Global With Knowledge Exchange Partners

Knowledge Exchange partnerships were formed with international organization such as the World Travel and Tourism Council (WTTC); the Pacific Asia Travel Association (PATA); World Tourism Organisation (WTO); the International Hotel and Restaurant Association (IH&RA); the United Nation Economic and Social Commission for Asia and the Pacific (UN-ESCAP); the South Asia Association of Regional Countries (SAARC), the World Health Organisation (WHO) and the European Union's South Asia Integrated Tourism Human Resource Development Programme (EU-SAITHRDP)

Inter-sectoral Linkages with Apex National Fora

At the National level working partnerships were established with apex industry for a like the Federation of Indian Chamber of Commerce and Industry (FICCI); Associated Chamber of Commerce and Industry of India (ASSOCHAM); Confederation of Indian Industry (CII); to provide hospitality industry perspective in the formation of national industrial policies and development.

Affiliation with World Health Organisation (WHO)

HAI's pioneered the concept of 'Healthy Hotels' in line with WHO's 'Healthy Cities' campaign by initiating programmes for the hospitality industry on 'Hygiene Management in Hotels' at Agra in 1997. The WHO representative in India delivered the keynote address at the First Hygiene Management Seminar.

Innovative-"India Quiz Contest" at ITB Berlin 2002

A new promotional first was scored by the HAI at ITB Berlin, held from 16th to 20th March 2002. This was the first time 25 leading Indian hotels were brought together by HAI on the industry net to sponsor prizes of FAM Holiday Tours to Travel Trade visitors at the ITB.

The India Quiz Contest brochure of HAI provided a high visibility to the Indian hospitality industry products among visitor to the ITB, Berlin. The participating hotels received excellent marketing exposure of their properties in the Quiz brochure. This also offered unique opportunities for prospective agents and operator for the familiarization and experience of the hotels.

Guidelines for Provision of Disabled Friendly Facilities in Hotels

The Association undertook a pioneering role in formulating a comprehensive set of Guidelines for provision of Disabled Friendly facilities in Hotels, especially in parking and Approach Areas, Lobbies, Public Areas, Lifts, Rooms, Bathrooms and to install special Fire Prevention measures for the disabled.

Promoting Public-Private Partnership

The Association in a step towards promoting the public-private partnership called upon its members to extend their full corporation to the Archeological Survey of India in the maintenance of the National monuments, which has translated into following public-private sector partnership:-

(i) Illumination of Humayun's Tomb at Delhi by the Oberoi Group of Hotels.

(ii) Development of facilities for visitors at the Agra Fort by the ITC Hotels Ltd.

(iii) Main entrance of the Jantar Mantar observatory at New Delhi by the Apeejay Surrendra Park Hotels Pvt. Ltd.

(iv) Illumination of the Safdarjung Tomb, New Delhi by the Grand Group of

Special Promotional Packages in Hotels

A major initiative undertaken by HAI galvanized the entire Indian hospitality industry to come together under the Association's banner to offer for the first time in the history of the industry as many as 62 special promotional packages in hotels for marketing averages in association with Air India.

Memorandum of Undertakings Signed With the Hotel Association of Nepal and the Uganda Investment Authority

The Hotel Association of India signed two Memorandum of Understanding which aimed at fostering and promoting tourism in their respective countries by inter alia agreeing to exchange information in respect to development and trend in the fields of tourism, hospitality and hotel sectors and encourage interaction between their respective hotels and Hospitality Association of India for Tourism Promotion and exploring investment opportunities in these sectors.

India Quiz Contest Brochure at 51st PATA Annual Conference

Encouraged by the overwhelming response received from the ITB Berlin, HAI launched its exclusive India Quiz Contest at the 51st PATA Annual Conference held in New Delhi from 14.04.2002 to 18.04.2002 offering opportunities of FAM Holiday in 14 leading Hotels.

Study Project on Management of Cross-cultural Tourists Movements in Hospitality Sector

HAI initiated a study project on Management of cross-cultural tourism movements in hospitality sector to assess and promote awareness among staff in smaller hotel and upgrade their knowledge and skills for handling of foreign tourists.

Grant of Fiscal Benefits to the Hospitality Industry

For the first time the tourism industry's aspirations elaborated in the Hotel Association of India's various memoranda to the Central Government were translated into "tourism-friendly", measures in the Union Budget of 2003-04. These measures were aimed at making India more affordable destination, fuelling growth of hospitality infrastructure, facilitating business re-organisation, re-structuring hospitality industry and motivating State Governments to rationalize tourism tax regime. The major incentives extended to hospitality industries included and exemption of Service tax in hotels relating to Conference and Banquet business, which have been excluded from the service tax net.

Encouraging Investments

Hotel Association of India orchestrated the strategy leading to announcement in the Union Budget 2003 of benefits under Section 10(23) (g) on loans to hotels (3 star and above categories) for increasing the availability of funds for the hotel industry.

This provision has allowed lending institutions to make available funds to hotel projects at reduced rates of interest. The financial institutions will get a tax break on the interest income they earn on loans extended to such borrowers. Inclusion of finance to the hotel projects of three star category and above for the first time under Section 10 (23)(g) of the Income Tax Act "signals" the positioning of hotels on the threshold of securing full infrastructure status as granted to other industries. HAI is now carrying this agenda forward to securing the wider benefits of infrastructure under Section 84 I/A of Income Tax Act.

Restructuring Hospitality Business

Amalgamation and Merger

It is at the behest of HAI that the Finance Ministry constituted a Working group under Chief Commissioner of Income Tax Mumbai which recommended the grant of benefits under Section 72 A of the Income Tax Act (which relates to the set-off of accumulated losses and depreciation on amalgamation), for the hotel industry to help loss-making hotel companies in re-organising their business.

The facility of mergers and acquisitions was hitherto available only to industrial undertakings and manufacturing units. With its extension to hotel companies, it has facilitated moves towards consolidation with the hospitality industry and releasing of resources blocked in non-performing assets.

This measure has now enabled smaller hotel units to enter into franchisee arrangements with established hotel groups/chains which in turn has led to improvements in occupancy levels and service standards.

Zero Duty Facility for Imports by Hotels

HAI pursued with the Ministry of Commerce, Government of India for grant of the zero duty import facility to hotels and stand alone restaurants. The Industry has now been granted under the "Served from India Scheme", the zero duty facility to all hotels including one star, two star hotels for import of food items and alcoholic beverages sell which would make India an affordable destination.

HAI Directory of Hotels Going Global

The exclusive HAI Directory of Hotels is an annual publication promoted with a singular aim of fulfilling the promotional need for tourists and visitor coming to India for an authentic compendium of leading Indian hotels recognized by the Ministry of Tourism. For the first time in 2005 the Directory was utilized by the Ministry of Tourism for distribution among foreign travel agents and tour operators in 12 countries through the Government of India's Tourist Offices abroad.

World Tourism Day Celebartion

A new promotional first was scored by HAI for creating awareness about the World Tourism Day on 27th Sept. 2005 amongst not only the member-hotels but also the school children. To encourage and facilitate the member-hotels in celebrating the World Tourism Day on 27th September 2005, HAI outlined a bouquet of activities to be organized by the member-hotels. The member-hotels came forward in large numbers and organized the activities with enthusiasm and excitement. In New Delhi, HAI collaborated with the Sanskriti School to launch a Quiz Contest on Tourism for school children on the World Tourism Day.

Members Services

Variety of professional member-services are provided by HAI to its members these include:-

(i) INFORMATION BULLETINS sent out regularly with updates on latest developments concerning hotel industries, policy changes and pronouncements by Ministry of Tourism, Ministry of Finance, Ministry of Commerce, CBEC, CBDT, State Governments and affiliate international organizations such as WTTC, IH&RA, WTO etc.;

(ii) HAI TODAY-the first hospitality industry magazine of its kind in India;

(iii) HAI DIRECTORY OF HOTELS-an exclusive high quality reference manual of recognized hotels in India;

(iv) HAI PRIVILEGE CARDS which are offered to members in the Gold and Silver Categories entitling them to

discounts on hotel room tariffs and restaurants outlets in all member hotels on reciprocal basis;

(v) HAI LEGAL SERVICES which enables members to avail benefits of highest calibre legal advice on issues of concern them and interventions on their behalf in courts.

Green Weeks of the HAI

HAI has successfully institutionalized the concept of celebrating annual green weeks in hotels to exhibit its commitment to conservation of environment through use of bio-degradable and environment-friendly products by efficient management of waste generated and by adopting measures for efficient utilization of day light to conserve upon electricity etc. HAI has this year celebrated its ninth annual green week, reaching out to large number of tourists, employees, their families, school children and society with its environment message.

Fundamentals Of Revenue Management Will Be Revealed In A Special Report Commissioned By HSMAI Special Interest Group

MCLEAN, VA The Hospitality Sales & Marketing Association International (HSMAI) Revenue Management Special Interest Group has taken on an ambitious project to produce the first-ever comprehensive "Fundamentals of Revenue Management" special report.

The report will be a practitioner-friendly publication that addresses the fundamentals of revenue management for a broad audience of hospitality professionals. With comprehensive content that is both readable and actionable, it will deliver tools and information for revenue management education, incorporating expert advice from interviews with industry executives and educators, case studies, and practical checklists for implementing successful revenue management strategies at the property level.

"Creating relevance for members and the industry at large through ground-breaking initiatives such as this Revenue Management Special Report is in keeping with HSMAI's mission to be the leading source for sales and marketing information, knowledge and business development for professionals in tourism, travel, and hospitality," states Robert A. Gilbert, CHME, CHA, president and CEO of HSMAI.

"We are very excited about this debut project, and expect it will be a springboard for other initiatives including certification and revenue management research," notes Tim Wiersma, vice president of revenue management for Host Marriott and chair of HSMAI's Revenue Management Tangible Resources Committee.

The publication will be produced in a manner similar to the recent special report produced by HSMAI and TIG Global entitled DeMystifying Distribution, widely praised by the industry for its insight, accuracy and comprehensive coverage of the topic.

The commissioned report, which will be released at the third annual HSMAI Revenue Management Strategy Conference on June 19, 2005 in Minneapolis, will be co-authored by Caryl Helsel and Kathleen Cullen of the Solutionz Group, a business development and strategic consulting group based in Florida. Helsel heads the hospitality practice and previously held executive positions with Kimpton Hotels, Pegasus Solutions and Mandarin Oriental Hotel Group, and is the former president of the Hotel Electronic Distribution Network Association (HEDNA). Cullen is a lead consultant on the hospitality team and is a hospitality revenue management and distribution veteran, holding executive positions with Swissotel and Raffles Hotels, as well as past vice president of HEDNA. Delving deep into the fundamentals, nuances and specifics of revenue management, the special report will address the following:

- Ideas and initiatives to maximize revenue opportunities, optimize profits by managing revenues and develop an infrastructure (strategies, policies, procedures, reports, etc.) to make informed decisions about accepting or rejecting business.
- An overview of the external market such as segmentation, demand forecasting, revenue strategy, operational forecast, interdepartmental integration, strategic pricing, inventory control strategies and internal performance analysis.
- Tactics including rate-level maintenance, inventory management and rate offer assessment (for group and negotiated rates).
- The optimal environment, characteristics and descriptors.

The Revenue Management Special Interest Group is made up of a group of HSMAI members who advance the revenue management discipline through education, certification, participation, resources and guidance, enabling leaders to optimize revenue and performance within their own organizations. The SIG Advisory Board includes corporate revenue management executives from Accor North America, Destination Hotels & Resorts, Host Marriott Corporation, Hilton Hotels, InterContinental Hotels Group, Outrigger Hotels & Resorts, Peabody Hotels, Preferred Hotel Group, and TravelCLICK.

Among the Board's strategic intentions are:

- Provide education on all levels through programs, events, and an annual strategy conference as well as provide education for senior executives through publications, press releases and conference participation.
- Develop and manage a revenue management certification program.
- Develop a sense of community and participation.
- Provide tangible resources through a fundamentals publication that defines the discipline of revenue management and includes a glossary of terms, maintain a website portal, create a self-auditing system and encourage industry internships.

Bibliography

Airey, D. and Nightingale, M. : *Tourism Occupations, Career Profile and Knowledge*, Annals of Tourism Research, 1981.

Brunt, Paul: *Market Research in Travel and Tourism*, Oxford, Butterworth Heinemann, 1997.

Carl H. : *Internet Distribution of European Travel and Tourism Services*, Research Centre of Bornholm, Denmark, 1999.

Cukier, J. : *Tourism Employment in Bali: Trends and Implications*, London: Thompson, 1996.

Donald E. : *Public Personnel Management: Contexts and Strategies*, Upper Saddle River, NJ: Prentice Hall, 1998.

Douglas C: *Practical Tourism Forecasting*, Oxford, Butterworth Heinemann, 1996.

Eberts, Marjorie: *Careers in Travel, Tourism, and Hospitality*, Lincolnwood, VGM Career Horizons, 1997.

Foster, Douglas: *Travel and Tourism Management*, London, Macmillan Educational, 1985.

Ghimire, Krishna: *The Native Tourist*: Mass Tourism within Developing Regions, London, Earthscan, 2001.

Graham M S: *Language of Tourism*, The, Wallingford, CAB International, 1996.

Harrison, Lyndon: *Tourism Means Jobs*, Chester, Lyndon Harrison, 1996.

Ireland, Lewis: *Quality Management for Projects and Programs*, Upper Darby, PMI, 1991.

Jennings, Gayle: *Tourism Research*, Chichester, Wiley, 2001.

Judi Radice: *Restaurant & Food Graphics*, Glen Cove, PBC International, 1994.

Karski, A: *Urban Tourism* - A Key to Urban Regeneration?, 1990.

Klein, S. : *Information & Communication Technologies in Tourism*, Springer-Verlag, Wien-New York, 2000.

Kotler, Philip: *Marketing for Hospitality and Tourism*: New Jersey, Prentice-Hall, 1998.

Larkham, P J: *Building a New Heritage: Tourism, Culture & Identity in the New Europe*, London, Routledge,1994.

Leivadi, S: *Sociology of Tourism, The: Theoretical And Empirical Investigations*, London, Retailed, 1996.

Lewis, Robert C.: *Cases in Hospitality Marketing and Management*, New York, John Wiley, 1997.

Madhukar Manoj : *Hospitality Industries in Next Millennium*, Rajat, Delhi, 2001.

Margaret Wade: *Medieval Travellers: The Rich and Restless*, London, Hamish Hamilton, 1982.

Marjorie, E.: *Careers in Travel, Tourism, and Hospitality*, Lincolnwood, VGM Career Horizons, 1997.

McNicol, B.J. : *Views of Residents, Developers and Government Planners About Tourists and Tourism Resort Developments in Canmore, Alberta*, The University of Galgary, Alberta, 1996.

Morrell, J. : *Employment in Tourism*, London: British Tourist Authority, 1985.

Murphy, P.E. : *Tourism: A Community Approach*, London: Methuen, 1985.

Nancy N.: *Choosing a Career in Hotels, Motels, and Resorts*, New York, Rosen Pub. Group, 1997.

Norman G.: *Hotel, Restaurant, and Travel Law: A Preventive Approach*, Albany, Delmar Publishers, 1993.

Paajanen, M. : *Assessing Local Income and Employment Effects of Tourism: Experience using the Nordic model of tourism*, Wiley, 1999.

Pearce, Douglas: *Tourism Today: A Geographical Analysis*, Harlow, Longman, 1995.

Peter J.: *College & University Foodservice Management Standards*, Westport, AVI Pub. Company, 1985.

Peters, M: *International Tourism*, London, Hutchinson, 1969.

Richards, G. : *Culture, Crafts and Tourism: A Vital Relationship*, Tilburg: Atlas, 1999.

Robert C.: *Cases in Hospitality Marketing and Management,* New York, John Wiley, 1997.

Rocco, M.: *An Introduction to Hospitality Today,* Orlando, Educational Institute, 1998.

Rosemary E.: *Managing Employee Relations in the Hotel and Catering Industry,* London, Cassell, 1995.

Scottish Tourist Board: *Visitor Attractions: A Development Guide,* Edinburgh, Scottish Tourist Board, 1991.

Sharma Sunil : *Planning and Development of Tourism and Hospitality,* Rajat Pub, Delhi, 2007.

Slinn, Judy A: *Tourism: Management of Facilities,* London, Pitman: M & E, 1993.

Smith, G. : *International Tourism and Hospitality Careers through Education and Training,* CHRIE Annual Conference, Washington DC, 1996.

Swarbrooke, J.: *Marketing Tourism, Hospitality and Leisure in Europe,* London, International Thomson Business Press, 1996.

Thomas, F.: *Introduction to Management in the Hospitality Industry,* New York, Wiley, 1995.

Timothy, R.: *Cases in Hospitality Management: A Critical Incident Approach,* New York, Wiley, 1995.

Index

O

P

S

T

❑❑❑